IFIP Advances in Information and Communication Technology 333

T0224001

IFIP – The International Federation for Information Processing

IFIP was founded in 1960 under the auspices of UNESCO, following the First World Computer Congress held in Paris the previous year. An umbrella organization for societies working in information processing, IFIP's aim is two-fold: to support information processing within its member countries and to encourage technology transfer to developing nations. As its mission statement clearly states,

> *IFIP's mission is to be the leading, truly international, apolitical organization which encourages and assists in the development, exploitation and application of information technology for the benefit of all people.*

IFIP is a non-profitmaking organization, run almost solely by 2500 volunteers. It operates through a number of technical committees, which organize events and publications. IFIP's events range from an international congress to local seminars, but the most important are:

- The IFIP World Computer Congress, held every second year;
- Open conferences;
- Working conferences.

The flagship event is the IFIP World Computer Congress, at which both invited and contributed papers are presented. Contributed papers are rigorously refereed and the rejection rate is high.

As with the Congress, participation in the open conferences is open to all and papers may be invited or submitted. Again, submitted papers are stringently refereed.

The working conferences are structured differently. They are usually run by a working group and attendance is small and by invitation only. Their purpose is to create an atmosphere conducive to innovation and development. Refereeing is less rigorous and papers are subjected to extensive group discussion.

Publications arising from IFIP events vary. The papers presented at the IFIP World Computer Congress and at open conferences are published as conference proceedings, while the results of the working conferences are often published as collections of selected and edited papers.

Any national society whose primary activity is in information may apply to become a full member of IFIP, although full membership is restricted to one society per country. Full members are entitled to vote at the annual General Assembly. National societies preferring a less committed involvement may apply for associate or corresponding membership. Associate members enjoy the same benefits as full members, but without voting rights. Corresponding members are not represented in IFIP bodies. Affiliated membership is open to non-national societies, and individual and honorary membership schemes are also offered.

Ryohei Nakatsu   Naoko Tosa   Fazel Naghdy
Kok Wai Wong   Philippe Codognet (Eds.)

Cultural Computing

Second IFIP TC 14
Entertainment Computing Symposium, ECS 2010
Held as Part of WCC 2010
Brisbane, Australia, September 20-23, 2010
Proceedings

 Springer

Volume Editors

Ryohei Nakatsu
National University of Singapore, Interactive and Digital Media Institute
7 Engineering Drive 1, Singapore 117574, Singapore
E-mail: idmdir@nus.edu.sg

Naoko Tosa
Kyoto University, Kyoto Laboratory for Culture and Computing
134 Minamimachi Chudoji, Shimogyo-ku, Kyoto 600-8813, Japan
E-mail: tosa@mm.media.kyoto-u.ac.jp

Fazel Naghdy
University of Wollongong
Wollongong, NSW 2522, Australia
E-mail: f.naghdy@uow.edu.au

Kok Wai Wong
Murdoch University, School of Information Technology
South St., Murdoch, WA 6150, Australia
E-mail: k.wong@murdoch.edu.au

Philippe Codognet
CNRS/UPMC, Campus Gérard-Mégie
3 rue Michel-Ange, 75794 Paris Cedex 16, France
E-mail: philippe.codognet@lip6.fr

CR Subject Classification (1998): H.5.2, H.1.2, H.5, H.4, I.4, I.3

ISSN   1868-4238
ISBN-10   3-642-42315-9 Springer Berlin Heidelberg New York
ISBN-13   978-3-642-42315-4 Springer Berlin Heidelberg New York

springer.com

© IFIP International Federation for Information Processing 2010
Softcover re-print of the Hardcover 1st edition 2010

Typesetting: Camera-ready by author, data conversion by Scientific Publishing Services, Chennai, India
Printed on acid-free paper   06/3180

IFIP World Computer Congress 2010 (WCC 2010)

Message from the Chairs

Every two years, the International Federation for Information Processing (IFIP) hosts a major event which showcases the scientific endeavors of its over one hundred technical committees and working groups. On the occasion of IFIP's 50th anniversary, 2010 saw the 21st IFIP World Computer Congress (WCC 2010) take place in Australia for the third time, at the Brisbane Convention and Exhibition Centre, Brisbane, Queensland, September 20–23, 2010.

The congress was hosted by the Australian Computer Society, ACS. It was run as a federation of co-located conferences offered by the different IFIP technical committees, working groups and special interest groups, under the coordination of the International Program Committee.

The event was larger than ever before, consisting of 17 parallel conferences, focusing on topics ranging from artificial intelligence to entertainment computing, human choice and computers, security, networks of the future and theoretical computer science. The conference History of Computing was a valuable contribution to IFIPs 50th anniversary, as it specifically addressed IT developments during those years. The conference e-Health was organized jointly with the International Medical Informatics Association (IMIA), which evolved from IFIP Technical Committee TC-4 "Medical Informatics".

Some of these were established conferences that run at regular intervals, e.g., annually, and some represented new, groundbreaking areas of computing. Each conference had a call for papers, an International Program Committee of experts and a thorough peer reviewing process of full papers. The congress received 642 papers for the 17 conferences, and selected 319 from those, representing an acceptance rate of 49.69% (averaged over all conferences). To support interoperation between events, conferences were grouped into 8 areas: Deliver IT, Govern IT, Learn IT, Play IT, Sustain IT, Treat IT, Trust IT, and Value IT.

This volume is one of 13 volumes associated with the 17 scientific conferences. Each volume covers a specific topic and separately or together they form a valuable record of the state of computing research in the world in 2010. Each volume was prepared for publication in the Springer IFIP Advances in Information and Communication Technology series by the conference's volume editors. The overall Publications Chair for all volumes published for this congress is Mike Hinchey.

For full details of the World Computer Congress, please refer to the webpage at http://www.ifip.org.

June 2010   Augusto Casaca, Portugal, Chair, International Program Committee
Phillip Nyssen, Australia, Co-chair, International Program Committee
Nick Tate, Australia, Chair, Organizing Committee
Mike Hinchey, Ireland, Publications Chair
Klaus Brunnstein, Germany, General Congress Chair

Preface

Welcome to the Second International IFIP Entertainment Computing Symposium on Cultural Computing (ECS 2010), which was part of the 21st IFIP World Computer Congress, held in Brisbane, Australia during September 21–23, 2010. On behalf of the people who made this conference happen, we wish to welcome you to this international event.

The IFIP World Computer Congress has offered an opportunity for researchers and practitioners to present their findings and research results in several prominent areas of computer science and engineering. In the last World Computer Congress, WCC 2008, held in Milan, Italy in September 2008, IFIP launched a new initiative focused on all the relevant issues concerning computing and entertainment. As a result, the two-day technical program of the First Entertainment Computing Symposium (ECS 2008) provided a forum to address, explore and exchange information on the state of the art of computer-based entertainment and allied technologies, their design and use, and their impact on society.

Based on the success of ECS 2008, at this Second IFIP Entertainment Computing Symposium (ECS 2010), our challenge was to focus on a new area in entertainment computing: cultural computing.

In the 21st century we are entering the era of "cultural computing" where computers would be able to handle specific forms and human characteristics that hide behind each culture. In this symposium we introduced and discussed still-unveiled possibilities of cultural computing, analyzing and visualizing substantial cultural issues such as sensitivity, memory, spirituality, storytelling, cultural diversity, etc. that have not been dealt with in computer science and engineering so far.

There are various possibilities in this area. From the point of view of art, cultural computing could go beyond the present media art by treating various kinds of cultural issues. From a technology viewpoint, it would open up a new area in computer technologies that so far have only been treating the digitization of cultural heritages/contents to preserve them.

The Second IFIP Entertainment Computing Symposium attempted to focus on this emerging and challenging area by bring various fields together and exploring boundaries and new frontiers. This symposium comprised a single track, with a highly selective set of presentations and discussions of visionary concepts, advanced technology, interactive demonstrations/installations, etc.

The topics discussed in this symposium included, but were not limited to, the following:

1) Preservation of cultural heritage using computers
2) Preservation of traditional technologies using computers
3) Treating models and types in cultural contents
4) Education of cultures using computers
5) Interactive installation treating cultural contents

As this is a totally new and challenging area, in addition to the normal submission and reviewing process of papers, we carefully tried to select several researchers who have been doing pioneering research in these areas and asked them to contribute to this challenging area. Happily to us, most of them accepted our invitation and prepared papers despite their busy schedule. All the submitted papers went through rigorous peer review process with two reviewers for each paper. Our sincere gratitude goes to these people who contributed to this symposium by submitting their papers and responding to our requests.

On behalf of the Organizing Committee, we would like to extend our personal thanks to all the members of the International Program Committee who reviewed and selected papers. The success of this symposium is credited to them, as well as to Session Chairs, presenters and attendees.

Ryohei Nakatsu
Naoko Tosa
Fazel Naghdy
Kok Wai Wong
Philippe Codognet

Organization

Second IFIP Entertainment Computing Symposium (ECS 2010) Cultural Computing

Organizing Committee

Symposium Co-chairs

Naoko Tosa   Kyoto University, Japan
Hyun S. Yang   KAIST, Korea
Fazel Naghdy   University of Wollongong, Australia

Program Co-chairs

Kevin Wong   Murdoch University, Australia
Paolo Ciancarini   University of Bologna, Italy
Matthias Rauberberg   Technical University of Eindhoven, The Netherlands
Ryohei Nakatsu   National University of Singapore, Singapore

Program Committee

Christoph Bartneck   Technical University of Eindhoven, The Netherlands
Brad Bushman   University of Michigan, USA
Marc Cavazza   University of Teesside, UK
Adrian Cheok   National University of Singapore, Singapore
Tony Brooks   Aalborg University, Denmark
Sidney Fels   University of British Columbia, Canada
Nahum Gershon   The Mitre Corporation, USA
Stephane Natkin   CNAM/ENJMIN, France
David Obrazalek   Charles University, Czech Republic
Zhigeng Pan   Zhejiang University, China
Claudio Pinhanez   IBM, Brazil
Ben Salem   Technical University of Eindhoven, The Netherlands
Andy Sloane   University of Wolverhampton, UK
Bill Swartout   USC, USA
Naoko Tosa   Kyoto University, Japan
Gino Yu   Hong Kong Polytechnic University, China

Table of Contents

Multiple Format Search and Rescue Robot as a Competitive Arena

Andrew Chiou

School of Computing Sciences, CQUniversity Australia
Rockhampton Campus, 4702 QLD, Australia
a.chiou@cqu.edu.au

Abstract. Current robot competition provides both students and researchers a platform to experiment with related technology and skills to solve challenging problems. However, the entry point for participation requires very demanding prerequisites of the participants. Even though robot competition is gaining popularity as a form of digital entertainment, it still remains a very specialised domain catering to academia. This paper presents on-going work in specifying, designing and developing a multiple format search and rescue robot to provide continuity for primary age participants to postgraduate researchers.

Keywords: robot, competition, search, rescue, arena.

1 Introduction

Competitive robots as entertainment and educational platform have been a popular domain in research. Several competitive formats have gained ever increasing followers, such as FIRA, RoboCup and RoboCup Jr. [1, 2]. The format of these competitions have a fundamental focus, that is, of providing a platform as a challenge whereby the motivation to do well at these competition inadvertently drives the participants to discover and use new knowledge. These formats, however, are constant instances of similar test *arenas* (i.e. the defined physical operational environment for the robot's operation) that is found in competition to competition. This raises a challenge to potential participants with various degrees of knowledge and ability. As these competitions are mainly patronised in academia, the participants are mostly undergraduates or postgraduates. These competition are used as a research and learning platform. However, the prerequisite for such participation is demanding as it requires that they have background knowledge in engineering to computer programming. That is, the entry point to become involved in this form of competition is too prohibitive to most. The current work presented here details a multiple format for competitive robots that provides continuity to allow participants from primary school ages to postgraduate researchers, in graduated phases. This allows participants to progress from one phase to the next as their technical knowledge and skill improves.

R. Nakatsu et al. (Eds.): ECS 2010, IFIP AICT 333, pp. 1–8, 2010.

2 Background

Competitive robots can be divided into three categories to include (1) intelligent autonomous robots, (2) remote controlled robots, and (3) passive or sympathetic (peripheral) robots. Each category provides different level of challenges to different age groups. These challenges provide specific problems for participants to solve or attempt to their best to overcome the challenges.

2.1 Intelligent Autonomous Robots

Intelligent autonomous robots are deployed in arenas to interact with objects or other robots to overcome specific problems. This includes soccer-playing robots and search and rescue (SAR) robots. Robots in this category employ exo-shells that resemble actual organic forms such as bipedal and quadpod creatures (e.g. Sony Aibo canine robots and Lynxmotion range of bipeal robots). Other forms are wheeled or track autonomous vehicles (e.g. Fischertechnik, Lego NXT and FIRA-based robots) [3, 4]. In order to address specific challenges such as scoring a goal in the opponent's goal, the autonomous robots must demonstrate a very high-level of intelligence. To accomplish this, computational intelligence methods need to be programmed into embedded microprocessor controllers, which further controls motors, sensors, servos and other type of actuators. Hence, a very high level of knowledge is required to build, program and operate robots in this category.

2.2 Remote Controlled Robots

Remote controlled robots within this category may be physically similar to intelligent autonomous robots. They may employ the same type of exo-shell and mechanics to resemble forms that would best help to overcome challenges within the competition. However, they do not demonstrate or have very little in-built intelligence. They are mostly tele-operated using wireless or tethered remote controllers. The primary purpose of this type of competition is to test and challenge the physical, mechanics and electronic aspects of the robots. Remote controlled robots are used in full-scale SAR urban test arenas and popular in competitive categories such as sumo-bot and battle-bots [5].

2.3 Passive or Peripheral Robots

Passive or peripheral robots neither demonstrate intelligence or are remote controlled. Their function is primarily to play the sympathetic role of ornamentation. With the exception of pre-programmed mobility and movement, it has very limited 'aware-ness'. Even though this may seem superfluous, their very appearance in the arena is inherent in a competition involving robots. Peripheral robots are employed in the dancing robots category in competition such as RoboCup Jr [2]. Categories such as this provide very young children with limited technical knowledge the opportunity to participate in robot competitions.

3 Multi Format Robot Search and Rescue (SAR) Arena

The development of the multi format robot competition adopts SAR arena as it provides the best platform and potential for extension [10]. The purpose of a multi format SAR arena is to provide accessibility to all participants ranging from young age children to postgraduate researchers. Each category provides continuity from one phase to the next, in turn providing increasingly more challenging problems for the participants to overcome. In this way, participants are not required to have comprehensive prerequisites to participate in a robot competition. For the purpose of the multi format robot SAR arena competition, only intelligent autonomous robots are considered. The format begins as a 2-dimensional flat arena, subsequently upgrading to a 3-dimensional arena and then finally to a problem-based arena.

4 2-Dimensional Arena

The 2-dimensional arena is based on the RoboCup Jr rescue robot format. Participants are to design, build and program an intelligent autonomous robot that could navigate across an arena following a pre-defined marked path to arrive at a pre-destined 'disaster' area to 'rescue' a victim. The arena is composed of 50x50cm flat surface platform tiles arranged edge-to-edge in a continuous path. The complexity depends on the age group of the participants. Fig. 1 shows an actual competition in progress, the 2-dimensional arena arranged in the desired path.

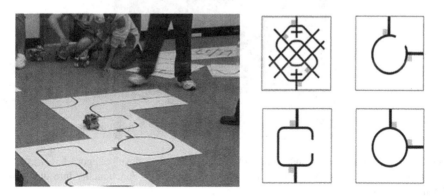

Fig. 1. 2-dimensional search and rescue robot arena based on RoboCup Jr (http://www. robocup.org/). Platform tiles are arranged edge-to-edge to provide a continuous path. Four samples from a possible pool of approximately 15 -18 different tiles are shown above. Tiles are designed with straight paths to increasingly complex paths.

In this category, the intention of the competition is to provide challenges to participants to demonstrate their competence in construction and programming. In most cases, the use of construction kits such as Lego NXT and Fischertechnik are commonplace. For more advanced participants, pre-fabricated embedded systems are used such as Arduino and Parallax Propeller microprocessors. In the advanced version of the 2-dimensional arena, participants are not only required to follow a pre-destined path to arrive at a destination, the robots must be sufficiently intelligent to avoid simple obstacles and slightly raised surfaces – a prelude to what is expected in the challenges expected in the follow up found in subsequent 3-dimensional arenas.

5   3-Dimensional Arena

5.1   Entry Level Competition Arena

The 3-dimensional arena is based on the 2-dimension version with added complexity. Obstacles in a variety of material is added to provide scaled-down version of possible real-life scenarios. Understandably, the 3-dimensional arena is a huge leap from the 2-dimensional version. Hence, in order to provide continuity in terms of gradual difficulties of the challenge, two version of the arena is employed. The first has a marked path (Fig. 2). The autonomous robot is only required to overcome the physical obstacles minimising the need to intelligently traverse in the arena. Autonomous navigation is a complex study in itself, therefore by reducing this requirement, the 3-dimensioanl arena is now made more accessible to participants with moderate background knowledge and skills.

Fig. 2. 3-dimensional search and rescue robot arena. The entry-level category has a marked path to simplify the necessity to program complex navigational functionality into the scaled down SAR robots.

5.2   Advanced Level Competition Arena

The advance version of the 3-dimensional arena is similar to the entry-level arena without the marked path. Also, based on the possible geomorphic arrangement, the test arenas can be arranged in any configuration depending on the requirements of the competition.

The purpose of this category (entry and advanced level) is to provide challenges that allow participants to demonstrate their ability in not only constructing and developing advanced robots that are capable of overcoming physical obstacles, participants should also be able to demonstrate their programming skills. It is expected that

Fig. 3. 3-dimensional search and rescue robot arena. Four platform tiles arranged in a geomorphic configuration. The arena is populated with scaled-down effigies of victims, debris and moveable objects.

programming skills would require a high level of proficiency in intelligent computational methods [6].

The arena will be populated with effigies depicting victims in real life scenarios [7]. The goal of each SAR robots in the test arena is to locate, and if possible, retrieve the victims. Secondary goals for the robots are to map the area and provide environmental data to the human operators. Overall, the competition is to address each of the following requirements:

- The ability to assess a structure and assist in shoring it for increased stability.
- The ability to enter and travel around small confined spaces that cannot be accessed by humans or rescue dogs (to scale).
- The ability to carry supplies, such as extra oxygen tanks (to scale) and tools for rescuers to use.
- The ability to monitor the critical signs of a victim and provide first aid or food and water or both, until the victim can be removed from the area.
- The ability to process images quickly and extensively, often coupled with infrared sensing capabilities, which allow them to do a more complete survey of their surroundings.
- The ability to check and monitor different environmental factors, such as temperature and atmospheric gases continuously. This would allow them to provide early warning of problems that might otherwise go unseen by rescue workers until too late.
- The ability to detect harmful materials. These robots can be programmed to discover the hazardous material and inform rescuers or take recourse to neutralise it.

6 Problem Based Arena

The problem based arena in robot competition is the outcome resulting from cumulative concepts inherited from the 2- and 3-dimensional arenas. The goal of the problem based arena is to progress into real life case studies modeled on its predecessors. Even though this may move away from the *search and rescue* principle inherent in such competitive robots, the technology and skills required remains unchanged. The purpose of this arena is to allow the participants to apply their expertise in a known problem area [9]. By deploying this as a competition, it inevitably support a solution based approach expeditiously. In the following experimental arena, an example is presented to show how the SAR multi format is applied to one of the many problem based arena representing real-life challenges.

6.1 Problem Based Scenario

Despite on-going attempts and current research to utilise intelligent systems technology to both provide advice on pest control strategies and to monitor mobile pests, the actual execution of the control and management task is ultimately manual driven and labour intensive [8]. In the attempt to substitute human labour with automated mechanised devices, autonomous mobile robots have been one of the most popular choices (Fig. 4). Ideally, robots are the mechanical-electronic embodiment of human functions. Even though this functionality has only been partially realised in specific challenges, the robots ability to perform task repetitively far outweighs many of its disadvantages. However, the utmost benefit of using autonomous robots over human labour is the minimising of risk and injury commonly encountered by its human counterpart.

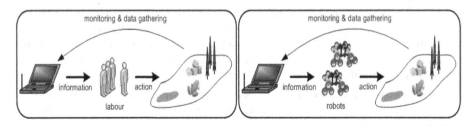

Fig. 4. Labour vs. Autonomous Robotics. Despite utilisation of computerised intelligent and monitoring systems, subsequent follow up action to control invasive pest is ultimately labour intensive. The capability to deploy autonomous robots to substitute human labour should be further investigated.

6.2 The Challenge

The SAR robot must be developed in a suitable operational environment. This environment is critical in facilitating the investigation, development and testing of functional components that comprises the hunter (i.e. SAR) robots. Fig. 5 illustrates the operational environment consisting of four entities and one staging area:

1. Hunter robots. This is the core component of the problem based arena.
2. Data collection station (for hunter robots and prey robots).

3. Working models to mimic stationary threats, i.e. obstacles, water, debris as Prey Type T-1).
4. Working models to mimic mobile threats, i.e. cane toad (designated as Prey Type T-2). This can be quickly built using construction kits.
5. The staging area is a collection of test arenas that itself comprise of different obstacles to simulate natural habitat of T-1 and T-2. The test arenas are isometric and geomorphic, that is, it allows the arenas to be setup in different configurations to allow almost any type of habitat to be replicated economically. The segmented test arenas can also be conveniently stored away or transported.

Overall, the competition (i.e. investigation) is to address each of the following requirements:

1. Pioneering the concept of using a singular hunter robot type to seek and control multiple types of threats and prey.
2. The use of electro-mechanical devices to mimic pests in order to test the performance of hunter robots is in itself significant innovation. The ability to model known pests accurately contributes directly to the ability in identifying the actual pests.
3. The utilisation of test arenas to artificially simulate a known habitat is significant. The ability to simulate a habitat accurately contributes directly to the ability to extract features from background noise. That is, differentiating specific specie from its surroundings.
4. Improving and refining the hardware devices used in robots. This may include the development of better tactile sensors, actuators, power supply and efficient locomotion.
5. A robot is only as good as the software that controls it. A functioning robot that successfully addresses the challenges proposed in this project should inevitably lead to better software techniques such as artificial intelligence methods, image processing algorithm, smart software and software architecture.

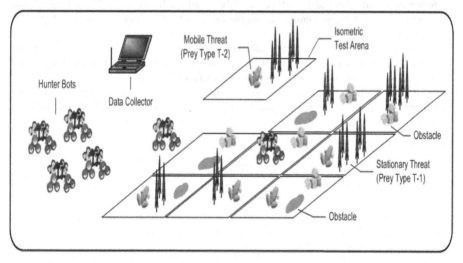

Fig. 5. Operational environment to facilitate the research, development and testing of hunter robots

7 Summary

Current robot competition provides both students and researchers a platform to experiment with related technology and skills to solve challenging problems. However, the entry point for participation requires very demanding prerequisites of the participants. Even though robot competition is gaining popularity as a form of digital entertainment, it is however a very specialised domain catering to academia. This has presented on-going work in specifying, designing and developing a multiple format search and rescue robot to provide continuity for primary age participants to postgraduate researchers.

References

1. http://www.fira.net/ (accessed on: May 10, 2010)
2. http://www.robocup.org/ (accessed on: May 10, 2010)
3. Tominaga, H., Onishi, Y., Hayashi, T., Yamasaki, T.: LEGO Robot Programming Exercise Support for Problem Solving Learning with Game Strategy Planning Tools. In: First IEEE International Workshop on Digital Game and Intelligent Toy Enhanced Learning (2007)
4. Asada, M., D'Andrea, R., Birk, A., Kitano, H., Veloso, M.M.: Robotics in Edutainment. In: IEEE International Conference on Robotics and Automation 2000, ICRA 2000 (2000)
5. http://www.battlebots.com/ (accessed on: May 10, 2010)
6. Kitano, H., Tadokoro, S., Noda, I., Matsubara, H., Takahashi, T., Shinjou, A., Shimada, S.: Robocup Rescue: Search and Rescue in Large-Scale Disasters as a Domain for Autonomous Agents Research. In: Proc. IEEE Conf. on Systems, Man, and Cybernetics, vol. 6, pp. 739–743 (1999)
7. Jacoff, A., Messina, E., Evans, J.: A Standard Test Course for Urban Search and Rescue Robots. In: Proc. of Performance Metrics for Intelligent Systems Workshop (2000)
8. Chiou, A., Yu, X.: A large-scale Agro decision support system: framework for (physical) fusion of a multi-input and multi-output hybrid system. In: Proc. the Third International Conference on Intelligent Sensors Sensor Networks and Information Processing, Melbourne (2007)
9. Chiou, A., Wynn, C.: Urban Search and Rescue Robots in Test Arenas: Scaled Modeling of Disasters to Test Intelligent Robot Prototyping. In: The Sixth International Conference on Ubiquitous Intelligence and Computing, Brisbane (2009)
10. Jacoff, A., Messina, E., Weiss, B.A., Tadokoro, S., Nakagawa, Y.: Test arenas and performance metrics for urban search and rescue robots. In: IEEE/RSJ International Conference (2003)

An On-Line Classification Approach of Visitors' Movements in 3D Virtual Museums

Kingkarn Sookhanaphibarn and Ruck Thawonmas

Intelligent Computer Entertainment Laboratory
Department of Human and Computer Intelligence
Ritsumeikan University
Kusatsu, Shiga 525-8577, Japan

Abstract. Recommender systems, in virtual museums and art galleries, providing the personalization and context awareness features require the off-line synthesis of visitors' behaviors therein and the off-line training stage of those synthetic data. This paper deals with the simulation of four visitors' styles, i.e., ant, fish, grasshopper, and butterfly, and the classification of those four styles using an Adaptive Neuro-Fuzzy Inference System (ANFIS). First, we analyze visitors' behaviors related to a visit time and an observation distance. Then, the proposed synthesis procedure is developed and used in the off-line training stage of ANFIS. The training and testing data are the average and variance of a set of visitors' attention data computing by the proposed function of the visit time and observation distance variables. Therefore, the trained ANFIS can identify the behavior style of an on-line visitor using the training set of synthetic data and its memberships can describe degrees of uncertainty in behavior styles.

Keywords: 3D virtual environment; Recommender system; Visitor movement; Visitor behavior; Visualization; Adaptive Neuro-Fuzzy Inference Systems (ANFIS).

1 Introduction

Currently, the number of existing virtual museums in Second Life (SL) is greater than 150 locations, characteristics of which vary tremendously in terms of scale and size, artifact types and exhibitions, media technologies, and target visitors, as reported by Urban [1]. An immersively interactive feature embedded in SL can attract the attention of up to 30 official organizations existing in Real Life (RL). One of them is the Smithsonian Latino Center opened the Smithsonian Latino Virtual Museum (LVM) in March 19, 2009 which provides the vast and rich collections, research and scholarship, exhibitions and educational activities related to U.S. Latinos and Latin America. This trend leads to the need of a conceptual framework of digital museums in the 3D virtual world, which was designed, developed and evaluated in [2,3].

Recommender modules, such as, guide avatar and personal route generation modules, were designed in the conceptual framework proposed by Sookhanaphibarn

R. Nakatsu et al. (Eds.): ECS 2010, IFIP AICT 333, pp. 9–20, 2010.

and Thawonmas [3] to achieve high visitors' satisfaction. The guide avatar addressed in [4] can create a new text for an individual visitor, at each time when he/she views an object. The guide avatar never repeats information which it has already expressed. For example, if a visitor moves from one artifact to another artifact, both of which belong in the classical period; the guide avatar will not repeat the description on classical period at the latter location. A personal route for a museum tour assists visitors in making a decision where they should stop over at and how long they should take. Since visitors in SL can teleport to any place with a constantly short time, the personal route generation module for a museum tour is a novel concept in the personalization issue.

Visitors in an art gallery have their stereotypical movement, which is categorized in four styles as proposed by Veron and Levasseur [5]. Four visiting styles based on an animals' behavior metaphor are ant, fish, grasshopper, and butterfly styles. The ant visitors spend quite a long time to observe all exhibits by walking closer to exhibits but avoids empty spaces. The fish visitors prefer to move to and stop over at empty spaces but avoid areas near exhibits. The grasshopper visitors spend a long time to see selected exhibits but ignore the rest of exhibits. The butterfly visitors observe all exhibits but spend varied times to observe each exhibit. Identifying their visiting styles can take advantage of recommender systems in virtual museums as mentioned in [6,7,8,9].

In this paper, we propose an on-line classification system of four visitor styles based on their definitions, which are summarized in [5,10]. This is based on our hypothesis that a visiting style can be simulated by using mathematic functions. To validate our hypothesis, we conduct an adaptive neuro-fuzzy inference system (ANFIS) trained by the synthetic visitor data in the off-line stage and tested by the new visitor data in the on-line stage. ANFIS is a hybrid learning algorithm to identify the membership function parameters of four visiting styles. The contributions of this work are (a) the novel simulation method of visiting styles in art galleries and museums in SL, (b) the proposed function to measure the visitors' attention of each exhibit, (c) the classification using ANFIS based on the average and variance of a set of visitors' attention data of all exhibit, and (d) our implications to applications of these findings.

2   Four Visiting Styles

2.1   Definition

Chittaro and Ieronutti [10] described four visiting styles based on results from their visualization tool, where black highlights areas more traveled, white identifies the areas less traveled and different shades of gray are used to identify intermediate previous situations, as shown in Table 1. Corresponding to four visiting styles, the aforementioned researches [5,7,10] described them beneficial to a physical environment design in museums as shown in Table 1. Note that Fig. 1 shows the visualization of a visitor in the art gallery, where all exhibits are placed on the wall. Without loss of generality, an art gallery shown in Fig. 2 is used as the museum map in our synthetic data with 12 exhibits hanging in three sides of the room.

Table 1. Visualization and recommended environment design of four visiting styles

Styles	Visualization	Recommendation
Ant	The center of most space on the map is colored in black, and there are no large differences in the time different exhibits have been seen as shown in Fig. 1 (a).	They need to be guided by a powerful rationale and this is the reason why they usually follow the path proposed by the museum curator.
Fish	The areas near all exhibits on the map are colored in black as shown in Fig. 1 (b) .	They prefer a holistic observation area, such as the center of the room.
Grasshopper	The areas near some exhibits are colored with highly variable shades of gray due to the fact that this visitor spends a variable time to observe different exhibits and ignores the rest of them as shown in Fig. 1 (c).	They move directly to their selective exhibits.
Butterfly	The areas near all exhibits are colored with different shades of gray and some are colored with black, but less regularly than those of the ant visitors as shown in Fig. 1 (d).	They refuse to follow the given path designed by other people and prefer their own route.

(a) Ant style   (b) Fish style   (c) Grasshopper style (d) Butterfly style

Fig. 1. Visualization of visitor styles

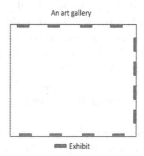

Fig. 2. The plan of an art gallery which all exhibits are hung on the wall

2.2   Algorithms of Data Synthesis

To synthesize the visit map, there are two input data as follows: a plan of museum, which illustrates the location of all exhibits, and his/her visitor type. We propose a synthesis approach for four visiting styles through the following steps:

1. Selective exhibit randomness
2. Preference weight randomness
3. Visit time distribution
4. Noise synthesis
5. Smoothing filter

There are four proposed synthesis procedures, i.e., ant, fish, grasshopper, and butterfly styles as described in Fig. 3 and their notations as defined in Table 2. All four synthesis procedures have one input argument, H or a set of exhibits, and one output, V or a visit map. Our synthetic visit maps have darkest colored pixels equal to 1 and brightest colored pixels equal to 0. The difference between the grasshopper and the butterfly styles is the number of stopovers at exhibits, i.e., the former stops fewer than the latter does. The selective exhibit randomness step is used in these two visiting styles using a β probability density function since two parameter γ and β can control the PDF curve corresponding to the grasshopper and butterfly paradigm of the number of stopovers. The β PDF of a sample x is written below:

$$f(x; \gamma, \beta) = \frac{1}{B(\gamma, \beta)} x^{\gamma-1} 1 - x^{\beta-1} x, \tag{1}$$

where $B(\cdot)$ is the Beta function as defined in [11]. In cases of both ant and fish styles, the selective exhibit randomness are not applied because the ant visitor stops at all exhibits and moves following the exhibit path proposed by a museum curator and the fish visitor stops at none of exhibits and moves only to the center of the room.

The preference weight randomness step generates varying stopover times at exhibits. Both ant and fish styles show no significant difference among their preferences of exhibits. Second, the visit time distribution functions are different among visiting styles. Third, noise synthesis is conducted using a Gaussian PDF. The implication of noise is randomly short stops in the exhibition area. Then, the smooth filtering such as a low pass filter is applied in order to discard the sharp detail and remove the noise. An example of the ant, fish, grasshopper, and butterfly visit maps derived by using the procedure is shown in Fig. 1 (a)-(d), respectively.

The aforementioned synthesis procedures require to construct a Voronoi partition of the set of pixels in a museum area. This is a division of the museum area into regions around each exhibit; a region is the set of pixels that are closer to that exhibit than to any other. Let $\mathbf{h}_k$ be the position of exhibit k and let $H = \{\mathbf{h}_k | 1 \leq k \leq M\}$ be a set of all positions of exhibits, where M is a total exhibit. Let $\mathbf{u}$ be the position of a visitor. The exhibit $\mathbf{h}_{k^*}$ nearest to a visitor $\mathbf{u}$ is calculated by the following

$$k^* = \operatorname{argmin}_k \|\mathbf{h}_k - \mathbf{u}\| \quad where \quad 1 \leq k \leq M \tag{2}$$

where $\|\mathbf{h}_k - \mathbf{u}\|$ is the Euclidean distance between exhibit $\mathbf{h}_k$ and visitor $\mathbf{u}$.

Table 2. Notations used in the synthesis procedures of four visiting styles

$U = \{(i_1, i_2)\|1 \leq i_1 \leq m,\ 1 \leq i_2 \leq n\}$:	The set of pixels in a museum area
$V = \{v(i)\|i \in U\}$:	Visit map
$H = \{h(k)\|1 \leq k \leq M\}$:	A set of all positions of exhibits
$v(i)$:	The visitor's stopover time at pixel i, called *Visit time*
h_k:	The position of exhibit k
M:	A total exhibit
$S(h_k)$:	A set of pixels **i** belonging to h_k
w_k:	The preference weight of exhibit h_k

3 Classification System of Visitors' Behaviors in 3D Virtual Museums

3.1 Proposed Function of Visitor's Attention at Each Exhibit

Considering the visualization scheme of visiting styles in [10,12], we can discard the temporal information in trajectories data of visitor movement in a museum. Given a visit map, V, it is obvious that a dark colored area is a key role to identify the visiting styles because it illustrates a long stopover. However, the dark colored area near or far from an exhibit is considered as a parameter to measure the visitors' attention to the exhibit. Given a museum area, U, the observation distance and map are defined as follows.

1. Observation distance $o(i)$ is defined as the visitor's fuzzy distance from the nearest exhibit
2. Observation map is defined as a set of $o(i)$, where $i \in U$

To compute the observation distance, the observation distance function $\Psi(h_k, u)$ is defined as an exponential function of the distance from an exhibit h_k to a visitor u as follows:

$$\Psi(h_k, u) = e^{-\rho\|h_k - u\|^2} \tag{3}$$

ρ is a weighted constant. In the same manner of an Gaussian-based activation function, this weighted constant is obtained from the variance of the Euclidean distance between exhibit h_k and pixel **i**, for all h_k and **i**, as shown in Eq.(4).

$$\mu = mean\left\{\bigcup\nolimits_{h_k \in H \,\wedge\, i \in U} \|h_k - i\|\right\} \tag{4a}$$

$$\sigma^2 = mean\left\{\bigcup\nolimits_{h_k \in H \,\wedge\, i \in U} (\|h_k - i\| - \mu)^2\right\} \tag{4b}$$

$$\rho = 2\sigma^2 \tag{4c}$$

Fig. 4 shows a graph plotting of $\Psi(h_i, u)$ and $\|h_k - v\|$ where σ^2 is 0.07. The observation distance is calculated as follows:

$$o(i) = \Psi(h_k, i) \quad where \quad i \in S(h_k) \tag{5}$$

Procedure: Synthesis of *Ant* visiting style
Input: H
Output: V
Step 1: Preference weight randomness is set by using the Gaussian PDF with the mean closer to 1 and smallest variance.
Step 2: Visit time $v(\mathbf{i})$ at pixel $\mathbf{i}$ is defined by using the following equation:
$$v(\mathbf{i}) = w_k e^{-\rho\|\mathbf{h}_k - \mathbf{i}\|^2} \text{ where } \mathbf{i} \in S(\mathbf{k})$$
Step 3: Smoothing filter is applied to the visit map obtained from Step 2.

Procedure: Synthesis of *Fish* visiting style
Input: H
Output: V
Step 1: Preference weight randomness is set by using the Gaussian PDF with the mean closer to 1 and smallest variance.
Step 2: Visit time $v(\mathbf{i})$ at pixel $\mathbf{i}$ is defined by using the following equation:
$$v(\mathbf{i}) = w_k(1 - e^{-\rho\|\mathbf{h}_k - \mathbf{i}\|^2}) \text{ where } \mathbf{i} \in S(\mathbf{k})$$
Step 3: Smoothing filter is applied to the visit map obtained from Step 2.

Procedure: Synthesis of *Grasshopper* visiting style
Input: H
Output: V
Step 1: Selective exhibit randomness is decided by using Beta PDF with $\gamma = 1$ and $\beta = 5$.
$$P(\eta) = \frac{\eta^{\alpha-1}(1-\eta)^{\beta-1}}{\Gamma(\alpha)\Gamma(\beta)}\Gamma(\alpha + \beta)$$
where Γ is the gamma function and the parameters α and β are related through
$\alpha = \mu\gamma$ and $\beta = (1 - \mu)\gamma$ where $\gamma = \frac{\mu(1-\mu)}{\sigma} - 1$.
The output of the PDF is the number of selected exhibits, as denoted by L.
Then, then selective exhibit is defined as a binary vector where f_i is an element of the binary vector and $\sum_i f_i$ must be L.
Step 2: Preference weight randomness is set by using the Gaussian PDF with the mean closer to 1 and small variance.
Step 3: Visit time $v(\mathbf{i})$ at pixel $\mathbf{i}$ is defined by using the following equation:
$$v(\mathbf{i}) = \begin{cases} w_k e^{-\rho\|\mathbf{h}_k - \mathbf{i}\|^2} & \text{if } \mathbf{i} \in S(\mathbf{k}) \text{ and } f_k = 1 \\ 0 & \text{otherwise} \end{cases}$$
Step 4: Noise synthesis is performed by using Gaussian PDF.
Step 5: Smoothing filter is applied to the visit map obtained from Step 4.

Procedure: Synthesis of *Butterfly* visiting style
Input: H
Output: V
Step 1: Selective exhibit randomness is decided by using Beta PDF with $\gamma = 5$ and $\beta = 1$.
$$P(\eta) = \frac{\eta^{\alpha-1}(1-\eta)^{\beta-1}}{\Gamma(\alpha)\Gamma(\beta)}\Gamma(\alpha + \beta)$$
where Γ is the gamma function and the parameters α and β are related through
$\alpha = \mu\gamma$ and $\beta = (1 - \mu)\gamma$ where $\gamma = \frac{\mu(1-\mu)}{\sigma} - 1$.
The output of the PDF is the number of selected exhibits, as denoted by L.
Then, then selective exhibit is defined as a binary vector where f_i is an element of the binary vector and $\sum_i f_i$ must be L.
Step 2: Preference weight randomness is set by using the Gaussian PDF with the mean closer to 1 and variance higher than the ant's.
Step 3: Visit time $v(\mathbf{i})$ at pixel $\mathbf{i}$ is defined by using the following equation:
$$v(\mathbf{i}) = \begin{cases} w_k e^{-\rho\|\mathbf{h}_k - \mathbf{i}\|^2} & \text{if } \mathbf{i} \in S(\mathbf{k}) \text{ and } f_k = 1 \\ 0 & \text{otherwise} \end{cases}$$
Step 4: Noise synthesis is performed by using Gaussian PDF.
Step 5: Smoothing filter is applied to the visit map obtained from Step. 4.

Fig. 3. Synthesis procedures of four visiting styles

The visitor's attention at exhibit $\mathbf{h}_k$ is computed by using the visit time and the observation distance belonging to $S(\mathbf{h}_k)$, as shown below:

$$A(\mathbf{h}_k) = mean \left\{ \bigcup_{\mathbf{i} \in S(\mathbf{h}_k)} \{o(\mathbf{i})\, v(\mathbf{i})\} \right\} \tag{6}$$

where $S(\mathbf{h}_k)$ is a set of pixels $\mathbf{i}$ belonging to $\mathbf{h}_k$, as defined by Eq.(2), and $o(\mathbf{i}) \geq \delta$. δ is a threshold in the range from 0 to 1, which its implication is a observation distance limit.

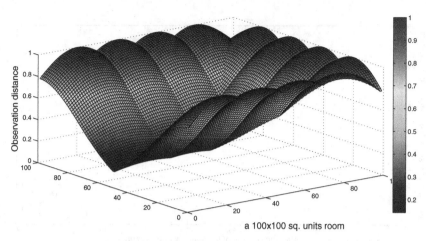

Fig. 4. Observation distance function of Eq.(3) where $H = \{(1, 20), (1, 40), (1, 60),$ $(1, 80), (20, 100), (40, 100), (60, 100), (80, 100), (100, 20), (100, 40), (100, 60), (100, 80)\}$

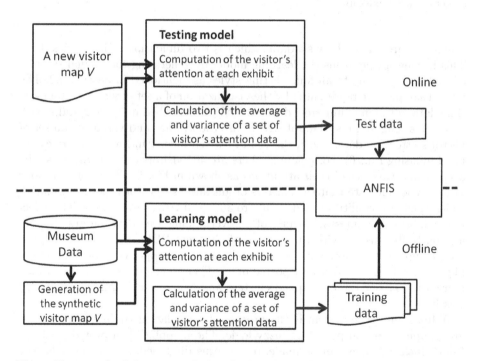

Fig. 5. Framework of the proposed classification system in off-line and on-line stages

3.2 Framework of Classification System

An overview of the proposed classification system is divided into on-line and off-line stages corresponding to learning and testing models, respectively. These models deal with the museum data, which is a set of the exhibits' positions in

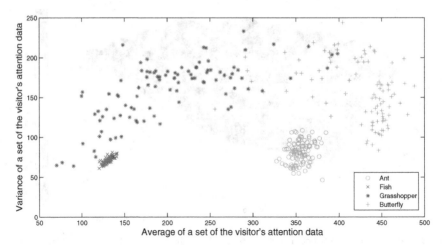

Fig. 6. 400 visitors of four clusters are plotted on the average and variance of their attention at all exhibits

a museum area, and the visit data, which is two dimensional time-series data. This framework performs the learning model by generating the virtual samples of visitors belonging to all four visiting styles as mentioned in Section 2.2. The virtual samples are represented by the visualization of a set of visitors' stopover-time data in the museum area, denoted by V as described in Table 2 and Fig. 3.

The training and test data of ANFIS are the average and variance of a set of visitor's attention data, which the visitor's attentions $A(\mathbf{h}_k)$ for all k are calculated by using Eq.(6). For example, there are 400 visitors each of which has the average and variance of their attentions as shown in Fig. 6. The clusters of four visitor types indicate that the clusters of ant and fish visitor types are isolated, which their probabilities found in [6] are 30% and 20%, respectively. The selective exhibit randomness is a cause of an overlapping area between grasshopper and butterfly clusters with the result that the Beta PDFs of both visitor types are a common area. However, the probability of grasshopper visitors found in the physical world is only 10% as reported in [6]. Therefore, a fuzzy inference system is used to classify the overlapped clusters and generate a linguistic rule-based classfier.

A fuzzy inference system is the process of formulating the mapping from a given input to an output using fuzzy logic. The mapping then provides a basis from which decisions can be made, or patterns discerned. ANFIS includes the neuro-adaptive learning method that works similarly to that of neural networks. The neuro-adaptive learning techniques provide a method for the fuzzy modeling procedure to learn information about a data set. The training data set is a set of input-output data, which the input data is the average and variance of a set of attention data obtained from the synthetic visit maps and the output is their visiting styles in the off-line stage, whereas the test data is from a new visitor in the on-line stage.

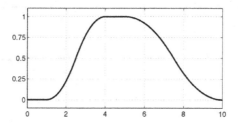

Fig. 7. Spline-curve-based membership function with the parameters $[a, b, c, d] = [1, 4, 5, 10]$

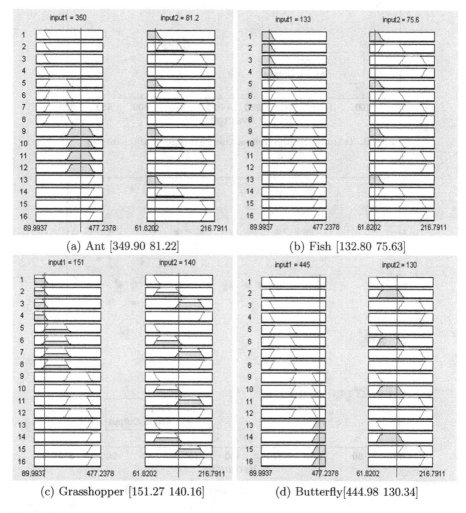

Fig. 8. Four examples of 16 spline-curve-based rules combining of two ANFIS inputs, [average variance]: (a) Ant, (b) Fish, (c) Grasshopper, and (d) Butterfly

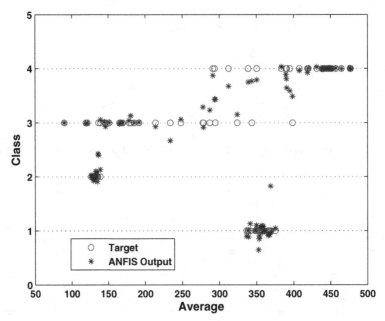

Fig. 9. Training results versus their average of 100 samples

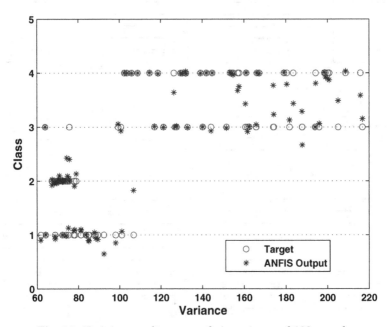

Fig. 10. Training results versus their variance of 100 samples

4   Experimental Results

In our experiment, we generated the total of 100 synthetic data by using the aforementioned procedures. Using the uniform distribution to generates the data portion, the percentages of the four styles are 21, 22, 25, and 32, respectively. In the off-line stage, we used the spline-based curve, i.e., a built-in membership function in MATLAB. Its parameters a and d locate the feet of the curve, while b and c locate its shoulders as shown in Fig. 7. The number of membership functions are four per variable; therefore, four by four rules are produced from two variables, i.e., the average and variance of a visitor's attention. The ANFIS outputs are four classes corresponding to ant, fish, grasshopper, and butterfly styles. In the off-line stage, we trained the ANFIS against the synthetic data and obtained the training error of 4%. Fig. 8 shows 16 produced rules built by spline curves. The degree of color intensity in spline curves indicate the fuzzy degree of the average or variance in according to rules. Fig. 9 and 9 show the ANFIS outputs comparing with their targets versus their averages and their variances, respectively.

The on-line stage is tested against 36 avatars in RDAP (Ritsumeikan Digital Archiving Pavilion). RDAP is a virtual gallery displaying the kimono textiles of 19 objects. All avatars intentionally explored the gallery following their assigned styles. In this experiment, the number of ant, fish, grasshopper, and butterfly visitors are equally set to 9. Then, the classification accuracy of on-line stage is 83%.

5   Conclusions and Discussions

In this paper, we propose the on-line classification system that its off-line stage can be trained by using the synthetic data. We, also, introduce the algorithms of generating the synthetic data of four visiting styles as defined in [5,10]. We, then, conduct an adaptive neuro-fuzzy inference system (ANFIS) trained by the synthetic visitor data in the off-line stage and tested by the new visitor data in the on-line stage.

Since the overlapping between two clusters of grasshopper and butterfly, we exploit fuzzy paradigm for dealing with continuous and imprecise variables. Two reasons of using ANFIS are the followings. First, fuzzy inference system (FIS) employing fuzzy if-then rules that can model the qualitative aspects of human knowledge and reasoning processes without employing precise quantitative analyses. Second, ANFIS uses a hybrid learning algorithm to identify parameters of Sugeno-type fuzzy inference systems.

In our future work, we will implement the on-line classification in Second Life in order to investigate user behaviors in 3D virtual museums comparing with those in real museums. A recommendation of personal route map is one of applications when a 3D virtual museum can classify the visitor style of a user. The system can recommend new artifacts, exhibitions, and events and navigate a route direction by using our proposed function of measuring the visitors' attention of each exhibit.

References

1. Urban, R., Marty, P., Twidale, M.: A second life for your museum: 3d multi-user virtual environments and museums. In: Museums and Web 2007. Archives & Museum Informatics, Toronto (March 2007)
2. Sookhanaphibarn, K., Thawonmas, R.: A framework for design and evaluation of digital museums in second life as learning institutions. In: Proceedings of International Conference on Information Hiding and Multimedia Signal Processing (IIH-MSP). IEEE, Los Alamitos (2009)
3. Sookhanaphibarn, K., Thawonmas, R.: A content management system for user-driven museums in second life. In: Proceedings of International Conference on Cyberworld. IEEE, Los Alamitos (2009)
4. Oberlander, J., Karakatsiotis, G., Isard, A.: Androutsopoulos: Building an adaptive museum gallery in second life. In: Proceedings of Museum and the Web, Montreal, Quebec, Canada, pp. 749–753 (2008)
5. Veron, E., Levasseur, M.: Bibliothque publique d'Information. Centre Georges Pompidou, Paris (1983)
6. Bianchi, A., Zancanaro, M.: Tracking users' movements in an artistic physical space. In: The i^3 Annual Conference, held in Siena, Italy, October 20-22, pp. 103–106 (1999)
7. Gabrielli, F., Marti, P., Petroni, L.: The environment as interface. In: The i^3 Annual Conference, held in Siena, Italy, October 20-22, pp. 44–47 (1999)
8. Zancanaro, M., Kuflik, T., Boger, Z., Goren-Bar, D., Goldwasser, D.: Analyzing museum visitors behavior patterns. In: Conati, C., McCoy, K., Paliouras, G. (eds.) UM 2007. LNCS (LNAI), vol. 4511, pp. 238–246. Springer, Heidelberg (2007)
9. Hatala, M., Wakkary, R.: Ontology-based user modeling in an augmented audio reality system for museums. User Modeling and User-Adapted Interaction (3-4), 339–380 (2005)
10. Chittaro, L., Ieronutti, L.: A visual tool for tracing users' behavior in virtual environments. In: AVI 2004: Proceedings of the Working Conference on Advanced Visual Interfaces, pp. 40–47. ACM, New York (2004)
11. Kotz, S., Balakrishnan, N., Johnson, N.L.: Continuous Multivariate Distributions, Models and Applications, 2nd edn. Wiley Series in Probability and Statistics, vol. 1 (2000)
12. Sookhanaphibarn, K., Thawonmas, R.: A movement data analysis and synthesis tool for museum visitors' behaviors. In: Proceedings of Pacific-Rim Conference on Multimedia. IEEE, Los Alamitos (2009)

A Machine That Daydreams

Graham A. Mann

School of Information Technology
Murdoch University
South St. Murdoch, Western Australia
g.mann@murdoch.edu.au

Abstract. Some aspects of human cognitive processing across experiential cases in episodic memory seem quite different from conventional artificial reasoning by logical rules, such as that seen in CBR systems. One difference is that in
humans, linkages between particular experiences can apparently be made in a
number of qualitatively different ways, forming recollective chains of memories along different dimensions. Data-driven, creative, free-association from one
memory to the next does not appear to be economically described by rules. Efforts to enable computers to deal with cultural content such as narratives in new
ways could benefit from sequential indexing of this kind, provided that the conceptual representations are rich enough, and that a way can be found of modeling the emotional impact each elicits. A conceptual-graph-based FGP (Fetch,
Generalise, Project) machine using a knowledgebase of archetypical narratives
enhanced with affect is described, which demonstrates how such emotive
"memory-walks" can be computed.

Keywords: cultural computing, narratives, conceptual graphs, affective
computing.

1 Introduction

If computer scientists are to a stake any further claim on cultural content, it will be
because i) their representations begin to include new forms, whether traditional expressions of culture that had never before been captured or entirely novel forms that
had never before been conceived and ii) they discover ways to go beyond today's
replay of cultural forms using linear, prescriptive representations for passive mass
consumption, to entirely new paradigms of cultural expression, manipulation and engagement. Such a shift began with the manifestations of interactive computer-based
artforms such as games, simulations and video performances. It can now progress to
more sophisticated forms of interaction, particularly through very close attention
to user's aesthetic experience, adding more sensory modalities, in-depth character
depiction and very flexible user involvement in the generation of and interplay with
storylines. Thought of this way, *cultural computing* involves not only the storage,
manipulation and playback of cultural content such as personal histories, minority
languages, myths, belief systems, poetical traditions etc. for human use, but also lays

R. Nakatsu et al. (Eds.): ECS 2010, IFIP AICT 333, pp. 21–35, 2010.

the foundations of enriched cultural processes which enable human and machine systems to create, experience and appreciate these forms in new ways.

Computer-based models of narrative processes, such as storytelling, have long been a staple of cognitive science. Even the early programs at the Yale University group lead by Roger Schank and his students such TALESPIN [1] and BORIS [2] showed that special purpose heuristic rules applied to properly-designed conceptual representations can achieve a remarkable degree of commonsense understanding of stories, in question-answering, summarization and translation tasks. More recently, Henrik Scharfe has demonstrated Prolog programs capable of identifying complex actantial roles and functions in the deep content of narratives such as Biblical texts, represented as conceptual graphs [3], while Elson and McKeown have developed SCHEHERAZADE, a promising platform for abstract conceptual processing in this domain [4]. Yet programs of this ilk seem to be missing a certain kind thinking familiar to humans. A good part of our understanding evidently draws on our store of experiences in episodic memory, through which our attention makes more of less controlled excursions that are sometimes called "memory-walks". Whether in well-organised, goal-oriented, rational trains of thought or in free associations with one idea recalling another almost at random, variations on these memory-walks are a familiar part of mental life. The mechanisms by which one experiential pattern may summon another, somehow similar pattern has also been of interest to the computing community since at least the origins of case-based reasoning (CBR) in the 1970s. "Reminding" is a recurring topic in memory-oriented views of conceptual processing [5]. In 1994, David Gelernter articulated a theory of "musing" to account for the memory walk phenomenon [6]. The theory conjectures that human minds link ideas together in different ways according to a continuum of mental focus, ranging from strictly constrained and quite logical operations on specifically selected ideas at the high end, through looser, more idiosyncratic and general connections between groups of related ideas in the middle range, to affect-linked or random "daydreaming" across the entire episodic memory at the low end.

To ratify part of the theory, a data-driven algorithm called the FGP (Fetch, Generalise, Project) machine was written to test the high-focus mode of reasoning [7]. In one experiment, the machine is tested on a series of room descriptions encoded as simple attribute pairs (e.g. ((oven yes) (computer no) (coffee-machine yes) (sink yes) (sofa no)). The program is to describe the kind of room which has a particular attribute or attributes, and is given an appropriate probe vector (e.g. (oven yes)). The FGP machine first fetches all the cases which closely match the probe attributes. It places these into a "memory sandwich" and examines this longitudinally for common attributes. If all cases in the sandwich have a common attribute, the program generalises, guessing that all cases with the probe attribute will also have the common attribute. If many of the cases have some attribute, the program "projects", or speculates that this attribute could be characteristic, and recursively uses this attribute as a probe. If the memory sandwich returned by this recursive probe is a good match to the characteristic pattern of attributes built up so far, the program accepts the putative attribute; if not, the attribute is discarded and the next attribute considered. The process continues this *fetch-generalise-project* cycle until all attributes have been accounted for, returning a composite room description.

An FGP machine may be described formally as follows: Let T be a feature tuple, M be an unordered database of feature tuples and L be a list of Ts, ordered by a suitably defined proximity metric to some arbitrary T. Then let the following functions be defined:

- *fetch* $(T, M) \longrightarrow L$ Given a single pattern T, returns an ordered list L of patterns from M which are closer than some threshold to T in the problem space.
- *generalise* $(L) \longrightarrow T$ Given a list L of patterns, generate a new pattern T, which captures general features of all patterns in L. The contribution of each element of L to the new gene-ralised pattern depends on its ordinal position in L and on the element's status as either a prototype or an ordinary case.
- *project* $(T) \longrightarrow T'$ Given a single pattern T, returns a new pattern T', which contains a sub-set of the most "evocative" features of T, and which thereby shifts subsequent processing in-to new regions of the problem place.

The basic aim is to answer a query input by the user. Queries can be either a pair $(T_0, a?)$ consisting of a test feature tuple and a single attribute, or else a single tuple T_0. An answer to the first query will be value of a for T_0, while the second query examines the cases for a prototypical redescription of T_0. In effect, it summons the memory walk process, asking "what does T_0 bring to mind?". From the initial T_0, the following two-step executive cycle calls the functions:

repeat (T_i, M)

    1) Extend: *generalise* $(fetch (T_i, M)) \longrightarrow T$
    2) Refocus: *project* $(T) \longrightarrow T'$
        for each feature of T'
            generalise $(fetch (T', M)) \longrightarrow T_{i+1}$

The cycle iterates until either a) a value for a is discovered or b) an iteration produces no new conclusions. Gelernter and Fertig's tests of the FGP machine on two databas-es show a predictive or diagnostic performance level close to or better than human domain experts in the same task (65% vs. a human expert's 53% correct predictions of the nationality of folkdances from a database of descriptive features, and 70% com-pared with a medical specialist's 60% correct differential diagnoses from descriptions of mammograms). Qualitatively, the behaviour of the program is interesting, as it interacts with the user, reporting its progress through the cycle of reminding, generali-sation and speculation in a very lifelike fashion.

The ability to find logical relationships in data without any explicit rules is valua-ble enough, but Gelernter wanted to improve the FGP machine in two ways. First, he argued that more and better relationships could be found if the cases were better re-presentations of real situations. This might also allow interactions with the machine to be carried out in natural language, making it easier to use. Second, he wanted a method by which affective states - emotions - can be represented in cases. These could be used to perform a kind linking at lower focus levels. In affect, the machine could make connections between situations which had the same emotional connota-tions. His own experiments apparently never pursued these in practice, but in Gelernter's hypothetical dialogues about such linking [6, p.145-146], a low-focussed FGP machine recognises the displeased state of a user, is reminded of a literary character by the plaintiff of a legal case study, and refuses to obey a request for financial help because the subject matter is boring!

The point of the current work is to pursue this line of development, and show how affective associations might be used to make computer reasoning more suited to cultural computing - more lifelike, more creative, and better grounded in emotions. Could a modern representation system, such as conceptual graphs [8], overcome the first problem? How can the design of the FGP machine be updated so that it functions with structured propositional forms instead of unstructured collections of features? And could the improved representations also incorporate emotional patterns, thus enabling affect-linking? In this paper, I answer these questions in the course of redesigning the FGP machine and making it work at lower focus levels.

2   Encoding of Aesop's Fables

For the current experiments, Townsend's translation of Aesop's fables [9] was chosen as an example of cultural content. Originating in approximately 600BC these are, of course, far from a new form, but here they will be encoded as conceptual representations so that they be dealt with and experienced in a new way – in a machine that meditates on their meanings and can mimic, at least in a simple form, some of the elements of human daydreaming. Practically speaking, the fables of Aesop were chosen for two reasons. First, it is difficult to overstate the impact of these narratives on the modern imagination of many societies. They form a fundamental wellspring of moral principles, animal archetypes and cautionary entertainment in both the Western and (since they were translated in Japan in the 16th century and China in 17th century) the Eastern traditions alike. Second, although the fables represent important cultural ideals, most are simple and short enough to make the task of encoding them into a consistent framework a practical proposition. For example, the following fable

The Wolf and the Crane

A Wolf who had a bone stuck in his throat hired a Crane, for a large sum, to put her head into his mouth and draw out the bone. When the Crane had extracted the bone from the throat of the Wolf and demanded the promised payment, the Wolf, grinning and grinding his teeth, exclaimed: "Why, you have surely already had a sufficient recompense, in having been permitted to draw out your head in safety from the mouth and jaws of a wolf." Moral: In serving the wicked, expect no reward, and be thankful if you escape injury for your pains. - Adapted from [9]

may be represented using a list of five conceptual graphs to encode the body of the story and one to represent the moral. The representations are composed of concept and relational instances from a catalogue of formal objects and are semantically "deep", in that they are invariant with respect to variations in surface expressive form; paraphrases, even in different languages, should map to identical graphs. For more detail on conceptual representations of this kind, see [10]. Building working conceptual structures at this level presents many difficulties. For one, a consistent ontology in the form of a conceptual and relational catalogues, containing all elements appearing in the fables is must be built, a substantial and ongoing task. Then once the elements are available for modeling, many questions remain about how best to compose logical representations of the actions, events, states, situations and juxtapositions that arise in the fables, simple as they are. Such structural ambiguity is probably inevitable with any truly expressive conceptual language. Although the encodings of the meanings underlying the fables provided for this experiment are still crude in many ways, they are sufficient to illustrate the principles and explore some of the potential of this sort of play.

A proper demonstration of the daydreaming effect with the new FGP machine will require a good many fables to be codified. The easiest way to produce these would be to use a conceptual parser, such as SAVVY - part of the author's larger conceptual graph processing toolkit written in Common Lisp [11] - to automatically convert Townsend's natural language sentences into conceptual graph form. For example, the phrase

> *"...the crane extracted the bone from the throat of the Wolf..."*

will, if input to the parser, generate the following graph in linear form (which is easiest for conventional computer input/output):

$$[PTRANS] -$$
$$(AGNT) \rightarrow [CRANE:\#]$$
$$(OBJ) \rightarrow [BONE:\#]$$
$$(SRCE) \rightarrow [THROAT] \leftarrow (PART) \leftarrow [WOLF:\#]$$
$$(DEST) \rightarrow [PLACE]$$
$$(INST) \rightarrow [PHYSOBJ]$$

This is a case-role representation organised around the action primitive [PTRANS], which was retrieved from SAVVY's lexicon by the principal verb "extracted". In accordance with Schank's primitive action theory [12], PTRANS covers all instances involving the physical transfer of a object from one location to another, and carries with it a set of five thematic case roles as slots to be filled from other elements of the input expression during parsing, if possible. These are represented by the relations (AGNT), (OBJ), etc. each attached to a concept enforcing a type selection constraint for the give role e.g. the agentive role (AGNT) is attached to [ANIMATE], which can only be restricted to a more specific concept that can serve that role (of type PERSON or ANIMAL). As parsing continues, actors connected to the prototype [PTRANS] template search the input stream right and left for concepts capable of filling each role. When one is found, a restrict operation to replace the general concept is placed on the parser's recommendation list (the concept [CRANE:#], retrieved earlier from the noun phrase "the crane" replaces [ANIMATE] in the example). At the end of each textual unit, the recommendations are examined by a simple algorithm which resolves any competing claims on each role and executes a series of join operations to form the final conceptual graph. If a role's slot cannot be filled from the available information, it simply remains unspecified. Thus the ultimate destination of the bone is not specified by the above sentence, and so remains at the general but meaningful concept [PLACE], which might be read as "some unspecified place", pending further information.

The SAVVY parser can handle several kinds of phrasal structure and multi-sentence paragraph-length texts, but it cannot build very complex, nested graphical structures with subtle contexts and relationships of the kind needed for many of the sentences in Aesopian texts. Therefore, in creating the knowledgebase $\mathcal{M}$, most of the conceptual graphs were actually hand-crafted, a laborious and time-consuming process. The inadequacy of today's conceptual parsers is not especially problematic for the present experiments (except that it takes longer) though of course the problem is generally an important one; of more immediate concern is the need to convert conceptual graphs into English expressions, so that the results of processing them can be expressed in a lifelike way. The author's existing Lisp toolkit had no such generator, so one had to be built for these experiments. So far, the GRAVY English generator performs only a simple analysis on an input graph, recognises it as one or more stereotyped grammatical forms, usually organised around a principal verb or contextual form. Thematic role cases and their extension graphs are located, and a textual expression is opportunistically assembled, using words created from the conceptual type labels. This is done because although the program's lexicon contains definitions in conceptual graph form, indexing it in reverse to find suitable words for conceptual graphs is theoretically and practically troublesome. The problem with the shortcut of using type labels is that they are not really words, and choosing an apt verb phrase or noun phrase for complex aggregations is a non-trivial recognition task. Thus the above conceptual graph, when processed by the generator, produces the somewhat awkward

"The crane ptransed the bone from the throat of the wolf to a place."

Once again, although graphs of great subtlety cannot be properly expressed, GRAVY is still sufficient to add some realism to the CG-FGP machine's fragmentary day-dreams.

3 Rational Linking

What modifications need to be made to *fetch*, *generalise* and *project* to make them work in the CG-FGP machine? To begin with, they should be renamed *CG-fetch*, *CG-generalise* and *CG-project*, to distinguish them from the existing functions. We must deal with each function in turn to make it perform the equivalent function over the knowledgebase of fables, but this time at a medium or low focus. Before that, however, it is necessary to discuss some general obstacles to this development. One obstacle is that the original $\mathcal{T}$ feature tuples contained numerical weightings indicating their frequency of occurrence in generalisations, or their importance in prototypes, which information was needed by the *generalise* function. For example, if in a barrel of 100 apples half were red and the other half green, this would be represented as

((name apple 100) (type fruit 100) (colour (red 50) (green 50))).

How may this be done in a conceptual graph i.e. what is the equivalent of an attribute-value pair, and where should the weight be stored? While numerical values can easily be represented in conceptual graphs, the position advocated here is that since the numbers could mean relative importance as well as frequency counts, it is better not to try to explicitly represent them in the graph. Instead, the weights will be invisibly annotated to the concepts using an internal mechanism at implementation level, so that they do not appear explicitly the following graph, thus avoiding a commitment at the knowledge level:

[APPLE: {*}] -

(CHRC) -> [COLOUR:Red]
(CHRC) -> [COLOUR:Green]

With this kind of representation, the "scope" of the weights can be restricted to the concepts themselves, which seem to encompass both attribute and value. But with most representations, as above, relation-concept pairs are attached to a main stem as cases. To correspond strictly to attribute-value weighting, a weight would have to apply to the linkage of relation and concept only, but the picture is complicated by the realisation that the colours of apples should not be confused with the colours of other objects, though their relation-concept pairs appear the same. So perhaps the weights should cover concept-relation-concept triples. Yet this argument applies recursively, threatening to demand that weights must only apply to entire graphs, which is clearly going too far. Moderation here seems appropriate: triples seem to have enough structure to avoid confusion during weight summation, yet not so much as to blur the distinction between separate features.

The richer, more complex conceptual structures pose other problems for finding commonalities across cases, compared to the simple feature tuples in Gelernter's representations. For one, the fables are partitioned into four separate contexts. Should longitudinal comparisons across cases be made only through corresponding contexts, or should relationships to different contexts be sought? It could be argued that the value of reminding lies in its power to discover unexpected relationships across cases, so that restricting the possibilities is defeating the purpose of the exercise. On the other hand, the point of contexts is to establish boundaries of relevance, and restricting processing to only corresponding contexts greatly reduces computation during each cycle. So if only for feasibility's sake, the corresponding-context-only policy may be forced.

Furthermore, each context may contain more than one graph. How can corresponding contexts be directly compared if they have different numbers of graphs? A strict policy would forbid any such matching as potentially invalid. A more liberal approach seems preferable here. If total structure is not regarded as essential for a match, triples from any graph within a context should still probably be permitted to match pairs or triples from any graph in the corresponding context of another case. The more structure there is in a match probe, the less likely this is to lead to an invalid result, and not to permit within-context graph confusion would be to risk missing important relationships.

Better opportunities to find commonalities across cases could be had if their graphs were entered into the database in standardised forms. (Put more strongly, adequate methods have yet to be created to run all functions of the CG-FGP machine on non-standardised graphs). Though this creates an additional expressive constraint, that is not necessarily a bad tradeoff. The task might even be automated: Mineau [13] has suggested that excess variability in conceptual graphs - a range of ontological choices and structural compositions beyond that which is strictly necessary to encode different meanings - might be reduced by automatically *normalising* the graphs. He outlines eight basic methods for normalisation, including checking against a graph grammar, restriction of choice to "privileged" relations and the use of rewrite rules. If these were applied to a database immediately after input, runtime performance would not be compromised.

Consider now the modifications required for the three basic functions.

• *CG-fetch* must now take a conceptual graph T and return a short list of graphs L from M which are semantically close to T and to each other. The semantic distance measure used must take account of similarity in, but not depend on, graphical structure. Furthermore, in the high-focus mode, it must take into account the "evocative-ness", or ability to add informative value, of the features within the graphs with respect to the query, which takes the form of a request to instantiate variables in T with one or more specific concepts.

Since this mapping is expected to be far more computationally expensive than that of *fetch,* an effort must be made to define an efficiently computable measure D of distance between conceptual graphs. Traditionally, this has been done by taking the sum over corresponding concepts in the two graphs of the distances on the type hierarchy between each concept's type and the most specific type which subsumes them both (minimal common generalisation). However, Wuwongse and Niyomthai [14] have that cogently argued that because concepts are not regarded as equally salient in human intuitions of similarity, so the orthodox semantic distance (SD) sum should be influenced by perceived importance values (IV) associated with the concepts:

$$D = \Sigma_{i=1}^n (IV_i - SD_i)$$
(1)

Normally the salience term IV presents a problem, because it requires a number to be assigned to each concept in the system manually, based on psychological data. Here we have the opportunity to automatically weight each distance measure by the "evo-cativeness" of T with respect to a query. This is a measure of how strongly and clearly T brings to mind a distinct value for the query. Fertig and Gelernter [7] used an in-formation-theoretic formula in which the information gain (negative entropy) on the query from T is defined as:

$$S = \frac{1}{\ln N} \left(-\frac{\Sigma_i n_i \ln n_i}{T} + \ln T \right)$$
(2)

where
N is the total number of possible values for the goal in M
n_i is the number of times goal value i appears in the top-cluster
T is the total number of goal values found in the top-cluster

S ranges from a 0 (maximum evocativeness) to 1 (minimum evocativeness). An equivalent computation can be made over conceptual graphs. Evocativeness E can then be included as a weight for each difference in our graph-matching measure with respect to the goal:

$$D = \Sigma_{i=1}^n SD_i (1-S_i)$$
(3)

Note that unlike Wuwongse and Niyomthai's importance values these measures of salience are automatically computed with respect to a given goal, then multiplied by the semantic distance measure. We might also require a way of ensuring that the graphs in L form a tight 'top-cluster', delineated from others in $\mathcal{M}$ by a discernable natural gap in semantic distances. Such a gap can be detected by performing a crude cluster analysis on the elements of the summed semantic distances. It results in a small number of close graphs being included in L each time *CG-fetch* is run.

• *CG-generalise.* The requirement to collapse the ordered list L of $\mathcal{T}$s into one which captures essential elements of each presents a real problem if multiple graphs are allowed in case contexts. While it is possible to imagine techniques which find the correct correspondences for longitudinal coalescence across multi-graph contexts, the problem is formidable, and when taken together with the other problems this causes, a good case emerges for requiring contexts to be standardised (or normalised) single graphs as discussed above. With that constraint the problem simplifies to the extraction of high-frequency or weighty features and the elimination of contradictory features. These features are then instantiated into a template for this context's standard graph form. Since $\mathcal{T}$s which are ranked higher on L exert a greater influence than later $\mathcal{T}$s, this is best organised as an iterative process.

> Begin $\mathcal{T}$ as a new copy of the template for the current context
> For each $\mathcal{T}_i$ in L
>   For each concept j in $\mathcal{T}$
> $\text{Weight}_j = \max \dfrac{\text{count}(j, \mathcal{T}_i) * \text{position}(\mathcal{T}_i, L) * \varepsilon}{\text{length}(L)}$
> Eliminate all features of $\mathcal{T}$ with a weight $< \theta$

This algorithm adds new features to the evolving generalisation, but records agreements and disagreements in later graphs, allowing features with contradictory values to eliminated at step 4. ε and θ are arbitrary thresholds which are easily set to properly detect commonality or contradiction, respectively, across small lengths of L.

• *CG-project.* This function must take a single graph and return a subgraph containing its most evocative features. Evocation has been discussed already; the feature's attribute must be evocative with respect to the query For a given relation-concept pair, the possible different concept attachments could be simply counted. A feature can then be excluded from $\mathcal{T}$ if

$$(1 - S) < \alpha \qquad (4)$$

where
  α is arbitrary threshold selected to allow interesting features to prevail.

The structure of the returned subgraph must resemble something of the original. With stem-and-case structures, this is simply a matter of preserving the stem, and pruning some of the relation-concept cases away. Theoretically, any substructure may contain regularities for future processing, so it is not essential; it may simply help with higher level processing, such as natural language description.

4 Affective Linking

A key aspect of human cognition which must now be brought into the picture is emotional reaction, which are commonly experienced from (indeed, are much of the essence of) stories. By so doing, we can hope to provide for i) the evaluation of otherwise unclassifiable objects, events and situations ii) distinctive signaling of important bodily and mental states for behaviour control and iii) positive and negative reinforcement for learning. Here, we focus on the value of affect as an important linkage between recalled memories. While any kind of content would serve, the basic idea is that at medium or low focus, the connections between one episode and the next could be essentially that they made the experiencer "feel the same", and thus allow them to form successive recollections as in a day-dream.

Emotional states could be simulated in our CG-FGP machine in two basic ways. Given a model of what (human) emotional states exist and how they relate to each other, a modeler could read each fable in the knowledgebase, and try to model his or her own reactions, creating a new conceptual graph and attaching it as special context within the episode. Given a good theory of emotions, this has the advantage of simplicity, and the machine's reactions should be at least recognisable to another human. But it requires extra human effort at the point of input of all new cases, and is essentially derivative. Alternatively, one could wish for a method of having the machine generate its own emotional graphs in response to cases. To do that, the model would need an attitudinal policy, which maps objects, events and situations onto a set of affective states. The mapping could be based on "survival-value" or other machine-oriented teleological principle. Though they could be difficult to create, and the resultant reactions are not guaranteed to be recognisable to a person, but it requires no extra effort at input.

The reader might wonder what justifies any effort at including affective states at all. Are these not simply more features of input for the CG-FGP machine to process? In a way, that is all they are. But emotions do not originate in the external state of affairs represented in the cases. They arise in a classificatory mechanism, whether in the human emoter or inherent in the system itself. They add important information about the relationship between a cognitive agent and a particular aspect of the world. If systematically assigned, affective commonalities might be discoverable between objects, events and situations which were otherwise unrelated, provided only that similar emotive representations were semantically close. For example, suppose a machine could capture and express reactions to situations in a fable where, despite a righteous act on the part of an actor he had not been well treated by others, or by the gods. Then one case of injustice could bring to mind another, even if the narratives had little else in common.

Here we experiment with two specific objects of each narrative, the protagonist and the antagonist. (Actually, not all of Aesop's fables have an animate antagonist; in many the protagonist is a victim of circumstance, or learns a lesson through misadventure. In such cases, the general concept [SITUATION:#] has been used to fill the objective case role.) This will be a hand-crafted data structure expressing the author's compassion, trust, aggressiveness, etc. toward each of them, and stored as two distinct contexts which can be longitudinally searched in the CG-FGP process.

Affective states are modeled by adapting Plutchik's circumplex model of emotions [15]. Essentially, this holds that four primary dimensions, or scales, of affect can be recognised in humans. At any instant, an emotional reaction toward a target object can be described by four points: one on each scale. The extremities of these scales form bipolar opposites, so that naturally competing emotions may not be experienced

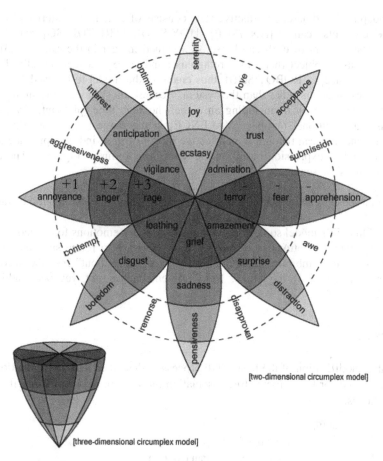

Fig. 1. Robert Pluchick's Wheel of Emotion (after Plutchick, 1980) represents affective states as four scales of polar opposites arranged around a circle based on the similarity of the states. The wheel can be folded into a 3D cone. The radial axis represents the intensity of arousal on each scale from maximum at the top of the cone to a minimum at the bottom, regardless of polarity (shown on one scale), which distinguishes the states on one side of each scale from those of the opposite.

simultaneously. The states can be arranged in a circle by similarity, like the colors on a color wheel (Figure 1). If integers are assigned to represent the intensity of each pair along the radial axis, the magnitude must represent intensity of the state, while sign must reflect which pole of the scale is chosen. Such a state might be:

[AFFECTIVE-STATE] –
　　　　(EXPR) ← [ROBOT:Self]
　　　　(OBJ) → [CRANE:#]
　　　(CHRC) → [ANT/SUP:2]
　　　(CHRC) → [JOY/SAD:-2]
　　　(CHRC) → [TRUST/DISG:2]
　　　(CHRC) → [ANG/FEAR:-1]
　　　(CHRC) → [VALENCE:0]

In the adaption used here, an affective state consists of a stem characterised by number-type concepts, called [ANT/SUP], [JOY/SAD], [TRUST/DISG] and [ANG/FEAR]. The referent of each can be set to a signed integer in the range [-3,3]. The graph also has an object (here, the protagonist) and an experiencer (usually the machine's self-concept, [ROBOT:Self]), thus enabling the model to be used for the affective states of actors other than the system. Because most models of emotion (and Gelernter) call for way of including an overall hedonic tone (pleasantness/ unpleasantness), an additional number, [VALENCE] in the range [-3,3] was added. The GRAVY generator can recognise an affective model of this kind, and produce an appropriate English expression based on the descriptive terms in Figure 2. The above graph produces the sentence:

"I feel a sense of anticipation for sad about trust toward and fear about the crane."

Since in Plutchik's model some combinations of primary emotions form recognisable, named compound emotions, it would be straightforward to refine such expressions by, for example, combining "anticipation for" and "fear about" into the secondary emotion "anxiety for" the crane. This refinement has not yet been added to GRAVY.

5 Results

A suitable modification of the basic FGP process as described in the Introduction was then developed for lower focus, free-association through (one context from) the database of fables:

repeat (T_i, M)

1)   Extend: $(cg\text{-}fetch\ (T_i, M)) \longrightarrow L$

$T \longleftarrow \min\ (\text{sort}(L))$

2   Refocus: $cg\text{-}project\ (T) \longrightarrow T'$

3   Query:

exit: break

why: compose response from T_i and T'

what: express affect (T')

next: remove T_i from M

$T_i \longleftarrow T'$

Because there is no goal in daydreaming, the role of evocativeness cannot be used in the semantic distance calculation of CG-fetch, but only to find features of interest in *CG-project* (where each feature in turn becomes the "goal"). Note also that according to theory, *CG-generalise* is not used here, since as Gelernter remarks, at lower focus the machine "does not build a memory sandwich" [6, p.132]. After Refocus, the algorithm breaks to allow some interaction with the user so as to demonstrate the value of accessing the fables in this way, as shown in the following fragment:

```
(daydream wolf&crane_ap)
  Free associating... It feels like The Cat and the Cock.
  Interesting...ROBOT
  Interesting...ANT/SUP
  Interesting...JOY/SAD
  Interesting...TRUST/LOATH
  Interesting...ANG/FEAR
  Interesting...VALENCE
>what do you feel most strongly?  .
  I feel a sense of anticipation for a little pensive about acceptance of
  and apprehensive about the bird. Not good.
>next .
  Continue.
  Free associating... It feels like The Thirsty Pigeon.
  Interesting...ROBOT
  Interesting...ANT/SUP
  Interesting...JOY/SAD
  Interesting...TRUST/LOATH
  Interesting...ANG/FEAR
  Interesting...VALENCE
>why did you recall that one?  .
  As with the cock, I felt sad about the pigeon. That's bad.
>next .
  Continue.
  ...
```

The algorithm searches $\mathcal{M}$ for close matches to the affective-state relating to the protagonist of the fable – the crane. Finding 16 close matches that are tightly clustered, it examines the closest – "The Cat and the Cock" for interesting features which might explain the association. It discovers that all the features of the affective state except the object are sufficiently evocative to re-enter the cycle in this case. Rather than completely abandon the selectional constraint of the object ("the cock") in the first instance, however, the program relaxes the constraint on this concept by generalising to the next level ("a bird"). When asked what it feels most strongly, the program actually describes the emotional referents of $\mathcal{T}$, so the optional exclamation expressing displeasure about the predicament of the crane is expressed as 'the bird'. Using $\mathcal{T}'$ as the next probe, the free association locates "The Thirsty Pigeon", another fable in which a bird protagonist comes to grief. When queried as to the reason for recalling that episode, the program compares the previous affective state with the current state and produces a comparative statement based on the closest features between the two, which will have been mostly responsible. Note that, although the program gains access to all the conceptual content describing the contents of the fable, and could potentially answer questions about it using well-proven conceptual reasoning methods, it could not as it stands find those particular events (the cheating of the crane, the capture of the pigeon) which lead to the emotions it is describing, because those were assigned by proxy and with respect to the whole fable, leaving no connection with particulars. (In the case of a policy-driven attitudinal system, such an explanation should be possible, though.)

What do we really gain from such a memory walk? Critics might object the above excursion is nothing more than a sequence of arbitrarily close matches through a database of cases based on an elaborate semantic distance measure. In such a small collection of cases, they might say, it is inevitable that apparently meaningful connections could easily be found. True, only a handful of cases are currently included in $\mathcal{M}$, though more are being added as quickly as time permits. But there are important differences between the current demonstration and, say, conventional reminding in the first part of on conventional CBR cycle. First, each narrative visited begins the entire refocus cycle anew, resulting in a chain of contextually evoked reminiscences, rather than just the top n matches with a single case on a simple distance metric. This is more like the operation of human memory. Second, the representation of the fables is unusually rich, episodic and able to be converted to and from natural language, making it possible to stop off and further ruminate over, or answer questions about, the currently indexed fable. Third, as mentioned in Section 4, affective-states are not inherent in the cases themselves, but represent reactions to them from a consistent cognitive agent (although this point is not as clear as it would be if the machine generated its own emotions to each fable as outlined in [16]).

Perhaps more importantly, the same basic FGP mechanism that can, without any domain-specific rules, perform logical reasoning at high focus has been demonstrated to function at low focus as a free-association system able produce emotion-like behaviour, just as Gelernter suggested it could. Therefore this simple mechanism may be of interest to anyone interested in more lifelike computing on ever richer representations of cultural episodic experiences. Imperfect as it is, the lower-focus CG-FGP process represents a subtle drifting indexation of narratives, which may have something in common with a human daydream.

References

1. Meehan, J.R.: TALE-SPIN, An Interactive Program that Writes Stories. In: Proceedings of IJCAI 1977, pp. 91–98 (1977)
2. Dyer, M.G.: In-depth Understanding. MIT Press, Cambridge (1983)
3. Scharf, H.: Searching for Narrative Structures. In: Proc. of the AAAI Spring Symposium on Mining Answers from Texts and Knowledgebases. AAAI Press, Menlo Park (2002), Technical Report SS-02-06
4. Elson, D.K., McKeown, K.R.: A Platform for Symbolically Encoding Human Narratives. In: Proc. of the AAAI Fall Symposium on Intelligent Narrative Technologies. AAAI Press, Menlo Park (2007), Technical Report FS-07-05
5. Kolodner, J.: Case-Based Reasoning, ch. 4. Morgan Kaufmann, San Mateo (1993)
6. Gelernter, D.H.: The Muse in the Machine. Fourth Estate, London (1994)
7. Fertig, S., Gelernter, D.H.: The Design, Implementation and Performance of a Database-driven Expert System. Technical Report #851, Department of Computer Science. Yale University (1991)
8. Sowa, J.F.: Knowledge Representation: Logical, Philosophical, and Computational Foundations. Course Technology, Boston (1999)
9. Townsend, G.F. (translator): Aesop's Fables (1867),
   http://classics.mit.edu/Aesop/fab.html
10. Scharfe, H.: CANA A study in Computer Aided Narrative Analysis Ch.12. PhD dissertation, Dept. of Communication Aalborg University (2004),
    http://www.hum.aau.dk/~scharfe/CANA.pdf

11. Mann, G.A.: Control of a Navigating Rational Agent by Natural Language. PhD Thesis, School of Computer Science & Engineering, University of New South Wales (1996), http://wwwit.murdoch.edu.au/~S850124d/NL/Mann_PhD_Thesis.pdf

12. Schank, R.C.: The Primitive Acts of Conceptual Dependency. In: Proc. of the 1975 Workshop on Theoretical Issues in Natural Language Processing, Association for Computational Lingusitics, Morristown, pp. 34–37 (1975)

13. Mineau, G.W.: Normalizing Conceptual Graphs. In: Nagle, T.E., et al. (eds.) Conceptual Structures: Current Research and Practice, pp. 339–348. Ellis Horwood, Chichester (1992)

14. Wuwongse, V., Niyomthai, S.: Conceptual Graphs as a Framework for Case-based Reasoning. In: Proc. of the 6th Annual Workshop on Conceptual Graphs, pp. 119–133 (1990)

15. Plutchik, R.: A General Psychoevolutionary Theory of Emotion. In: Plutchik, R., Kellerman, H. (eds.) Emotion: Theory, Research and Experience, vol. 1, pp. 3–33. Academic Press, New York (1980)

16. Mann, G.A.: Rational and Affective Linking Across Conceptual Cases – Without Rules. In: Delugach, H.S., Keeler, M.A., Searle, L., Lukose, D., Sowa, J.F. (eds.) ICCS 1997. LNCS (LNAI), vol. 1257, pp. 460–473. Springer, Heidelberg (1997)

Cluster Analysis for Personalised Mobile Entertainment Content

Worapat Paireekreng, Kok Wai Wong, and Chun Che Fung

Murdoch University, South Street, Murdoch,
6150, Perth, WA, Australia
{w.paireekreng,k.wong,l.fung}@murdoch.edu.au

Abstract. There is much attention given to emerging technologies like mobile internet because of its increasing popularity. Much research has concentrated on hardware and some have focused on personalisation in terms of content visualisation. The focus of this paper is on mobile content personalisation, seeking to understand the user groups through clustering users based on their profile. This paper focuses on the implementation of a technique known as 'Zoning-Centroid', which is the evaluation technique used to determine the appropriate number of clusters required to best cluster the given users profile. The user profile used in this paper includes mobile content usage and their demographic factors. The clustering algorithm used in this paper is k-means clustering. The results show that the proposed technique could suggest appropriate number of clusters to be used with the k-values, in order to implement for mobile entertainment content personalisation.

Keywords: mobile content user clustering, mobile content personalisation, clustering, cluster analysis.

1 Introduction

Mobile devices have improved substantially over the past few years with many added features and attributes such as internet access. Besides provide communications and mobile services, it also allows users to access a wide range of information based on personal need or context. Relatively some improvements have been performed to enhance the delivering of the mobile internet content, an area of increasing importance [21]. However, there are still problems relating to information overload and the users' behaviour on their desire contents. This creates a challenge for researchers in the domain of identifying the user's segment, and the definition of these groups according to different demographic factors and user information rankings.

In this paper, we investigate and analyse mobile internet user using clustering analysis. The technique realised in this paper could be applied in the entertainment computing domain by assisting users when accessing mobile entertainment content. The feature selection for the number of clusters and content items for each cluster is implemented for clustering with the zoning of Centroid to examine the cluster of mobile internet content user.

R. Nakatsu et al. (Eds.): ECS 2010, IFIP AICT 333, pp. 36–45, 2010.

2 Background

2.1 Mobile Content Personalisation

Personalisation was defined as mechanisms to allow a user to adapt or produce a service to fit user's particular needs, and that after all subsequent services rendering by this service towards the user is tuned accordingly [14]. Mobile personalisation research has focused on how to facilitate the use of mobile internet. Application such as tourist guide, news update or classified information and services [7], [8] have been developed. Adaptive content which can be adjusted when the usage changed according to the context becomes important issues. It includes some researches that also looking into entertainment content and mobile games by catering different game genres for different group of users [10],[11].

Intelligent systems with machine learning and data mining play a vital role for personalisation system such as finding customer's needs[1]. Wu et al. [6] have shown that some commonly used algorithms in data mining are k-means, and SVM. Wu et al. also described k-means as a simple iterative clustering method. This is also a simple algorithm with the adaptation ability for different applications [2]. The clustering component in [16, 17] also show the mobile user clustering using demographic factors and information ranking to filter the cluster could enhance the system.

2.2 Mobile User Clustering

The research on mobile internet user can be observed from [24]. Yamakami [24] used Aging Analysis model to identify mobile internet user behavior. This model used statistical techniques to divide the users into four groups based on amount of access time. This research focused only on the frequency of the user using the mobile internet. In 2006, Okazaki [3] has includes attitudinal and demographic information for cluster analysis. It automatically determined the number of clusters which is four clusters based on Baysian Inference Criterion (BIC) techniques and TwoStep algorithm. Furthermore, [22,23] develop a formula to identify the appropriate number of clusters using a method known as 2, 3 and 4 cluster. These researches implemented k-means clustering technique to know how long they spent their time in each time zone (Always on, Morning, Daytime and Night). In another research [4], they used factors analysis related to call usage, payment behavior and additional service usage clustered by k-means and Association Rule.

K-means and determining number of clusters. K-means has been introduced by Tou and Gonzalez since 1974 [12]. K-mean can handle large data and is computational efficient with its simple implementation when compared to other techniques like hierarchical clustering [13], [24] and implemented in various areas [9], [19] such as image processing or information retrieval. Nevertheless, identifying the optimal number of cluster seems to be a problem. There are some research in identifying the number of cluster such as 'Gap Statistic' [5] which focused on well-separated cluster and uniform distribution dataset. In 2009, Muhr and Granitzer [15] proposed automatic cluster number selection by applying x-means with split and merge clustering method. They measure cluster validity with BIC and F-Score. This technique is also appropriate with known class or labeled data. Another cluster number determination technique is 'L method' [20]. However, this method did not work well with global evaluation metrics and it is unable to work with less number of clusters like 1 or 2 clusters.

Labelled clustering data. F-Score has been used in [15] to measure the quality of cluster. However, to measure the cluster analysis, prior information of the cluster is necessary. This problem is similar to Random Index (RI). Although there is research performed in using fuzzy C-means clustering with 'Induced Entropy' to evaluate the cluster, it also needs testing data for known classes such as visited and recommended web pages [18].

Cluster evaluation. Ray and Turi [19] proposed the method to evaluate the clustering techniques using k-means. It is validity ratio which is defines as

$$validity = \frac{Intra}{Inter}$$

The concept of this measurement is minimizing the sum of squared distance for intra-cluster and maximizing inter-cluster value. If the validity value is small, it can be implied that the cluster is compact compared with other k-values.

From the above, it can be observed that most of the researches have focused on the clustering in terms of mobile internet user behavior such as adoption or experience in mobile internet. Although, there were researches mentioned about number of cluster and clustering techniques, there are not used in clustering of mobile entertainment content users. In addition, with the limited computational resource user needs to get the response,. a simple algorithm should be considered for mobile computing. K-means and its acceptable k-values which are suitable for unlabelled mobile content user clusters will be carried out for this paper. This method helps to select the appropriate number of clusters with efficient computation.

3   Proposed Method and Experiment

The data source used for the experiment was obtained from the published research on the mobile internet content users in Bangkok [25]. This set of data consists of the user's content preference such as multimedia, news or information services on mobile internet. 300 randomly selected records were used as training data for clustering. There are several factors and attributes in the dataset. In this research, we have selected the key demographic factors of gender, age, income and occupation to find potential groups or clusters. These attributes were chosen in acquiring the requisite data from the mobile internet users as well as the ease of classification for further analysis.

The cluster analysis is performed using the k-means cluster technique. K-means clustering technique was selected as it provides a simple algorithm that can be used to determine cluster sizes. This allows the implementation of a clustering model at the server of the content provider in order to know the customers' characteristic and provide appropriate content to each cluster based on the cluster characteristic.

The aim of the experiment is to analyse the group based on demographic factors. The analysis should generate the appropriate number of clusters for mobile content users, leading to the identification of contents which these clusters of users will be accessing. The experiments are conducted with k-means where k=4,5,6,7 and 8 consecutively.

Zoning-Centroid. The evaluation method called '*Zoning-Centroid*' is proposed in this paper. The distance from the centre of each cluster should be used to determine the cluster's members in each cluster, and to ensure that they are appropriately distributed.

'*Zoning-Centroid*' will use the distance between centre of cluster and data to calculate the zone that this data is sought. It measures how far from the centre of this data. The zone will be divided into 5 zones. Each zone is computed from *Zone-Distance* which is derived from the difference between the maximum distance in the cluster and the minimum distance in the cluster

$$\text{ZoneDistance}_{(n,i,k)} = (\text{MaxDistance}_{(n,i,k)} - \text{MinDistance}_{(n,i,k)}) / 2^n . \qquad (1)$$

where, n=zone number of cluster i and k = k-values; $1 \le n \le 5$; $1 \le i \le 5$; $4 \le k \le 8$

Then, the '*Zone-Limit*' will be calculated from *Zone-Distance* as following

$$\text{ZoneLimit}_{(n,i,k)} = \text{ZoneLimit}_{(n-1,i,k)} + \text{ZoneDistance}_{(n,i,k)} . \qquad (2)$$

where, n = zone number of cluster i and k = k-values; MinDistance = n-1 for n=1.

After that, the distance of each data will be assigned to each zone according to its limits. For example, if cluster 1 and zone 1 limit is 0.924737, the data with distance below this limit will be in zone 1. In contrast, if the distance is over that limit, the data will be assigned to the subsequent zone. Figure 1 shows the concept of zoning.

We will measure the amount of cases that will fall in each zone and count the number and percentage of each zone to determine the data distribution based on '*Zoning-Centroid*'. This evaluation method will be applied in k-means between k=4 and k=8 for mobile content usage.

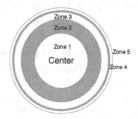

Fig. 1. The '*Zoning-Centriod*' diagram shows the data coverage for each zone

The 'Zoning-Centroid' separates each zone using exponential distance from the centre of each cluster. The main concept is based on proximity between data and centre. The first zone consumes 50% distance from the minimum to half of the maximum distance. This is because good quality cluster should contain data close to its centre as much as possible. Therefore, the first zone covers area larger than the next zone. In contrast, if the zone division implements linear zoning, the distance in each zone would be separated to be far from each other equally. As a result, the data will difficult to be separated as most data will appear to be near to its centre.

4 Experiment Results

4.1 Analysis of Cluster with k-Values

The characteristics of each cluster based on demographic factors and content usage are analysed and concluded by using difference k-values as follows;

k=4. The results show that gender and age do not have any effect on clustering except cluster 4. It shows unique characteristics are teenager, low income and studying. For income and occupation, they are different in 3 clusters, therefore they are unable to be determined precisely.

k=5. At this k-value, demographic factors, income, started to show some significance and separated more precisely. In addition, age has clearer influenced on the cluster than the previous k-value. The 'teenager' is still the dominating attribute in clustering while there is no effect to clustering with gender.

k=6. The cluster of 'teenager' is maintained and gender still has no effect towards clustering. Age and occupation seem to be clearer. There are different ages in each cluster such as more than 18 years old, more than 36 years old or between 19-35 years old. In addition, income begins to be separated into less income and above average income.

k=7. There is one cluster that has the proportion equal to 5% appeared in cluster 6 and age begin to influence to clustering. Then, income is also clustered more precisely in cluster 1 and 2 by less income and more income groups. Occupation shows the groups which are free-time and employed with low income in cluster 3 and 4. It is similar to other k-values that 'teenager' cluster is separated clearly compared to other clusters.

k=8. We stop at this k value by setting up cut off point when the small cluster which proportion less than 5% appeared. The teenager group together with gender has effect in cluster 1 and 8 by division between male and female with combination of age. Furthermore, occupation also determines the group characteristic by presenting employed or having more free time. In cluster 3,4,7 which there is age between 19-35 years old, show different among cluster by occupation and income.

4.2 Number of Cluster Using 'Zoning Centroid'

As can be seen from the table 1, the cases in Zoning-Centroid for each cluster (CZCC), as expected, the percentage of cases that fall in Zone 1 is the highest percentage in each k-value. The cumulative percentage of cases between Zone 4 and Zone 5 is around 5-8%. It can be implied that 92-95% of data approximately has not fallen over to zone 3 for every k-value. In addition, it shows the highest percentage in Zone 1 followed by Zone 2 and Zone 3 which means the data for k=5 is disseminated appropriately especially in the first 2 zones. The percentage and trends of each k-values and CZCC each zone are shown in Figure 2.

To consider the cumulative of dissemination of data compared to percentile of distance from the centre of the cluster to its limit, we sum data from Zone 1 to Zone 4 which are 93.75% of the percentile of distance. This shows that the data distribution is at around 94-96%. The highest is at k=4 and it decreases slightly when k-values is increased. However, the percentage rises again when k=8. When compared with cumulative 3 zones, the result still presents trends similar to 4 zones.

Table 1. Number of Cases in '*Zoning-Centroid*' in Each Cluster

Cluster	# Cases Zoning-Centroid	k=4	k=5	k=6	k=7	k=8
1	Zone 1 limit	58	22	66	25	9
	Zone 2 limit	21	21	0	2	4
	Zone 3 limit	3	0	2	0	0
	Zone 4 limit	0	1	0	0	0
	Zone 5 limit	2	1	4	3	1
2	Zone 1 limit	44	29	20	20	20
	Zone 2 limit	9	10	4	4	0
	Zone 3 limit	2	1	2	2	1
	Zone 4 limit	1	1	1	0	0
	Zone 5 limit	5	3	1	1	1
3	Zone 1 limit	57	66	33	67	43
	Zone 2 limit	20	0	2	22	25
	Zone 3 limit	4	0	0	0	7
	Zone 4 limit	2	0	0	0	0
	Zone 5 limit	3	3	1	11	4
4	Zone 1 limit	61	47	47	12	12
	Zone 2 limit	7	16	16	3	3
	Zone 3 limit	0	0	0	3	3
	Zone 4 limit	0	0	0	0	0
	Zone 5 limit	1	6	6	1	1
5	Zone 1 limit		68	43	63	63
	Zone 2 limit		4	0	6	6
	Zone 3 limit		0	1	0	0
	Zone 4 limit		0	7	0	0
	Zone 5 limit		1	3	1	1
6	Zone 1 limit			38	11	22
	Zone 2 limit			1	3	9
	Zone 3 limit			0	0	2
	Zone 4 limit			1	0	0
	Zone 5 limit			1	1	1
7	Zone 1 limit				27	19
	Zone 2 limit				9	13
	Zone 3 limit				2	0
	Zone 4 limit				0	1
	Zone 5 limit				1	2
8	Zone 1 limit					24
	Zone 2 limit					1
	Zone 3 limit					1
	Zone 4 limit					0
	Zone 5 limit					1
	Total	300	300	300	300	300
	CZCC - Zone 1	73.33%	77.33%	82.33%	75.00%	70.67%
	CZCC - Zone 2	19.00%	17.00%	7.67%	16.33%	20.33%
	CZCC - Zone 3	3.00%	0.33%	1.67%	2.33%	4.67%
	CZCC - Zone 4	1.00%	0.67%	3.00%	0.00%	0.33%
	CZCC - Zone 5	3.67%	4.67%	5.33%	6.33%	4.00%
	Total	100.00%	100.00%	100.00%	100.00%	100.00%

Table 2. The percentage sum of data dissemination in various zones

Zone	K				
	4	5	6	7	8
Sum 4 Zones (93.75%)	96.3333%	95.3333%	94.6667%	93.6667%	96.0000%
Sum 3 Zones (87.5%)	95.3333%	94.6667%	91.6667%	93.6667%	95.6667%
Sum 2 Zones (75%)	92.3333%	94.3333%	90.0000%	91.3333%	91.0000%

* In blanket means the percentile of distance from centre to its limit.

K=5 shows the cumulative percentage from Zone 1 to Zone 2 at approximately 94% which is significantly higher than the other k-values. The percentage comparison can be seen from the table 2.

According to CZCC, it seems that k=5 shows the most significant results compared to other k-values based on *Zoning-Centroid* consideration with less cumulative zones (2 zones). This can be implemented to choose the appropriate number of cluster for mobile content usage.

To evaluate the quality of cluster, the method to measure the number of cluster is used and the results are shown in table 3. We use TwoStep clustering techniques to compare the results of the number of clusters. This method was used in Okazaki's research for determining the number of clusters and mobile inter adopter cluster solution [3]. However, the TwoStep algorithm with BIC (Bayesian Information Criterion) and ratio of distance measure showed that the number of auto-clustering for this mobile content usage dataset is just 2 clusters. As a result, we will ignore this measurement because the results for the clustering are unable to implement in the further stage such as customer's pattern of content usage. It is too small a number of clusters. Our method can show most numbers of cluster compared reasonably to auto-clustering with TwoStep.

The quality of clusters is then measured. As in this case, we are using unlabelled data, we will use the fundamental concept of clustering to measure the quality. The concept is based on the measurement of the minimum distance within cluster and the maximum distance between clusters. Therefore, the validity metric from Ray and Turi [19] is used. The results are presented as following:

According to the validity metric, the intra cluster value is calculated from the sum squared of distance in the cluster while the inter cluster value is selected from the

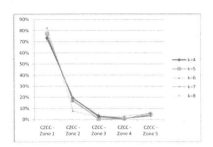

Fig. 2. Percentage of cases of 'Zoning-Centroid' in each zone in each cluster

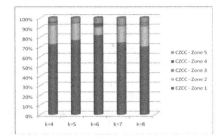

Fig. 3. Cumulative percentage of cases of 'Zoning-Centroid' in each zone in each cluster4.3 Cluster Evaluation

Table 3. The validity of clustering

k	Intra	Inter	Validity
4	499.4445	3.8780	128.7895
5	430.2511	3.9670	108.4574
6	372.2088	3.2829	113.3793
7	360.6455	2.7056	133.2981
8	298.2944	2.3483	127.0281

minimum value of distances between cluster centers which it is desired to be maximized. The validity can imply that if the value is small, it means the cluster quality is good. From the results, it implies that for this mobile content clustering problem, the appropriate number of clusters should be 5 because its validity is the smallest compared to other k-values clustering.

Table 4. The comparison of validity and 'Zoning-Centriod' using cluster k=5

	Normal Validity	Zoning-Centriod	% of calculation reduced
Number of cases	300	283	5.6667%
Percentile of distance	100%	75%	25%

To consider the concept of 'Zoning-Centroid', it can be seen from the Table 4 that this method can reduce the number of data or cases to be calculated for finding the number of clusters and at the same time ensuring the quality of cluster by at least 5.6667%. It also decreased the percentile of distance to consider to 75% from the cluster's centre.

5   Discussions and Conclusions

This research not only recommends the optimum number of clusters for mobile internet content user groups but also provides the techniques to cluster through the use of k-means and subsequent evaluation with *'Zoning-Centroid'*. This clustering is based on demographic factors with the data provided by the users allowing both the cluster analysis to be processed easily. The 'Zoning-Centroid' can assist in determining the appropriate k-values for the number of clusters, allowing the content providers to focus on individual clusters and deliver the right content to the right group at the right time.

The results of the research potentially increase business value by determining the optimal number of clusters to be grouped for mobile content personalisation. The appropriate number of clusters is determined by the combination of a clustering technique with fundamental demographic factors.

The k-means is a simple algorithm, and therefore suitable to be used for the mobile content personalisation. The model can be built at the content provider's server and predict the user's group from incoming user's profile faster. When the content provider knows the user's characteristics, it would be easier to provide appropriate content to them quickly.

References

1. Bose, I., Mahapatra, R.K.: Business Data Mining - A Machine Learning Perspective. J. Information and Management 39, 211–225 (2001)
2. Jain, A.K.: Data Clustering: 50 Years Beyond K-Means. J. Pattern Recognition Letters (2009)
3. Okazaki, S.: What Do We Know About Mobile Internet Adopters? A Cluster Analysis. J. Information and Management 43, 127–141 (2006)
4. Sohn, S.Y., Kim, Y.: Searching Customer Patterns of Mobile Service Using Clustering and Quantitative Association Rule. J. Expert Systems with Applications 34, 1070–1077 (2006)
5. Tibshirani, R., Walther, G., Hastie, T.: Estimating the Number of Clusters in a Data Set via the Gap Statistic. J. Royal Statistical Society 63, 411–423 (2001)
6. Wu, X., Kumar, V., Quinlan, J.R., Ghosh, J., Yang, Q., Motoda, H., Mclachlan, G., Ng, A., Liu, B., Yu, P., Zhou, Z.-H., Steinbach, M., Hand, D., Steinberg, D.: Top 10 Algorithms in Data Mining. J. Knowledge and Information Systems 14, 1–37 (2008)
7. Zhang, D.: Web Content Adaptation for Mobile Handheld Devices. J. Communications of the ACM 50, 75–79 (2007)
8. Zipf, A., Jost, M.: Implementing Adaptive Mobile GI Services Based on Ontologies Examples from Pedestrian Navigation Support. J. Computers, Environment and Urban Systems 30, 784–798 (2006)
9. Gonzalez-Barron, U., Butler, F.: A Comparison of Seven Thresholding Techniques with the K-means Clustering Algorithm for Measurement of Bread-crumb Features by Digital Image Analysis. J. Food Engineering 74, 268–278 (2006)
10. Paireekreng, W., Rapeepisarn, K., Wong, K.W.: Time-Based Personalised Mobile Game Downloading. In: Pan, Z., Cheok, A.D., Müller, W., Rhalibi, A.E. (eds.) Transactions on Edutainment II. LNCS, vol. 5660, pp. 59–69. Springer, Heidelberg (2009)
11. Rapeepisarn, K., Wong, K.W., Fung, C.C., Khine, M.S.: The relationship between Game Genres, Learning Techniques and Learning Styles in Educational Computer Games. In: Pan, Z., Zhang, X., El Rhalibi, A., Woo, W., Li, Y. (eds.) Edutainment 2008. LNCS, vol. 5093, pp. 497–508. Springer, Heidelberg (2008)
12. Tou, J.T., Gonzalez, R.C.: Pattern Recognition Principles. Addison-Wesley, Massachusetts (1974)
13. Bose, I., Xi, C.: Exploring Business Opportunities from Mobile Service Data of Customers Using Inter-cluster Analysis. In: The IEEE International Workshop on Data Mining for Design and Marketing, Hongkong (2006)
14. Jorstad, I., Thanh, D.V., Dustdar, S.: Personalisation of Future Mobile Services. In: 9th International Conference on Intelligence in Service Delivery, Bordeaux, France (2004)
15. Muhr, M., Granitzer, M.: Automatic Cluster Number Selection using a Split and Merge K-Means Approach. In: 20th International Workshop on Database and Expert Systems Application. IEEE Computer Society, Linz (2009)
16. Paireekreng, W., Wong, K.W.: Mobile Content Personalisation Using Intelligent User Profile Approach. In: The 3rd International Conference on Knowledge Discovery and Data Mining (WKDD 2010), Phuket, Thailand (2010)
17. Paireekreng, W., Wong, K.W.: Client-side Mobile User Profile for Content Management Using Data Mining Techniques. In: 8th International Symposium on Natural Language Processing, Bangkok, Thailand (2009)
18. Phatak, D.S., Mulvaney, R.: Clustering for Personalized Mobile Web Page. In: The IEEE International Conference on Fuzzy Systems (2002)

19. Ray, S., Turi, R.H.: Determination of Number of Clusters in K-Means Clustering and Application in Colour Image Segmentation. In: The 4th International Conference on Advances in Pattern Recognition and Digital Techniques (ICAPRDT 1999), Calcutta, India (1999)
20. Salvador, S., Chan, P.: Determining the Number of Clusters/Segments in Hierarchical Clustering/Segmentation Algorithm. In: 16th IEEE International Conference on Tools with Artificial Intelligence (ICTAI 2004), Boca Raton, Florida (2004)
21. Uribe, S., Fernandez-Cedron, I., Alvarez, F., Menendez, J.M., Nunez, J.L.: Mobile TV Targeted Advertisement and Content Personalization. In: 16th International Conference on Systems, Signals and Image Processing (IWSSIP 2009), Chalkida, Greece (2009)
22. Yamakami, T.: A User-Perceived Freshness Clustering Method to Identify Three Subgroups in Mobile Internet Users. In: The 2nd International Conference on Multimedia and Ubiquitous Engineering, Busan, Korea (2008)
23. Yamakami, T.: Exploratory Day-scale Behavior Assumption-Based User Clustering with the Mobile Clickstream. In: Eighth International Conference on Parallel and Distributed Computing, Application and Technologies, Adelaide, Australia (2007)
24. Yamakami, T.: Toward Understanding the Mobile Internet User Behavior: A Methodology for User Clustering with Aging Analysis. In: Fourth International Conference on Parallel and Distributed Computing, Application and Technologies, Chengdu, China (2003)
25. Paireekreng, W.: Influence Factors of Mobile Content Personalization on Mobile Device User in Bangkok (2007)

Auto-explanation System: Player Satisfaction in Strategy-Based Board Games

Andrew Chiou[1] and Kok Wai Wong[2]

[1] School of Computing Sciences, CQUniversity Australia, Rockhampton Campus,
Rockhampton Campus, 4702 QLD, Australia
a.chiou@cqu.edu.au
[2] School of Information Technology, Murdoch University,
Murdoch, Western Australia 6150
k.wong@murdoch.edu.au

Abstract. In computerised version of board games, player satisfaction can be augmented by providing explanation of what the computer based AI analytical processes are. This helps the players to understand the reasoning behind the action taken by the computer AI opponent. This paper proposes a method that provides the mechanism for a game AI to communicate its evaluation processes using descriptive auto-explanation through symbolic reasoning. A case study is presented in an implementation of a game AI opponent that is capable of describing its inferential processes in a tabletop war game.

Keywords: board games, player satisfaction, strategy, auto explanation.

1 Introduction

The primary purpose of games in any format, be it tabletop board game or its digital counterpart, is to provide entertainment and pleasure to the participants. There are games belonging to the serious game genre. These games, in addition to providing the entertainment and pleasure value, also impart the value of knowledge to the players involved in the current game's subject matter. In the game of chess, it is normal for players to undertake in-depth analysis of completed games. This is to elicit the reasoning behind what and why of specific moves were made during the game. In this way, players augment their pleasure they experience from the games played or being played. This paper will propose a method on how such information can be communicated to the players using its evaluation processes utilising descriptive auto-explanation through symbolic reasoning. This is followed by a case study involving a game AI in a tabletop strategy-based war game.

2 Background

Entertainment computing has becoming a significant area in the field of computing. Recently, it can be observed that there is a shift to focus on the design of the

R. Nakatsu et al. (Eds.): ECS 2010, IFIP AICT 333, pp. 46–54, 2010.

entertainment media for individual, so as to increase the perceived value [1]. In the following section, the concept of Player Adaptive Entertainment Computing (PAEC) has been re-examined. The fundamental of the PAEC is to provide personalised experience for each individual when interacting with the entertainment media [2]. The more common area in entertainment computing is digital games. To address the perceived value of players in games in addition to normal game play, this project attempts to implement an auto-explanation mechanism to provide symbolic reasoning to player participants.

2.1 PAEC Concept

Perceived value by the users has the power to determine the success of an entertainment media, and thus PAEC is introduced to address this important issue. There are three broad areas of focus in the PAEC: 1. the player, 2. the content and 3. the entertainment quality. The interaction between the content and player is driven primarily by the value the player perceives. PAEC can be modelled as follow:

$$perceived\ value_i = \frac{experience + entertainment\ quality}{price}. \tag{1}$$

We can see from (1) that the perceived value for player i has several components. The first component, which is experience, refers to the idea that players buy experience and not the particular entertainment products. To the extent, the content of a product enhances the experience and it then increases the player's perceived value. The content that normally enhances experience in entertainment computing includes game resources, platform and the delivery medium. The entertainment quality also increases player's perceived value. Entertainment quality refers to the ways in controlling the mind of the players so that the player feels entertained, which includes inherent interest of events, indirect control techniques, psychological proximity, and player modeling. The way in which a media is produced is often as important as the content itself. Price is also a component of the perceived value. Different components of the player's perceived value provide opportunities for enhancement and management of the interactive content with individual players. From (1), we can see that the perceived value is defined at the individual level (hence the subscript i). Therefore it is important to identify the components of perceived value that are unique to each player or player base.

2.2 Auto-explanation

Previous research has indicated that computerised solutions provided by intelligent systems accompanied by an explanation or justification can make the recommendations more acceptable to end users [3, 4]. In addition, descriptive recommendations using symbolic reasoning or schemas to describe its outcome can facilitate comprehension as compared to numerical-only data. It has been shown that end users require data to be charted or graphically presented to facilitate better understanding. The use of symbolic reasoning to visualise qualitative data and information gathering is well established in areas of ethnography [5]. The implementation of specific symbolic types were adapted from and structured around observations such as:

- Space – what are the boundaries of the playing area?
- Actors – what is the purpose of the players, avatars, counters and the playing pieces?
- Activities – what are the [above] activities?
- Events – what specific events is the activity attempting to achieve?
- Time – what are the sequence of events?

3   Implementation

The implementation of the auto-explanation mechanism is embedded in the SA³GE-GAIA game AI shell prototype [6]. The prototype shell, SA³GE (Shell for Self-Adapting, Self-Analysing and Self-Aware Game Exponent) was based on specifications of proposed framework in previous work. The purpose of the SA³GE production engine is to generate an AI opponent specific for geomorphic tabletop games and its digital variant. The resulting middleware is GAIA (Game AI Avatar). In Fig. 1, the application provides sockets where the core rules and knowledgebase components can be explicitly instantiated. The core rules are the set of rules specific to the game to function as a filter to ensure that the game play strategies operate within the valid [rule] boundaries of the game. In this experiment, the AI opponent, GAIA is then deployed as a standalone game AI entity where it is fielded against expert human participants to assess its performance in a real-life competitive environment.

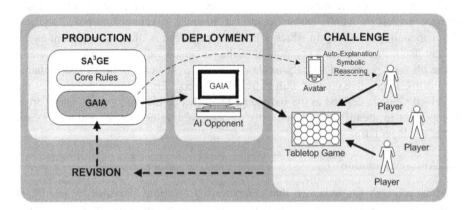

Fig. 1. The SA³GE-GAIA AI shell with embedded auto-explanation to provide player participants information on specific moves or action considered by the computerised AI playing the role of the avatar

4 Auto-explanation Using Symbols

Descriptive schemas are generated as a series of symbols. There are three types of symbols utilised by GAIA application in providing meaningful advice and suggestions to game players. These are *type S, T* and *A*. Their technical implementation has been presented in [7]. Each respectively represents *deployment strategy, confidence threshold* and *directed action*. The symbols and its purpose will be explained in the following section in the case study. In this way, complex advice such as, "Infantry units can be deployed surrounding, but not within the objective area", can be conveniently expressed. In contrast, a similar output using conventional numerically based data would have been complex and cumbersome.

5 Case Study

Tide of Iron is a strategy-based war game played on a hex tiled game board (Fig. 2) [8]. It is a turn-based game for two players. The objective of the game is for players to take the role of either an Axis or Allies military force in order to accomplish specific goals (e.g. secure area of conflict, destroy enemy forces, etc.). The hex-based playing board is geomorphic, allowing the same playing platform to be rearranged to allow different historical battlefield scenarios to be recreated. Different types of resources are available to both players. These are infantry, armour and artillery units. By judicious deployment of these units, players will attempt to defeat the opposition (or score the most points) with minimal lost to its own units.

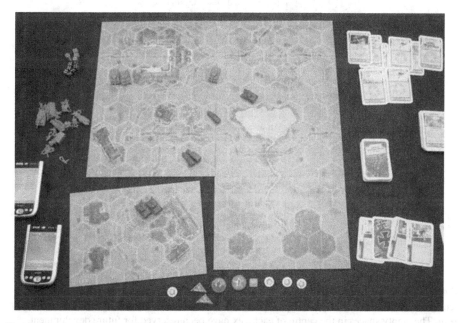

Fig. 2. Physical layout of *Tide of Iron* [8]. Game board is based on geomorphic arrangement depending on battle scenario. Auto-explanation is generated by GAIA, translated into a script file and transmitted to hand-held devices or netbooks via a web server.

In the scenario specifically created for the experiment, the objective of the Allied forces (human player) is to capture and hold the town square (in upper left hand corner in Fig. 3). The town is under the control of Axis forces (GAIA). Armour and infantry of the Axis forces surround the objective. The Allied forces should commence by inserting paratroopers in the clear zone (indicated by the three hexes in the lower left). For the Allied forces to gain victory in the confrontation, it has to control at least two hexes occupied by the town square after eight rounds of action. The Axis forces wins immediately if the Allied forces are unable control the required hexes after eight rounds. However, if the Allied forces are able to overrun the enemies after eight rounds but are unable to occupy the required hexes (i.e. the enemies retreat, leaving the town hexes unoccupied by neither forces), this is considered a minor win for the Allied forces.

5.1 Deployment Strategy, *Type S*

Deployment strategy refers to the type of possible action to be taken by the player controlling X force (the opposition is Y force). A selection of the symbols utilised to represent the strategies is explained in Fig. 3. Depending on the type of board game, the different number of possible strategies and variations appropriate to the type of

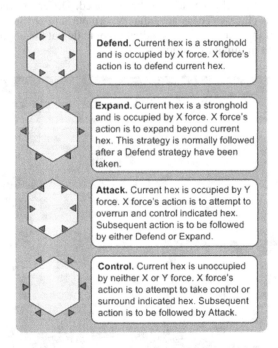

Defend. Current hex is a stronghold and is occupied by X force. X force's action is to defend current hex.

Expand. Current hex is a stronghold and is occupied by X force. X force's action is to expand beyond current hex. This strategy is normally followed after a Defend strategy have been taken.

Attack. Current hex is occupied by Y force. X force's action is to attempt to overrun and control indicated hex. Subsequent action is to be followed by either Defend or Expand.

Control. Current hex is unoccupied by neither X or Y force. X force's action is to attempt to take control or surround indicated hex. Subsequent action is to be followed by Attack.

Fig. 3. Legend for the different types of symbols used by GAIA to convey assessment of current game play meaningfully to human participants. There are nine strategies used in *Tide of Iron*. The empty spaces in the centre of each hex have been reserved for future development.

game play can range from 4 to 24. In Tide of Iron, nine strategies are utilised with two variations for each main strategy. After the fifth round (game play normally ends after the ninth round), GAIA generated the auto-explanation in the example output in Fig. 4 representing the lower left zone of the case study scenario. Four critical zones (hexes) were identified where immediate action is required of the human participant playing the role of X force, where X is the current player representing the force prepared to move in the current round. Y force is the opposing player. The critical zones were labelled *1, 2, 3* and *4*, corresponding to the legend in Fig. 5. The auto-explanation in Fig. 5 is in real time, displaying GAIA most recent evaluation of any particular position in the current game play. At present, GAIA is incapable of archiving historical data or keeping track of previous rounds. It is only capable of analysing and providing explanation of a given current position.

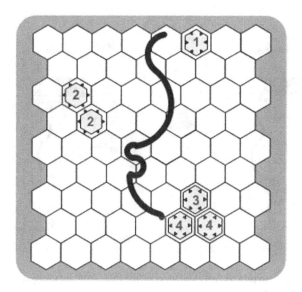

Fig. 4. The critical zone identified by GAIA AI avatar labelled *1, 2, 3* and *4* to correspond with the auto-explanation in Fig. 5. The critical zone are clusters of hexes requiring immediate action in the nth round during game play. In this case, this is the fifth round.

5.2 Confidence Threshold, *Type T*

In addition, each deployment strategy is complemented by an impact meter to indicate the confidence threshold. This meter provides the confidence level required by players to ensure that the deployment strategy expressed by GAIA is sound or unsound. Darker shade readings indicate that the effectiveness of the deployment strategy is guaranteed. The lighter shade indicates a probable level of effectiveness. The symbolic reasoning for confidence threshold is only meaningful when associated with the relevant deployment strategies inferred previously for each of the critical sectors in Fig. 4 and Fig. 5.

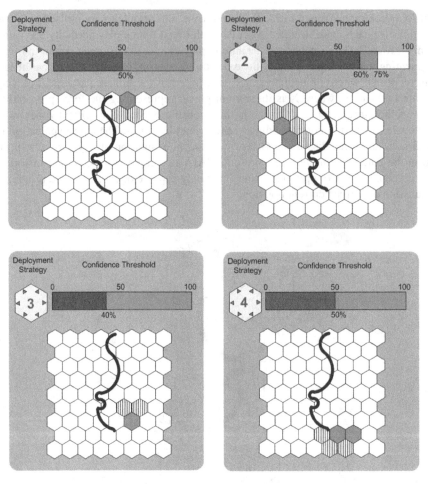

Fig. 5. A stylised and simplified representation of the auto-explanation generated by GAIA to communicate the current analysis for player X forces against its opponent, Y forces

5.3 Directed Action, *Type A*

Even though the location have been identified, GAIA requires the proper direction the actions taken should be targeted. An optimal deployment strategy does not necessarily guarantee a high level of success if a less appropriate action has been taken to implement it (e.g. expanding towards an inappropriate hex). Therefore, the application of each action needs to be indicated directionally to maximise the effectiveness of the deployment strategy and its combined actions. To simplify the representation of the recommended actions and to maintain the symbols at a practical and useable level, approximation of the concentration of force along each direction or particular hex corresponding to the critical zones is taken into account. For example, in Fig. 5, the auto-explanation critical zone 3 indicates that expansion be concentrated primarily towards northern hexes with minimal focus on the remaining directions.

6 User Satisfaction

In an initial study involving 22 participants were carried out to provide early indication if auto-explanation generated by a computerised avatar such as GAIA could improve satisfaction. The participants were all male adults in the age range of 16 to 19. All participants have played the game, *Tide of Iron,* at least five times in two months prior to the study being carried out. In the study, participants played the game two times over a course of three days. Each game requires an average of four hours to complete. This included the time in consulting the auto-explanation generated by GAIA. After the games were played, the participants were asked to complete a questionnaire. Of the 22 participants, 18 indicated that their level of satisfaction increased with auto-explanation. The remaining 4 indicated that their level of satisfaction remained unchanged or have decreased with auto-explanation. From the 18 that indicated satisfaction, 3 were mildly satisfied, 7 moderated satisfied and 8 highly satisfied as in Fig. 6.

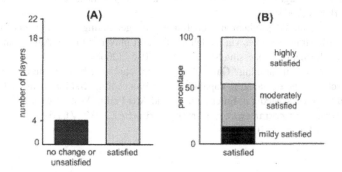

Fig. 6. (A) Participants feedback after playing *Tide of Iron* with auto-explanation. (B) Composite of participants' degree of satisfaction from those who responded positively.

Therefore, from this early study, it indicates that is feasible for an auto-explanation generated by a computerised avatar such as GAIA, to support and improve a game player's satisfaction during game play. Many factors have yet to be factored and considered. However, this early indication provides the stimulus to allow this proposal to be pursued in more depth.

7 Summary

In computerised version of board games, player satisfaction can be augmented by providing explanation of what the computer based AI analytical processes are. This helps the players to understand the reasoning behind the action taken by the computer AI opponent. This paper proposes a method that provides the mechanism for a game AI to communicate its evaluation processes using descriptive auto-explanation through symbolic reasoning. A case study has been presented in an implementation of a game AI opponent that is capable of describing its inferential processes in a tabletop war game. In an initial study, early results show that it is feasible that satisfaction of game players provided with auto-explanation can be augmented and improved.

References

1. Nakatsu, R., Hoshino, J.: Entertainment Computing: Technologies and Applications. Kluwer Academic Publishers, Dordrecht (2002)
2. Nykamp, M.: The Customer Differential: The Complete Guide to Implementing Customer Relationship Management. AMACOM, New York (2001)
3. Gregor, S., Yu, X.: Exploring the Explanatory Capabilities of Intelligent System Technologies. In: Second International Discourse With Fuzzy Logic In The New Millennium. Physica-Verlag, Heidelberg (2000)
4. Gregor, S.: Explanations from Knowledge-based Systems and Cooperative Problem Solving: An Empirical Study. International Journal of Human-Computer Studies 54(1), 81–105 (2001)
5. Crabtree, A.: Designing Collaborative Systems: A Practical Guide to Ethnography. Springer, Berlin (2003)
6. Chiou, A.: A game AI production shell framework: generating AI opponents for geomorphic-isometric strategy games via modeling of expert player intuition. Australian Journal of Intelligent Information Processing Systems 9(4), 50–57 (2008)
7. Chiou, A.: What is it thinking? Game AI opponent computer-human interaction using descriptive schema and explanatory capabilities. In: Proceedings 2nd International Conference on Digital Interactive Media in Entertainment and Arts Perth, Western Australia (2007)
8. http://www.boardgamegeek.com/boardgame/22825/tide-of-iron (accessed on: May 20, 2010)

Comparing Binarisation Techniques for the Processing of Ancient Manuscripts

Rapeeporn Chamchong, Chun Che Fung, and Kok Wai Wong

School of Information Technology, Murdoch University,
90 South Street, Murdoch, Western Australia 6150
rapeeporn.c@gmail.com, l.fung@murdoch.edu.au,
k.wong@murdoch.edu.au

Abstract. Ancient manuscripts have been preserved by many organizations so as to protect these documents and retrieve traditional knowledge. With the advanced computer technology, digitized media is now commonly used to record these documents. One objective of such work is to develop an efficient image processing system that could be used to retrieve knowledge and information automatically from these ancient manuscripts. Binarization is a preprocessing technique used to extract text and characters from the manuscripts. The output is then used for further processes such as character recognition and knowledge extraction. This paper compares different binarization techniques that could be used for processing of ancient manuscripts. The aim is to improve the binarization techniques with the main objective of developing an automated preprocessing technique for ancient manuscript recognition and knowledge extraction.

Keywords: Binarization, Image segmentation, Ancient Documents.

1 Introduction

Dried palm leaves have been used as one of the most popular written documents for over five hundred years in Thailand. Such materials have been used for recording Buddhist teaching and doctrines, folklores, knowledge and use of herbal medicines, stories of dynasties, traditional arts and architectures, astrology, astronomy, and techniques of traditional massages. Over time, most of these palm leaves, if left unattended, will deteriorate. This could be caused by dampness, fungus, bacteria, insects and bugs. This leads to many projects with the objectives to preserve and protect information from ancient manuscripts. Such projects are initiated and carried out by the Thai libraries, universities and institutes including medical departments and religion organizations. Three examples of these projects are the Digitisation Initiative for Traditional Manuscripts of Northern Thailand Project at Chiang Mai University Library [1, 2], the Palm Leaf Manuscript Preservation Project in Northeastern Region of Thailand at Mahasarakham University [3], and the Thailand Herbal Repository Access Initiative (THRAI) at Kasetsart University [4]. In particular, the THRAI project aims at developing a database for Thai traditional

R. Nakatsu et al. (Eds.): ECS 2010, IFIP AICT 333, pp. 55–64, 2010.
© IFIP International Federation for Information Processing 2010

medicine in order to preserve and propagate Thai medical knowledge from the ancient manuscripts.

The number of multimedia databases and the amount of information stored and captured digitally is increasing rapidly with the advances of computer technology. Although the availability of advance imaging tools and effective image processing techniques makes it feasible to process these documents in multimedia formats for future analysis and storage, there is no specific system that is capable to retrieve relevant information efficiently and to extract knowledge from them. It is therefore a key objective of this study to develop an efficient image processing system that could be used to retrieve knowledge and information from these historical manuscripts. However, it is recognized that the process of scanning a digital image of the ancient palm leaves could also presents some difficulties. Most of the original leaves are aged, leading to deterioration of the writing media, with seepage of ink and smearing along cracks, damage to the leaf due to the holes used for binding the manuscript leaves, dirt and other discoloration. These factors lead to poor contrast, smudges, smear, stains, and ghosting noise due to seeping ink from the other side of the manuscripts between the foreground text and the background. Digital image processing techniques are therefore necessary to improve the readability of the manuscripts.

Prior to the stage of knowledge extraction, characters or text on the images have to be recognized. There are three steps which need to be completed prior to the task of character recognition. First, a manuscript is scanned into a RGB image and then it is converted to a gray-scale image. Next, image enhancement is used to enhance the quality of the image. After this stage, binarization is applied and then text and character separation are carried out before character recognition. Binarization is an essential part of the preprocessing step in image processing, converting gray-scale image to binary image, which is then used for further processing such as document image analysis and optical character recognition (OCR). Consequently, both image enhancement and binarization of historical document are crucial to remove unrelated information, noise and background on the documents. If these steps are ineffective, the original characters from the image may be unrecognizable or more noise may be added. Therefore, these techniques are essential to improve the readability of the documents and the overall performance of the process.

Several binarization algorithms have been proposed in the literature [5-14]. However, it is difficult to select the most appropriate algorithm. The comparison of image qualities from those algorithms is not an easy task as there is no objective evaluation process to compare the results. In contrast, some researchers have proposed a quantitative image measurement of binarization. This performance evaluation of binarization algorithms is recognized to significantly dependent on the image content and on the methodologies of binarization. The common approach is to design a set of criteria and scores of criteria. The criteria may be computed by machine or may be decided by visual human. Within this domain, Badekas and Papamarkos [15], applied some binarization techniques with a standard database (Mediateam Oulu Document) [16]. However, these documents are not as complex as palm leaf manuscripts.

In this paper, a comparison of different binarization techniques of manuscripts is reported. In section 2, the binarization techniques are explained. Section 3 describes the framework of appropriate selection of binarization techniques by machine learning. The experimental results are then shown in section 4 and finally, a conclusion and discussion on future research are given in the last section.

2 Binarization Techniques

Binarization is the task of converting a gray-scale image to a binary image by using threshold selection techniques to categorize the pixels of an image into either one of the two classes. Most of studies [5-8, 14, 17] separated the binarization techniques into two main methods that are global thresholding and local adaptive thresholding techniques.

Global Thresholding Techniques. These techniques attempt to find a suitable single threshold value (Thr) from the overall image. The pixels are separated into two classes: foreground (text which is black color) and background (white color). This can be expressed as follows [5]

$$I_b(x,y) = \begin{cases} \text{black} & \text{if} & I_f(x,y) \leq \text{Thr} \\ \text{white} & \text{if} & I_f(x,y) > \text{Thr} \end{cases} \tag{1}$$

where $I_f(x,y)$ is the pixel of the input image from the noise reduction and $I_b(x,y)$ is the pixel of the binarized image.

Otsu's algorithm [11] is a popular global thresholding technique. Moreover, there are many popular thresholding techniques such as Kapur and et al [18], and Kittler and Illingworth [19].

Local Thresholding Techniques [14]. These techniques calculate the threshold values which are determined locally based on pixel by pixel, or region by region. A threshold value (Thr(x,y)) can be derived for each pixel in the image, and the image can be separated into foreground and background as given in expression (2) [5].

$$I_b(x,y) = \begin{cases} \text{black} & \text{if} & I_f(x,y) \leq \text{Thr}(x,y) \\ \text{white} & \text{if} & I_f(x,y) > \text{Thr}(x,y) \end{cases} \tag{2}$$

The conventional local adaptive thresholding techniques have been proposed by Niblack [10] and Sauvola [12].

In this paper, a comparison from nine binarization techniques are reported which are Otsu [11], Kittler and Illingworth [19], Kapur [18], Tsai [20], Huang [21], Yen and et al [22], Niblack [10], Sauvola [12], and Bernsen [14]. The first six techniques are global thresholding techniques and the last three techniques are local adaptive thresholding techniques.

These approaches are then applied to the palm leaves images and also the MediaTeam Oulu Document Database. The objective is to determine whether automated process could be developed in determining the optimal value of threshold for the binarization of the images. A collection of the techniques is given below.

Binarization Tecniques	Criteria
1.Otsu [11]	$\eta(\text{thr} *) = \sigma_B^2(\text{thr}*)/\sigma_T^2$, $\sigma_B^2(\text{thr}*) = \underset{0 \le \text{thr} < L-1}{\arg\max}\, \sigma_B^2(\text{thr})$ thr* is optimal threshold, η is separation criteria, $\sigma_B^2(\text{thr})$ is variance between group of histogram at threshold thr and σ_T^2 is variance of histogram
2.Klittler and Illingworth [19]	$T_{opt} = \arg\min\{P(T)\log\sigma_f(T) + [1 - P(T)]\log\sigma_b(T)$ $- P(T)\log P(T) - [1 - P(T)]\log[1 - P(T)]\}$ where $\sigma_f(T)$ and $\sigma_f(T)$ are foreground and background standard deviations.
3.Kapur [18]	$T_{opt} = \arg\max[H_f(T) + H_b(T)]$ where $H_f(T) = -\sum_{l=0}^{T} \frac{p(l)}{P(T)} \log \frac{p(l)}{P(T)}$ and $H_b(T) = -\sum_{l=T+1}^{L} \frac{p(l)}{P(T)} \log \frac{p(l)}{P(T)}$
4.Yen and et al. [21]	$T_{opt} = \arg\max[C_b(T) + C_f(T)]$ where $C_b(T) = -\log\left\{\sum_{l=0}^{T}\left[\frac{p(l)}{P(T)}\right]^2\right\}$ and $C_f(T) = -\log\left\{\sum_{l=T+1}^{L}\left[\frac{p(l)}{1-P(T)}\right]^2\right\}$
5.Huang [21]	$T_{opt} = \arg\min\{-\frac{1}{N^2\log 2}\sum_{l=0}^{L}[\mu_f(l,T)\log(\mu_f(l,T))]$ $+ [1 - \mu_f(l,T)\log(1 - \mu_f(l,T))]p(l)\}$ where $\mu_f[l(i,j),T] = \dfrac{L}{L + |I(i,j) - m_f(T)|}$
6.Tsai [20]	$T_{opt} = \arg\text{equal}[m_1 = b_1(T), m_2 = b_2(T), m_3 = b_3(T)]$ where $m_k = \sum_{l=0}^{T} p(l)l^k$ and $b_k = P_f m_f^k + P_b m_b^k$
7. Niblack [10]	$T(x,y) = m(x,y) \cdot + k * s(x,y)$ k=-0.2, window size =20x20
8. Sauvola [12]	$T(x,y) = m(x,y) \cdot \left[1 + k \cdot \left(\frac{s(x,y)}{R} - 1\right)\right]$ k=0.5, R=128, window size = 20x20
9.Bernsen [14]	$T(x, y) = (Zlow + Zhigh)/2$, $C(x, y) = (Z_{high} - Z_{low} <)$ e Window size (r x r) = 15x15 and e = 15

3 Framework of Appropriate Selection of Binarization Techniques

According to human knowledge, human may predict the performance of algorithms on the image and select the best one. However, it is not an easy selection task by computer. If the process of automated algorithm selection can be simulated, this will help people to choose the best one. This study attempt to investigate and propose desire algorithm from image features by using machine learning technique

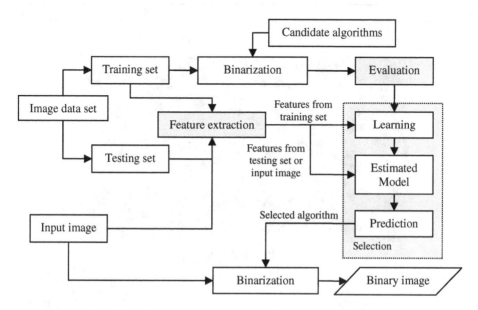

Fig. 1. Framework of appropriate selection of binarization techniques

The propose framework of this system composts of three modules: evaluation, feature extraction, and selection. Firstly, evaluation module is employed with binary image by using k-means algorithm [23]. Secondly, feature extraction module is automated by selecting some characteristics from image. In general, histogram can be used for non-texture image. In addition, average and standard deviation of histogram are used to explain image characteristic. Finally, main module of this system, selection module, is calculated by feeding features from image to learn from training set and then estimated module is generated for predicting the appropriate algorithm. The appropriate selection is done by using Backpropagation [23].

4 Experimental Results

In this experiment, the image data set is based on ancient palm leaf manuscripts. The data set is obtained from the Palm Leaf Manuscript Preservation Project in Northeastern Region, Mahasarakham University [3]. There are 330 palm leaf images which

Table 1. Performance of appropriate selection of binarization algorithms

Algorithm	True Positive Rate
1.Otsu	91.05%
2.Klittler and Illingworth	84.00%
3.Kapur	48.72%
4.Yen et al.	8.82%
5.Huang	0%
6.Tsai	71.05%
7.Bernsen	87.81%

a)   Palm leaf manuscripts

b)   MediaTeam Oulu Document Database

Fig. 2. Samples of original image from the two data sets

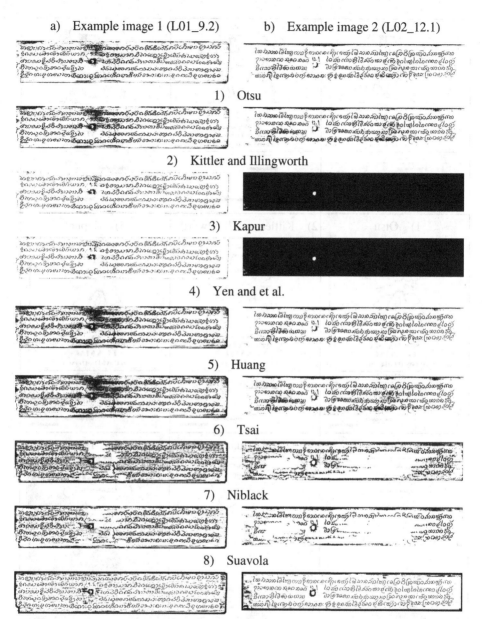

Fig. 3. Binary results of nine thresholding techniques on palm leaf manuscripts

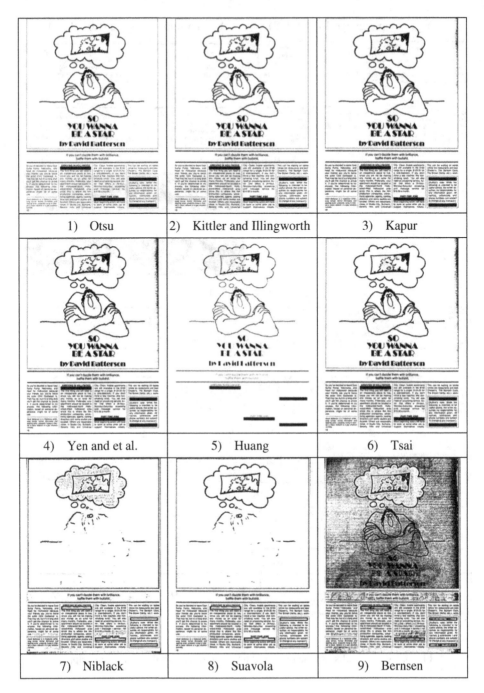

Fig. 4. Binary results of nine thresholding techniques on sample 1 from MediaTeam Oulu Document Database

have been scanned previously. The resolution of the input images is 200x200 dpi in RGB format. In addition, the documents from the MediaTeam Oulu Document Database [16], which is a standard database, is processed to compare binary results with palm leaf manuscripts. There are 158 documents 512 pages and the resolution of the input image is 300x300 dpi in RGB format. Samples of the original images from both data sets are shown in Fig. 2. The input images were converted to gray-scale images and then noise is reduced by Gaussians filtering technique. After that, binarization techniques have been applied. Fig. 3 and 4 show some example binarized results from ancient palm leaf manuscripts and from the MediaTeam Oulu Document Database respectively.

This experiment, 10 fold cross-validation is used for 330 images from palm leaf manuscripts to evaluate the appropriate selection of binarization techniques. According to evaluating by visual human with this data set, there is no best algorithm from Niblack and Suavola, so seven algorithms are selected. The performance of selection system is given in Table 1.

The results from this experiment have shown that Otsu's algorithm, Bernsen's algorithm, and Klittler and Illingworth gave better performance. In contrast, true positive rate of Huang's algorithm and Yean et al. are the lower performance algorithms.

Comparing the results from global thresholding techniques and local adaptive thresholding techniques, it was found that results from local adaptive thresholding techniques have adjusted the output among local areas so that characters will appear to have more stable appearance than the global techniques. The global thresholding techniques may have eliminated noise in some background areas, but the characters in other areas may become unreadable.

5   Conclusion and Future Work

Although many binarization techniques have been successfully applied to the MediaTeam Oulu Document Database [15], such techniques have difficulty in eliminating background noise on palm leaf manuscripts. Most of the reported work has been carried out on standard images that are not as complex and in poor quality as the ancient palm leaf manuscripts. From this study, it can be concluded that there is no single binarization technique that is suitable for all images in each domain. For this reason, how to choose the best binarization technique for the user is the key issue and currently, there is no automatic selection of the optimal binarization technique. At present, machine learning technique is being investigated in order to determine which algorithm is suitable for binarization techniques in different situations. This proposed framework can be applied for automatic selection system.

References

1. Information Heritage,
   http://www.emc.com/leadership/digital-universe/
   information-heritage-awards-2008.htm
2. Musiket, Y.: Scanning the Past (2009)

3. Mahasarakham University: Palm Leaf Manuscript Preservation Project in Northeastern Region. Reports for the Financial Year 2004 and 2005 (2005) (in Thai)
4. Thailand Herbal Repository Access Initiative (THRAI), http://thrai.sci.ku.ac.th/
5. Chamchong, R., Fung, C.C.: Comparing background elimination approaches for processing of ancient Thai manuscripts on palm leaves. In: 2009 Int. Conf. Machine Learning and Cybernetics, China (2009)
6. Chen, Y., Leedham, G.: Decompose algorithm for thresholding degraded historical document images. In: IEE Proceeding Visual Image Signal Processing p. 152 (2005)
7. He, J., Do, Q.D.M., Downton, A.C., Kim, J.H.: A comparison of binarization methods for historical archive documents. In: Proc. 8th Int. Conf. Document Analysis and Recognition, vol. 538, pp. 538–542 (2005)
8. Leedham, G., Chen, Y., Takru, K., Joie Hadi Nata, T., Li, M.: Comparison of some thresholding algorithms for text/background segmentation in difficult document images. In: Proc. 7th Int. Conf. Document Analysis and Recognition, pp. 859–864 (2003)
9. Sezgin, M., Sankur, B.: Survey over image thresholding techniques and quantitative performance evaluation. J. of Electronic Imaging 13, 146–168 (2004)
10. Niblack, W.: An introduction to digital image processing. Prentice-Hall, Englewood Cliffs (1986)
11. Otsu, N.: A threshold selection method from gray-level histogram. IEEE Trans. Systems Man Cybernet 9, 62–66 (1979)
12. Sauvola, J., Pietikainen, M.: Adaptive document image binarization. Pattern Recognition 33, 225–236 (2000)
13. Sezgin, M., Sankur, B.: Selection of thresholding methods for nondestructive testing applications. In: Proc. 2001 Int. Conf. Image Processing, vol. 3, pp. 763, 764–767 (2001)
14. Trier, O.D., Jain, A.K.: Goal-directed evaluation of binarization methods. IEEE Trans. Pattern Analysis and Machine Intelligence 17, 1191–1201 (1995)
15. Badekas, E., Papamarkos, N.: Document binarisation using Kohonen SOM. IET Image Process. 1, 67–84 (2007)
16. Suavola, J., Kauniskangas, H.: MediaTeam Document Database II, a CD-ROM collection of document images. University of Oulu, Finland (1999)
17. Gonzalez, R.C., Woods, R.E.: Digital Image Processing. Prentice-Hall, New Jersey (2002)
18. Kapur, J.N., Sahoo, P.K., Wong, A.K.C.: A new method for gray-level picture thresholding using the entropy of the histogram. Graph. Models Image Process. 29, 273–285 (1985)
19. Kittler, J., Illingworth, J.: Minimum error thresholding. Pattern Recognition 19, 41–47 (1986)
20. Tsai, W.H.: Moment-preserving thresholding: A new approch. Graph. Models Image Process. 19, 377–379 (1985)
21. Huang, L.-K., Wang, M.-J.J.: Image thresholding by minimizing the measures of fuzziness. Pattern Recognition 28, 41–51 (1995)
22. Jui-Cheng, Y., Fu-Juay, C., Shyang, C.: A new criterion for automatic multilevel thresholding. IEEE Transactions on Image Processing 4, 370–378 (1995)
23. Heijden, F.v.d., Duin, R.P.W., Ridder, D.d., Tax, D.M.J.: Classification, parameter estimation and state estimation: an engineering approach using MATLAB. John Wiley & Sons, Ltd., West Sussex (2004)

Complex Game Design Modeling

Viknashvaran Narayanasamy[1], Kok Wai Wong[1], Shri Rai[1], and Andrew Chiou[2]

[1] Murdoch University, School of Information Technology,
South St, Murdoch, Western Australia
viknash@hobbiz.com, k.wong@murdoch.edu.au, s.rai@murdoch.edu.au
[2] CQUniversity Australia, School of Computing Sciences,
Rockhampton, Queensland, Australia
a.chiou@cqu.edu.au

Abstract. This paper looks at the game design and engineering approach to model the game design. The game modeling framework discussed in this paper could be a systematic alternative for implementing in the game engine architecture. The suggested game modeling framework incorporates structural game component, temporal game component and boundary game component frameworks. It is suitable to model most complex games and game engines.

Keywords: game modeling framework, complex system, game component, game design and engineering approach.

1 Introduction

Many fields of computer science and engineering have been studied as complex system and thus modelling is an important area of research in many applications. In computer games, applications of complex system modelling has been utilised to facilitate the modelling of Artificial Intelligence in agent-agent and human-agent interaction research [1]. Recent computer games have often made use of multi-agent technologies for modelling cooperation, teamwork and character behaviour as well [2] in agents. Models are idealisations of a system in which certain aspects of the system are captured and other aspects are ignored. As a model should not be as complicated as the phenomenon it purports to describe the best models are usually the simplest possible model of the system [3]. Models that increase the complexity of a system and models that need to be updated constantly are not desirable. The main difficulty in constructing a model is identifying the important aspects of the system without compromising on features that are required to regenerate the actual system with sufficient detail. Since all models are abstractions of the modelled entity, information will be lost when the modelling is performed. Thus a variety of models representing different views of the system are often needed. These types of models used are driven by what aspects of the system the definers of the model want to expose [4].

In the context of the Game Engine Architecture, three modelling frameworks are proposed. Each of these frameworks models Game Design from a different point of view. The complete models can then be mapped onto elements in the Game Engine Architecture and be implemented easily.

R. Nakatsu et al. (Eds.): ECS 2010, IFIP AICT 333, pp. 65–74, 2010.
© IFIP International Federation for Information Processing 2010

2 Game Design and Engineering

This section introduces the Game Modelling and Designing and Engineering approach that is needed to design a game model that can be applied to the Game Engine Architecture so that a game can be built.

In the interest of clarity, this approach is best described from left to right. The High-Level Architecture (HLA) consists of the Game Modelling Framework and the Game Engine Architecture. The Game Modelling Framework itself consists of three Game Component Frameworks. The Game Modelling Framework is used to refine the above mentioned player-driven [5] Game Design into a more concrete and formalised model for applying a Game Design.

The complete Game Model would then be the result of numerous iterations and proto¬typing efforts, made with inputs from player-driven requirements and Game Design goals. The Game Architecture, which is described in this section and in the completed Game Model, is used to systematically develop the Game Engine in the Game Engineering phase. The high-level architecture is the result of the application of the Game Modelling Framework (consisting of the Game Design and the Game Model) and the Game Architecture. From then on the Game Engine can be configured and extended for different games by using a data-driven approach. Both the player-driven and data-driven approaches offer a greater level of flexibility to the Game Designer.

3 Modelling the Game as a Complex System

In [6], the authors define a system as a set of parts which are in a relationship to each other to create a complex whole. In that sense a system would fundamentally consist of four components, namely, objects, attributes, internal relationships and the environment. The game itself will be represented by a set of states, for which transition functions are required to move from one state to another. [7] describes games as a container of objects which change their state during the play, where the evolution of their state is governed by the rules and influenced by the players or other objects. These two definitions provide an abstract yet accurate representation of a simple game.

In this abstract representation, games consist of Game Objects that are part of a system that must contain attributes to define the properties of the objects; internal relationships to define the behaviour of objects and between objects; and the environment to govern objects with rules. Each game system can embody a control system. Each system can be a subsystem of a larger system. This will require hierarchical ordering of a number of state machines within game systems as well as composition of a number of control systems. The composition of a number of control systems will unintentionally turn into a complex system problem, as more and more Game Objects are added.

It is also important to note that games are not collections where objects can be added, removed or modified without affecting the relationships of other objects or the behaviour of the whole system [8]. As the majority of objects in an artificial environment respond better to discrete input it may be good to model games as discrete control systems.

Discrete control systems can be defined by making use of finite state automata, which can be represented by a triple (Q, Σ, δ) where [9]:-

> Q – defines a finite sets of states
> Σ - defines a finite set of input symbols
> δ - defines a mapping function that maps the current state to the state given a finite set of input symbols.
> i.e. $\delta: Q \times E \rightarrow Q'$

For each $q \in Q$, there exists a set of choices, such that elements $\sigma \in \Sigma$ are defined for $\delta(q, \sigma)$. As games tend to be mechanically deterministic and have a deterministic number of states [10], it is only necessary to model the controlled evolution of the state transitions in the game with the partial function δ [11].

It is also beneficial to look at this finite state automata representation from a different perspective that involves representing the list of states or inputs as strings. The string representation of sets of states simplifies the process of defining the allowable set of combinatorial actions on sets of states.

Let Σ^* denote the set of all finite strings obtained by concatenating elements in Σ, including the empty string ε.

As the concatenation of strings operation can be considered a map from $\Sigma^* \times \Sigma^*$ to Σ^*, Σ^* can be considered a monoid.

As the concatenation of strings is an associative operative operation, ε can be considered the monoid identity since it satisfies $s \cdot \varepsilon = \varepsilon \cdot s = s$ for any $s \in \Sigma^*$.

From basic automata theory, δ defines a unique partial map $Q \times E^* \rightarrow Q$, with the following properties:

$$\delta^*(q, \varepsilon) \rightarrow q$$
$$\delta^*(q, \sigma_1 \sigma_2) \rightarrow \delta^*(\delta^*(q, \sigma_1) \sigma_2)$$

From this, it can be concluded that δ^* is a partially defined action of the monoid Σ^* on the set Q.

Σ^* can also be represented as a disjoint union as follows:

$$\Sigma^* = \prod_{n \in N_o} \Sigma^n$$

Given a set of n elements, $\{1,2,3,.....,n\}$, the map u : $\{1,2,3,.....,n\} \rightarrow \Sigma$ defined by u(i) $= \sigma_i$ for i=1,2,3,...n, will be $(\sigma_1, \sigma_2, \sigma_3, ...\sigma_n \in \Sigma^n$.

The concatenation of strings and maps are related as follows:

$$\Sigma^n \times \Sigma^m \rightarrow \Sigma^{n+m}$$

$$(u(i), v(i)) \text{ a } (u.v)(i) = \begin{cases} u(i) & if \quad 1 \le i \le n \\ v(i-n) & if \ n+1 \le i \le n+m \end{cases}$$

However, the above operation is only well-defined in discrete systems where n is finite. This is because the concatenation operation n+m will not be possible if n is not finite. Also, since $u \cdot v \in \Sigma^{n+m}$, n+m and consequently m has to be finite.

In reality, however, control systems can either be discrete or continuous. The modelling of continuous control systems is similar to that of discrete systems, as they can be both modelled after monoids. However, the state space and input space of continuous control systems are modelled using smooth functions instead of discrete values [11]. Continuous control systems can also work with variables that are not finite.

It has been assumed that games have an unknown but finite number of states. The introduction of continuous input variables can introduce useful emergent behaviour. Continuous input variables can be introduced by making use of higher-level AI implementations such as Fuzzy Finite State Machines and Neural Networks. To allow for the emergence of emergent behaviour the game is best modelled after hybrid control systems that handle both discrete and continuous input.

The first step in modelling the game as a complex control system involves using a higher-level abstraction of control systems that is common to both discrete and continuous control systems. This is required as the composition of a number of discrete control systems can cause the control system of the game to exhibit properties that more closely resemble continuous control systems, especially when the game rules change with respect to time. Furthermore, a higher-level abstraction of a control system such as that based on abstract control systems can also be the basis upon which hybrid control systems can be built upon in future [11]. An abstract control system can be represented as follows:

A game utilising an abstract control system can be modelled as a triple (S, M, Φ).

S – is a Set representing the state space of the game, which is a collection of the states of all game objects.

M – is a monoid that represents a set of inputs.

Φ – is the abstract control system defines a map, that is, an action or partially defined action of the monoid M on the set S.

i.e. $\Phi : S \times M \to S$

Identity Property: ε represents a neutral element. So, $\Phi(s, \varepsilon) = s$

Semi-Groups: Given two consecutive inputs m_1 followed by m_2, and then applying the inputs in that particular order is the same as applying input m_2 to the resultant state after m_1 has been applied.

$\Phi(s, m_1 m_2) = \Phi(\Phi(s, m_1), m_2)$, where $s \in S$ and m_1 & $m_2 \in M$

The evolution or state transition of the abstract control system can be defined as follows:

$$s \xrightarrow{m} s'$$

The formal method of using an abstract control system to define systems in games is useful in defining the states of Game Objects and the interconnection between state spaces of Game Objects. However, this technique does not address the complexity issues involved in interconnecting various systems and subsystems of Game Objects.

4 The Game State

Playing a game can be described as making changes in quantitative game states, where each state is a collection of all values of all Game Elements and the relationships between them [12]. Game play can then be described as an action by which quantitative changes can be made to game states. Players would then be influencing the game state by performing actions on Game Elements to achieve goals in the game.

More importantly, the game state is not necessarily the same as the state of the running game program. The state of a program can include the state of all hardware register values, the state of data structures, the state of the rendering subsystem, etc. The states of these items and many other items are crucial for the proper functioning of the Game Engine and consequently the game while it is running. However, in a high-level architecture, the implementation details and the states of low-level platform-dependent features are irrelevant in analysing the state of the game.

The game state in this context will refer to the states in finite state machines (FSMs) and their variants in each object. It will also refer to the state of data in components of data-driven architectures; the running state of processes, threads and micro-threads used by a game; the state of responses to high-level function calls and events; and the mode of the game. Generally, this can be termed the game play state of a game.

The game when viewed as a system is made up of objects. Objects are made up of attributes and their functionality is described by behaviours. Attributes can be used to determine the result of behaviours while the relationships between objects can be determined by their behaviours [13]. There are three fundamental parts to defining a valid and functional Game Element. They include the definition of the Game Object; the presence of at least one control system to control the behaviour of an object; and progress conditions that can introduce cumulative emergent behaviour.

5 The Game Modelling Framework

The Game Component Framework as proposed by [12] consists of four possible categories, by which the activity of playing a game can be viewed. These categories are referred to as components and from the players' perspective represent the action of playing a game. [12] mentions that all four component frameworks are essential for describing the game. A thorough analysis of these component frameworks was done and their relation to the proposed architecture was mapped. It was found that the fourth and final component framework, i.e. the Holistic Component, was not useful as a tool to map informal techniques in Game Design to a formalised Game Architecture as it contrasts the activity of game play with other external activities, which is not relevant considering the design of a Game Engine Architecture.

The Game Modelling Framework was derived from the Structural, Temporal and Boundary Game Component Frameworks. As such, the following sections will describe three approaches for which elements in a game can be modelled and translated to a form that can be implemented in the Game Engine Architecture. The Structural Game Component Framework presents an opportunity to model Game Design Elements using a control view from a Complex Systems perspective. The Temporal Game Component Framework, on the other hand, enables Game Design Elements to be modelled and implemented using a bottom-up approach where the individual components are modelled before their higher-level structures. The Boundary Game Component Framework, in contrast to this however, models the rules and constraints of actions in the environment.

6 The Structural Game Component Framework Mapping

The Structural Game Component Framework consists of five essential components: Game Elements, Game Time, Players, Interface and the Facilitator. Games Design can be broken down into the following components and the components can be implemented by mapping the functionality of the components to their counterparts in the Game Engine Architecture:

Game Elements – In the Structural Game Component Framework, Game Elements are the physical and logical components that contain the game state, which are an abstract representation of the actual Game Object in the human domain. Game Elements will contain both attributes and actions. Attributes define the object types of Game Elements and the Ownership of a Game Element. In the Framework this would refer to the controller of a Game Element. In the Game Engine Architecture this will refer to the Game Object that has privileged and/or exclusive rights to the Game Object that implements the Game Element. Attributes can also be numerical attributes that are used in algorithms to determine the outcome of actions. The Environment in the Game Engine Architecture is a special Game Element that defines the spatial world in which other Game Elements reside.

Game Time – Game Time determines how changes in the game state (the progress of game) relate to real time. A change can be discrete or continuous and can be different for different modes of play. In the Game Architecture, the Game Objects are event-driven and react to messages passed to them by the scheduler or other Game Objects. Ultimately, all Game Objects rely on the clock module in the scheduler to generate periodic or time-based offset events. True representations of time can be simulated using the Scheduler. To make use of the Structural Game Component Framework, a time-dependent order of allowable actions has to be modelled so that it can be translated to a series of periodic events and implemented in the Scheduler. If strict time-based ordering is not required, then event-based actions can be modelled directly into the state machine representation using the temporal Game Component Framework.

Interface – The interface provides information to the players regarding the game state. It does this by providing an access point where players can query and perform available actions. The interface can also help to express the theme of the game, or rather define a protocol for interaction between heterogenous Game Elements. External interfaces are input devices like the keyboard or the mouse. However, their internal representations as input events are of more importance in this framework. An example of an interface in a game is the play grid in a turn-based strategy game. The Game Objects on the grid would then partially represent the Game State.

Players – Players can be defined as representation of entities that are trying to achieve the goals in the game. Players change the game state through actions. Players can either be human-controlled Game Entities or computer-controlled agents. They can either compete or cooperate with other players or agents.

Facilitator – The facilitator takes care of setting up the game and synchronises the game state and maintains the game time. Facilitators can also be ultimate arbitrating entities between the players and the game system. In the Game Architecture, facilitators are available to synchronise the Game States of client and server machines in MMP Games and all client nodes in a DIS. Facilitators in the form of Overseers are also available to arbitrate the allocation of system and Game Resources.

7 The Temporal Game Component Framework

The Temporal Game Component Framework was designed so that the flow of the game can be easily represented. The causality and the action-consequence behaviour of the game are of particular interest in this framework. This framework de-emphasises rule making and does not take into consideration the reasons for players' actions. In the Game Engine Architecture, the Temporal Game Framework most closely represents the microscopic views of state machines that exist for each and every Game Object in the Game Environment.

Actions will define the actions that are provided and the actions that can possibly be taken at particular states in the game. Actions in the context of this framework would mean through which players can make changes to the Game State. Actions can either be implicit or explicit and are associated with the interface provided for each player. Implicit actions are actions taken to find the actions that are possible. Actions in the Temporal Game Component Framework map onto the actions that are performed by a Game Object in response to an input event.

In contrast to Actions, Events are means by which the players can be informed of the consequence of their actions. In a way, events are the output of Game Objects and form part of the Game States perceivable by the player. Additionally, events can show the events generated by other players' actions. Events can also be generated by randomness, algorithms, etc. In the Game Engine Architecture, Events would translate to the Event-Based Messages generated after a successful change in state due to Actions taken by the Game Object.

Closures – Closures are quantifiable meaningful player experiences usually associated with changes in game state. Closures occur at points in time when a goal is met or when an end state is no longer reachable. Closures are not always associated with a milestone change in game state or significant progress. Closures can form on players' subjective experiences. Game state closures are usually non-reversible.

End Conditions – End Conditions define the set of conditions that need to be met for either a switch in mode of play, the completion of a closure, the end of a game instance, the end of a game or the end of a play session.

Evaluation Functions – Evaluation Functions are algorithms used to determine the outcome of end conditions or closures. Deterministic evaluation functions are desirable as they lead to consistent results.

By streamlining the list and sequence of allowable actions for each Game Element, a well-defined temporal structure can be defined in the Temporal Game Component Framework. This structure can then be translated and implemented in the event-based state machine in the Game Engine Architecture.

8 The Boundary Game Component Framework

The Boundary Game Component Framework was designed to implement constraints in the game to limit the activities that can be performed in a game. This can be done in several ways. It can be done by allowing only certain actions (i.e. by negative constraints) or it can be done by making certain activities more rewarding (i.e. by positive constraints). It can also be done by establishing social contracts between the players which have to be satisfied while playing through a set of limitations or by making use of rules of play [6], where boundaries between allowed and forbidden actions are clearly defined and enforced.

Rules – Rules are used extensively in this framework. They govern how components interact and determine the actions that are allowed, and the order in which they are allowed. They can also determine the choice and order of actions as they can limit a player's range of actions. Rules are also used to define and describe boundaries and govern how all other components are instantiated.

Although rules are necessary to define the Game Environment, their extensive use is undesirable in successful emergent systems. Rules can be classified into three categories [6]: Operational Rules are rules that define how the game is played by players. They also define how the game corresponds to explicitly written rules by players and define the physical implementation of constitutive rules. Constitutive Rules are more abstract and define the underlying formal structures that exist beneath operational rules. The last classification of rules is Implicit Rules. As Implicit Rules deal with the human and social aspects of playing the game, they will not be included in the design of the framework. These rules include Etiquette, Sportsmanship, etc. In Multi-tiered AI Frameworks different rule types are used for different tiers in the AI Architecture.

There are other rules that differ between game instances and these are usually optional. House rules are rules agreed to by players before the start of the game (e.g. Game Play Options for multiplayer maps in Real-Time Strategy Games, such as "Auto respawn", are one such example). These rules balance the game and introduce variance.

Non-Static Rules in games allow rules to change. Such rules allow for games where the game play is about changing rules. Such rules require high-order rules that are rules created to govern non-static rules.

Goals – Goals set predefine tasks for players to achieve. In the Game Engine Architecture goals are represented as favourable game states set for individual players to achieve. Goals give players motivation for their actions. Sub-goals can be introduced, too, if the process of achieving a goal is too lengthy. Diagrammatically, this can be represented by Composite and Sub-State machine. In some games the process of identifying goals can be part of a game, and in such games identifying a goal can in itself be a goal.

Modes of Play – Modes of play refers to sections of the game where perceivably different types of activities take place. For example, this can be in the form of having sub-games within games. These are considered sub-modes of play. Different players can have different action sets and each action set is associated with different modes of play. Role reversals can also be considered as a different mode of play.

Table 1. Rule types in a Multi-tiered Framework

	Operational Rules	Constitutive Rules	Implicit Rules
Strategic Intelligence		✓	✓
Operational Intelligence	✓		✗
Tactical Intelligence	✓		✗
Individual Unit Intelligence	✓		✗

Creating a game by making use of the Game Modelling Framework for the Game Engine Architecture requires the modelling of the Game using the three Game Component Frameworks. Firstly, structural modelling will have to be done on the individual Game Element using the Structural Game Component Modelling Framework and this will have to be implemented as a Game Object in the Game Architecture. Secondly, the state machine, (i.e. the states of the game) will have to be accurately modelled using the Temporal Game Modelling Framework and the abstract control system model for representing the game. The Boundary Game Component Framework can then be used to design the rules needed to govern the behaviour of Game Entities. This can be done by implementing the Boundary Game Components as Overseers in the Overseer Tier or other higher-level AI mechanisms. . A high fidelity prototype based on a sub-set of the framework presented in this paper has been developed by Chiou [14].

9 Conclusion

This paper has introduced the Game Design and Engineering approach to model a Game Design and implement it in the Game Engine Architecture. It has also shown how the Game can be modelled as a system of systems within the Game Component Framework. The Game State was modelled using Finite State Automata. This formulation can prove useful in consolidating and validating the list of possible Game States.

The Game Component Framework has also shown how a Complex system of systems can be achieved by mapping the various objects and associated game states by means of an abstract control system. If successfully applied, this methodology will be able to simplify the content generation task by allowing designers to define simple game objects and the rules to create more complex objects from simple game objects. On the other hand the Game Component Framework has shown how complex rules can be broken down into simpler rules that are manageable by entities in the game.

The suggested Game Modelling Framework incorporates the Structural Game Component, Temporal Game Component and Boundary Game Component Frameworks. By making use of a combination of these three frameworks, the Game Design can be formally captured into a format that can be easily translated to be implemented in the Game Engine Architecture.

References

1. Bezek, A.: Modelling Multiagent Games Using Action Graphs (2004), http://www.cs.biu.ac.il/~galk/moo2004/proceedings/poster/1.pdf
2. Orkin, J.: Constraining Autonomous Character Behavior with Human Concepts. In: AI Programming Wisdom, vol. 2. Charles River Media (2005)
3. Wolfram, S.: A New Kind of Science. Wolfram Media, Champaign (2002)
4. Little, R.: Architectures for Distributed Interactive Simulation, Software Engineering Institute, http://www.sei.cmu.edu/architecture/Architectures_for_DIS.html
5. Gaash, A.: Asian Game Markets and Game Development - Mass Market for MMP Games. In: Alexander, T. (ed.) Massively Multiplayer Game Development, vol. 2, pp. 481–494. Charles River Media, Hingham (2005)
6. Salen, K., Zimmerman, E.: Rules of Play - Game Design Fundamentals. The MIT Press, Cambridge (2004)
7. Grunvogel, S.: Formal Models and Game Design. Game Studies: The International Journal of Computer Game Research 5(1) (2005)
8. Fullerton, T., Swain, C., Hoffman, S.: Game Design Workshop - Designing, Prototyping, and Playtesting Games, CMP Books (2004)
9. Cassandras, C., Lafortune, S.: Introduction to Discrete Event Systems. Kluwer Academic Publishers, Boston (1999)
10. Crawford, C.: The Art of Computer Game Design. McGraw-Hill Osborne Media, New York
11. Tabuada, P., Pappas, G., Lima, P.: Compositional abstractions of hybrid control systems. In: Proceedings of the 40th IEEE Conference on Decision and Control, Orlando, Florida (2001)
12. Bjork, S., Halopainen, J.: An Activity-Based Framework for Describing Games. In: Patterns in Game Design. Charles River Media, Hingham (2004)
13. Barry, I.: Game Design. In: Rabin, S. (ed.) Introduction to Game Development. Charles River Media, Hingham (2005)
14. Chiou, A.: A game AI production shell framework: generating AI opponents for geomorphic-isometric strategy games via modeling of expert player intuition. Australian Journal of Intelligent Information Processing Systems 9(4), 50–57 (2008)

Haptic Carillon: A Computationally Enhanced Mechanical Performing Instrument

Mark Havryliv[1], Fazel Naghdy[1], Greg Schiemer[2], and Timothy Hurd[3]

[1] Faculty of Informatics, and
[2] Sonic Arts Research Network, University of Wollongong, Australia
[3] Olympic Carillon, Seattle

Abstract. This paper describes the development of a haptic device for emulating the sonic and haptic dynamics of a carillon, specifically the National Carillon in Canberra, Australia. The carillon is one of only a few instruments that elicit a sophisticated haptic response from the amateur and professional player alike. Force-feedback varies widely across the range of the instrument and developing an intuition for the heaviness of different bells is a critical part of carillon pedagogy. Unfortunately, rehearsal time available to individual carillonneurs is limited by competition from other carillonneurs and environmental factors like civic noise limits and carillon maintenance schedules. Rehearsal instruments do exist but they do not accurately display the haptic dynamics of the real carillon. Our device couples the notions of *entertainment* and *cultural* computing; while musical instruments are now regularly digitised for purposes of entertainment the haptic carillon is motivated by an awareness of the musicianship of carillonneurs and the public cultural space they inhabit with their instrument.

1 Introduction

The carillon is perhaps the most public of musical instruments. The development of its repertoire and sense of musicianship is entwined with the culture and politics of statehood and religion in Western Europe for a significant part of the past five hundred years. Even today individual carillons are dependant on civic, ecumenical or private patronage — or combinations thereof — and rehearsal and musical opportunities for their carillonneurs are constrained by a combination of competition from other performers and the resources of host bodies. Although practice instruments exist they share a critical shortcoming: an inability to replicate the *haptic* sensation of carillon performance, force-feedback felt by a carillonneur that varies across the range of an individual instrument and with further idiosyncratic variation from one instrument to another.

These variations range from the number of bells in a carillon, the size of the bells and their corresponding clappers, and the dimensions and positioning of the keyboard and pedals. The mechanism, or action, for each bell in a single carillon is subtly and not-so-subtly different, and the general design and construction of the carillon varies from one to the next. The magnitude of these variations

R. Nakatsu et al. (Eds.): ECS 2010, IFIP AICT 333, pp. 75–86, 2010.

is compounded by factors like the regularity with which a carillon is serviced and the extent to which it is exposed to the elements. This is entirely natural for an instrument that has been in development for over five-hundred years and the specifications for which have only very recently approached any level of uniformity [12].[1]

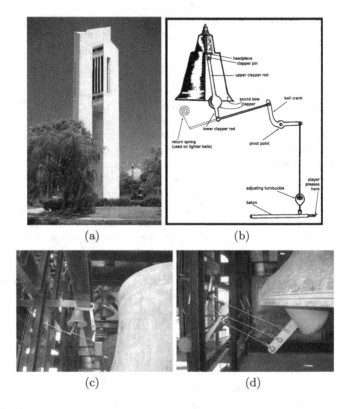

Fig. 1. (a) The National Carillon, Canberra, Australia is located on Aspen Island in Lake Burley Griffin (b) Simplified illustration of the carillon mechanism (c) Bell 54 (d) Bell 4

The application of synthesised force-feedback based on an analysis of forces operating in a typical carillon mechanism offers a blueprint for the design of an electronic practice clavier and with it the solution to a problem that has vexed carillonneurs for centuries, namely the inability to rehearse repertoire in private. The need for carillonneurs to develop musicianship and extend the instrument's repertoire offers a compelling musical reason to build a haptic practice instrument. Unlike other traditional instruments, the carillon always has an audience,

---

[1] And even that uniformity concerns only the dimensions of the keyboard, saying nothing of forces and/or dynamics.

willing or unwilling, even if the carilloneur is only trying to practice. The professional practise of concert carillonneurs provides another motivation: that one might prepare for a performance at a foreign carillon well ahead of actually having the chance to play it.

Measurements taken at the National Carillon in Canberra, shown in Figure 1(a), lay the groundwork and verification methodology for the design and construction of our haptic carillon prototype baton. As a prelude to a discussion on the role of haptics in musical instruments observe from Figure 1(b) that the carillonneur interacts with the instrument through a wooden baton which is linked to a crank that rotates and pulls a clapper against the inside of the bell wall. The mass of this clapper can be as great as 2 tonne and small as 600 gram, however the influence of this mass on the force felt at the baton is usually mediated by forward or return springs that respectively assist or resist the carillonneur's stroke. Figure 2(a) shows the range of forces felt at the baton tip across the National Carillon, along with the changing clapper stem lengths.

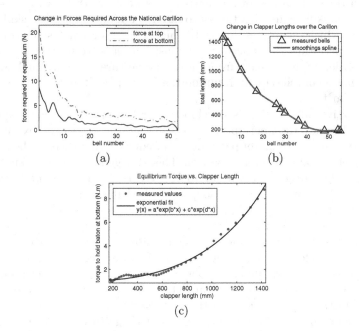

Fig. 2. (a) Force required to stabilise the baton over the carillon range (b) Measured and interpolated clapper lengths (c) Torque versus clapper lengths

This paper will focus primarily on the haptic aspects of simulating the carillon; the acoustics of carillons/bells are generally well-understood and regularly modelled. Fletcher and Rossing [5] is an excellent resource for understanding the physics of bell sounds while Karjalainen et al. [11] and Hibbert [10] discuss modern synthesis and modelling techniques.

2   Haptics and Musical Instruments

This project builds on advances in haptic engineering and design that permits the accurate display of the sensation of force-feedback. Haptically rendered instruments are designed to remove a major flaw in otherwise useful practise instruments; namely, the absence of an authentic sense of touch, or *feel*, which accompanies almost any instrumental interaction [16]. Feel can be simply defined as force felt by a player at the point of contact with an instrument; a brass player feels the vibration of his lips [19], a violinist experiences vibration and resistance at the point where the bow is held and where the string is depressed [1], a pianist feels different levels of resistance at the key [7] [8] and so on.

2.1   Musical Skill Acquisition

Together, the acoustic and haptic feedback from a musical instrument play a crucial part in the early stages of familiarisation with an instrument. O'Modhrain extends motor skill acquisition theory to develop a model of musical skill acquisition [16] in which she argues that at the higher levels of motor skill acquisition and musical performance proficiency the musician ceases to be actively (in real-time) concerned with feedback from individual gestures at individual keys; instead, the musician relies on an intuition that anticipates the instrument's state at a particular time.

This intuitive anticipation is developed over the course of much repetitive practise and is key to expert performance because it allows the execution of sequences of gestures, or motor patterns, at a frequency that exceeds the reaction time (RT) of the human motor system. This RT, generally determined to be between 120–180 mSec, or less than 10 Hz [17], is the upper limit for human motor system to work in a closed loop control; that is, in order for a gesture scheduled for time t_{later} to adapt or respond to some acoustical or mechanical feedback, that feedback must occur at a time $(t_{later} - 180)$mSec or earlier.

A corollary to the intuitive anticipation described above — greatly relevant to the instrument builder — is that an expert performance becomes unstable when learned interaction constraints are violated; this is the case whether a musician is performing on a traditional instrument, an electro-mechanical replica of a traditional instrument or a novel instrument, electronic or otherwise.

The principle of lawfully relating a performer's gesture to a consequent instrument state that is received in some form of sensory feedback, whether it be acoustic, visual, haptic or otherwise takes a second important, if abstracted, form when considering the haptic carillon. One of the principle aims of the project is to prepare a carillonneur for performance on a foreign instrument; in order to do so, a carillonneur must have confidence in the haptic carillon's ability to replicate the dynamics of a foreign carillon and this confidence will be eroded through experience over time if a set of intuitions developed in practice do not match foreign realities. This would undermine not only a single performance but the haptic carillon's artistic *raison d'être*. Carillonneurs also have historical reasons to be sceptical of technological 'advancements', to wit: "Finally there is the *computer*, but it will also be defeated" [13, p. 305].

It is possible to predict and recreate (at least, theoretically) forces felt by a player at the point of contact with an instrument by analysing its mechanical properties. This requires an understanding of how the mechanical components of a particular instrument interact, or a kinematic analysis, prior to considering the effects of user input.

2.2 Physical Modelling

This type of analysis is already being used to develop physically modelled synthesis algorithms; the interactions between physical components that contribute to sound production are expressed as equations that model an instrument's response to an excitation from a player. A physical model for the synthesis of a violin, for example, will consider the interaction of the bow against the strings, the width of the bow, the damping and resonance of the string, the transfer of energy through the bridge, and the resonance of the soundboard [6] [18].

A kinematic analysis with a view to haptically rendering an instrument, however, looks at the interactions between physical components that contribute to the force felt by the user. The kinematic constraints of a brass instrument include, for example, the width and depth of the mouthpiece, the length of the tube, and the type of metal used. In haptically rendered instruments such as the Nichol's vBow [14], Gillespie's Touchback Keyboard [8], Oboe's Multi-Instrument Keyboard [15] and Berdahl's Haptic Drumstick [3] physical models in the form of differential equations compute the behaviour of their respective traditional instrument's mechanical systems under different excitations, or gestures, performed by a player.

Using sensors (force, displacement sensors etc.) to monitor a player's gestures, the computational models are able to determine what a player might expect to feel in response, and then actuate this response using a motor. The means of generating haptic response need not be based on a physical model — Beamish's Haptic Turntable [2] uses a combination of simple linear analysis and user-programmable look-up tables for the display of assistive haptic feedback for DJs.

A thorough taxonomy of new instruments which are either originally conceived or emulate traditional instruments can be found in the author's previous work [9], and O'Modhrain [16] and Berdahl [4] present useful discussions and a framework for evaluating the effectiveness of haptic interaction in novel musical instruments.

3 The Carillon

Existing practise carillons make little effort to replicate the force-feedback of a real carillon. A typical practice instrument employs extension springs to emulate the resistance felt by the carillonneur as the baton is displaced from its détente position downward. As well as providing an inaccurate force-feedback this arrangement is unable to simulate the dynamic behaviour of a baton in free

Fig. 3. Chamber carillon with adjustable keyboard and pedal dimensions

motion. These limitations speak to the real purpose behind practice carillons: to familiarise a carillonnuer with the *geometry* of a particular carillon keyboard. Practice carillons are almost always associated with a particular carillon and help a performer rehearse for the dimensions of that carillon; to this end a new practice carillon has been built by Timothy Hurd that permits the manual adjustment of the batons and pedals in the x/y/z axes (Figure 3). This instrument, though, is still limited to the linear force-feedback of extension springs. Upon analysis of the carillon mechanism it is clear why a simple extension spring is unable to accurately simulate the force-feedback of the carillon. An immediate limitation of the spring is its lack of memory over time; Hooke's law for the restoration force of a spring

$$F(x, t) = -k(x(t) - x_0) \tag{1}$$

is simply the linear relationship between the spring's force constant k and displacement from its equilibrium at any time, $(x(t) - x_0)$. It has no capacity to 'remember' previous values of x as a function of time t.[2] However, not only is force-feedback in the carillon non-linear with respect to position but it is also dependant on the baton's velocity.

3.1   Non-linear Force Response

The haptic sensation felt by the carillonneur at the point of interaction, the *baton*, is the result of static and dynamic forces acting on mass components of the carillon mechanism. Along with haptic cues, the carillonnuer observes the baton's motion as an indicator of the mechanism's kinetic energy and adapts the force of the next stroke accordingly. For example, a baton for a low bell stays in periodic motion for as long as 3 seconds (see §3.3) and a carillonneur can reduce

---

[2] Oboe [15] showed this to be sufficient for modelling the force-feedback of a Hammond organ and many interesting haptic/musical applications use virtual springs exclusively or in concert.

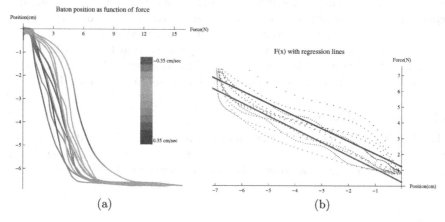

Fig. 4. Force, position and velocity relationships for bell 9, (a) Baton displacement as a function of player force at baton tip, (b) Regression lines for force as a function of position for downward (blue; $R^2 = 0.88$) and upward (red; $R^2 = 0.9$) motion

the amount of force they need to apply for a repeated note if they strike the baton while it is already in compliant motion.

The typical force profile for a low bell (here, bell 9) is shown in Figure 4, where user-applied force is measured at the tip of the baton with a finger pressure sensor and the resultant vertical position of the baton over time is recorded using a motion sensor[3] with a sampling rate of 50 Hz. After the method for capturing the force profile of switches outlined by Weir et al. [20], a player was instructed to depress the baton to its maximum displacement and then allow it to return to détente while staying in contact with the baton at all times; the procedure was repeated several times with increasing velocity.

Figure 4(a) shows that greater force is felt during a downward stroke than the return stroke; observing the rainbow spectrum as a visualisation of velocity one notes that 'hot' colours which indicate negative velocity (downward motion) are grouped to the right of 'cool' colours representing positive velocity. The adjacent Figure 4(b) combines two scatter plots grouped by the direction of baton motion (blue and red for downward and upward, respectively) showing the force felt by a player as a function of baton displacement. The regression lines show that the linear change $\beta \approx 0.8$ is very similar in both directions and there is a force offset of approximately $+1$ N for downward motion. This velocity- and position-dependant change in force is encapsulated in the following function:

$$F_{\text{off}}(\dot{x}, t) = \begin{cases} 1.2 & \dot{x}(t) < 0 \\ 0.2 & \dot{x}(t) > 0 \end{cases}$$

$$F(x, \dot{x}, t) = \beta x(t) + F_{\text{off}}(\dot{x}, t). \tag{2}$$

---

[3] Xsens MTi inertial motion sensor, http://xsens.com

Simple velocity-dependant linear regression, however, is clearly far from an ideal representation of the relationship between user input and carillon force-output. Further, the carillonneur's experience is not constituted of dynamic force interactions alone: the carillon is unique amongst musical instruments in that its dynamic state is strongly time-dependant and the connection between performer gesture and acoustic result is mechanically and temporally decoupled.

3.2   Carillon Mechanics and Dynamics

The plots in §3.3 demonstrate the persistent influence of the carillon's internal dynamics on the baton's state at any time; those particular bells also display the extent of dynamical variation even between nearby bells, like 4 and 7.

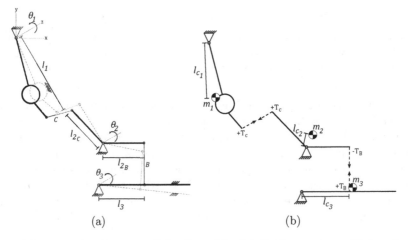

(a)   (b)

Fig. 5. Three rotational systems linked by cables (a) Carillon system with lengths and angles labelled (b) Centres of mass and tension forces

For the purposes of dynamic modelling the carillon mechanism is considered as three rotating sub-systems: the clapper, the crank and the baton systems. The three systems are linked by thin wound cables and forces exchanged between the systems are encapsulated in the tensions of the two cables. From Figure 5 we see the systems are linked in series, with a cable from the mid-length of the baton joined to the tip of the straight crank rod, and a cable from the tip of the L-shaped crank rod joined to the tip of the lower clapper rod.

The linkage cables impose velocity constraints on the motion of the three sub-systems: the two points at either end of a single cable exhibit uniform velocity, and therefore acceleration. The rotational accelerations of the three sub-systems are therefore constrained:

$$\ddot{\theta}_1 l_1 = \ddot{\theta}_2 l_{2_C} \tag{3a}$$

$$\ddot{\theta}_3 l_3 = \ddot{\theta}_2 l_{2_B} \tag{3b}$$

If we include the tension forces from the linkage cables along with the effective torques τ_i and moments of inertia I_i about the pivot point for each of the rotational systems, we derive equations for the respective rotational accelerations:

$$\ddot{\theta}_1 = \frac{\tau_1 + T_C l_1}{I_1} \tag{4a}$$

$$\ddot{\theta}_2 = \frac{\tau_2 + T_C l_{2_C} - T_B l_{2_B}}{I_2} \tag{4b}$$

$$\ddot{\theta}_3 = \frac{\tau_3 + T_B l_3}{I_3} \tag{4c}$$

where the torques are

$$\tau_1(t) = g l_{C_1} m_1 \cos \theta_1(t) + f_{\text{ext}}(\theta_1, \dot{\theta}_1, t) \tag{5a}$$

$$\tau_2(t) = g l_{C_2} m_2 \cos \theta_2(t) \tag{5b}$$

$$\tau_3(t) = g l_{C_3} m_3 \cos \theta_3(t). \tag{5c}$$

The function $f_{\text{ext}}(\theta_1, \dot{\theta}_1, t)$ in (5a) represents the external forces acting on the clapper system: impact with the bell, any forward or return springs, and impact with a rubber damper that prevents the clapper from swinging away from the bell past a certain threshold.

Impact Constraints. The carillon mechanism is constrained to rotate over only a small range; at the baton this is between an upper and lower felt-lined row of wooden beams, and at the clapper this is between the inside of the bell shoulder and approximately 3 cm away from the bell. The latter constraint is implemented by means of a fixed rubber damper mounted below the forward spring which is linked to the lower end of the clapper (the top cable in Figure 1(d)). The baton and clapper constraints are related such that the baton's lower beam stops the baton bringing the clapper into contact with the bell — like in a piano, the clapper is in free-flight, or 'let-off' just prior to impact with the resonating surface. Ideally, the upper beam is positioned to coincide with the impact of the rubber damper.

These relations are determined by the length of the cable linking the baton and crank; a turnbuckle attached to this cable allows non-invasive length adjustments and over the course of a single performance it is not unlikely for the carillonneur to do so. In our simulation, we assume that the impact constraints for the baton and clapper coincide perfectly and all position constraints are encapsulated as impact forces applied directly to the clapper in the f_{ext} function in (5a).

3.3   Simulation

We now reduce the three equations (4a) – (4c) into just one by finding a solution for either T_C or T_B; if we solve for T_B and eliminate T_C, for instance, we can

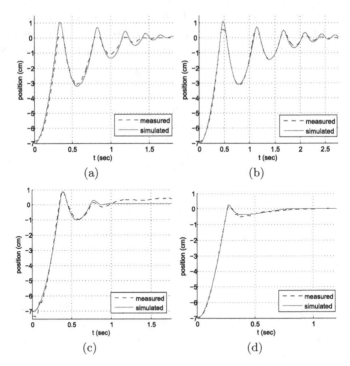

Fig. 6. Bell simulation responses (a) Bell 28 free motion (b) Bell 4 free motion (c) Bell 7 free motion (d) Bell 48 free motion

then solve (4c) and apply the relationships in (3) to determine accelerations for θ_2 and θ_1.

In the model presented above, the number of parameters that change over the range of the carillon is rather low; indeed, using principally the measured and estimated values for clapper length shown in Figure 2(c) we are also able to estimate a changing clapper mass and its rotational range. The baton mechanism is the same across the entire carillon, while the crank mechanism is slightly smaller for the upper twenty bells.

The remaining variables to be estimated are damping and springiness coefficients for the clapper impacts against the wall and rubber damper; variation in these values is responsible for the difference in 'bounciness' shown in the figures above as the baton returns to détente position.

3.4   Prototype

The mathematical model presented here is arranged such that it can be solved in real time using forward dynamics, the system's motion in response to forces. It is programmed in Simulink and compiled to run on a standalone target PC which connects to an electromagnetic linear actuator through a dedicated analogue I/O board. This actuator (Figure 7) controls the position of the baton, and

Fig. 7. Haptic prototype of single baton

back-EMF at the actuator windings is measured in order to close the feedback loop by determining the force applied by the player. The problem of generating appropriate sound synthesis is somewhat mitigated in this environment. Typically, a carillonneur only hears their instrument through loudspeakers amplifying the signal picked up by strategically-positioned microphones in the bell tower. The National Carillon, for example, provides only this type of aural feedback to the performer.

4 Summary and Future Work

This paper has demonstrated analytical techniques that permit the accurate simulation of batons of varying force-feedback and dynamic behaviour across the range of the National Carillon. Future user-testing will build on current haptic research to assess the nature of a performers perception of a traditional instrument against this haptically rendered one.

The construction of an electro-mechanical version of the carillon has ramifications beyond simply helping carillonneurs rehearse. A potential source of musical innovation lies in the construction of a 'remote' carillon that would allow a carillonneur to perform from outside the bell tower, and hear themselves as they are heard by their audience. The introduction of haptics into an otherwise normally functioning instrument also opens the door to novel ensemble performance opportunities for carillonneurs; haptic detents could be built into the performance of a musical work that helps the carillonneur stay in time, or receive cues from performers without them necessarily being in the same room as is required now.

References

1. Askenfelt, A., Jansson, E.V.: On vibration sensation and finger touch in stringed instrument playing. Music Perception 9(3), 311–350 (1992)
2. Beamish, T., Maclean, K., Fels, S.: Designing the haptic turntable for musical control. In: Proceedings of the 11th Symposium on Haptic Interfaces for Virtual Environment and Teleoperator Systems, Vienna, Austria, pp. 327–336 (2003)

3. Berdahl, E., Verplank, B., Smith, J.O., Niemeyer, G.: A physically-intuitive haptic drumstick. In: Proceedings of the International Computer Music Conference (August 2007)
4. Berdahl, E., Niemeyer, G., Smith, J.O.: Using haptics to assist performers in making gestures to a musical instrument. In: Proceedings of New Interfaces for Musical Expression (2009)
5. Fletcher, N., Rossing, T.: The Physics of Musical Instruments. Springer, New York (1998)
6. Florens, J., Henry, C.: Bowed string synthesis with force feedback gesture interaction. In: Proceedings of the International Computer Music Conference (2001)
7. Furuya, S., Kinoshita, H.: Organization of the upper limb movement for piano key-depression differs between expert pianists and novice players. Journal of Experimental Brain Research 185, 581–593 (2008)
8. Gillespie, B.: Haptic Display of Systems with Changing Kinematic Constraints: The Virtual Piano Action. Ph.D. thesis, Stanford University (1996)
9. Havryliv, M., Schiemer, G., Naghdy, F.: Haptic carillon: Sensing and control in musical instruments. In: Proceedings of the Australasian Computer Music Conference (2006)
10. Hibbert, W.A.: The Quantification of Strike Pitch and Pitch Shifts in Church Bells. Ph.D. thesis, The Open University (2008)
11. Karjalainen, M., Esquef, P.A.A., Vlimki, V.: Making of a computer carillon. In: Proceedings of the Stockholm Music Acoustics Conference, SMAC 2003 (2003)
12. Keyboard Committee, Word Carillon Federation: Consensus on Technical Norms for a World Standard Carillon Keyboard (2006)
13. Lehr, A.: The Art of the Carillon in the Low Countries. Lannoo, Tielt (Belgium) (1991)
14. Nichols, C.: The vbow: A virtual violin bow controller for mapping gesture to synthesis with haptic feedback. Organised Sound Journal 7, 215–220 (2002)
15. Oboe, R.: A multi-instrument, force-feedback keyboard. Computer Music Journal 30(3), 38–52 (2006)
16. O'Modhrain, S.: Playing by Feel: Incorporating Haptic Feedback into Computer-Based Musical Instruments. Ph.D. thesis, Stanford University (2000)
17. Schmidt, R.A., Lee, T.D.: Motor Control and Learning: A Behavioral Emphasis, 4th edn. Human Kinetics Publishers (2005)
18. Serafin, S., Vergez, C., Rodet, X.: Friciton and application to real-time physical modeling of a violin. In: Proceedings of International Computer Music Conference (1999)
19. Vergez, C., Rodet, X.: Model of the trumpet functioning: Real-time simulation and experiments with an artificial mouth model. In: Proceedings of the International Symposium on Musical Acoustics (1997)
20. Weir, D.W., Peshkin, M., Colgate, J.E., Buttolo, P., Rankin, J., Johnston, M.: The haptic profile: Capturing the feel of switches. In: IEEE Processings of the 12th International Symposium on Haptic Interfaces for Virtual Environment and Teleoperator Systems, pp. 186–193 (March 2004)

3D Geometric and Haptic Modeling of Hand-Woven Textile Artifacts

Hooman Shidanshidi[1], Fazel Naghdy[1], Golshah Naghdy[1], and Diana Wood Conroy[2]

[1] School of Electrical, Computer and Telecommunications Engineering, Faculty of Informatics,
University of Wollongong, Australia
[2] Faculty of Creative Arts, University of Wollongong, Australia
hooman@uow.edu.au, fazel@uow.edu.au, golshah@uow.edu.au,
dconroy@uow.edu.au

Abstract. Haptic Modeling of textile has attracted significant interest over the last decade. In spite of extensive research, no generic system has been proposed. The previous work mainly assumes that textile has a 2D planar structure. They also require time-consuming objective measurement of textile properties in mechanical/physical model construction. A novel approach for haptic modeling of textile is proposed to overcome the existing shortcomings. The method is generic, assumes a 3D structure textile artifact, and deploys computational intelligence to estimate textile mechanical and physical properties. The approach is designed primarily for display of textile artifacts in museums. The haptic model is constructed by superimposing the mechanical model of textile over its 3D geometrical model. Digital image processing is applied to the still image of textile to identify its pattern and structure. In order to deal with the non-linearities associated with the textile, a fuzzy rule-based expert system is deployed. This information is then used to generate a 3D geometric model of the artifact in VRML. Selected mechanical and physical properties of the textile are estimated by an artificial neural network with the textile geometric characteristics and yarn properties as inputs. The neural network learning and verification and validation processes are carried out by a sample data set. The mechanical properties are used in the construction of the textile mechanical model. The haptic rendered model is generated by superimposing the physical/mechanical model over the 3D geometric model. This model has been implemented and rendered in Reachin environment, provided an interactive Virtual Reality environment where the user can navigate the graphic 3D presentation of the textile and touch it by a haptic device. Different samples have been modeled and the whole approach has been validated. The interface can be provided in both in the physical environment and through the cyberspace. The validation of method indicates the feasibility of the approach and its superiority to other haptic modeling algorithms.

Keywords: Haptic, Fuzzy logic, Neural Network, Hand-woven textile.

1 Introduction

Haptic Modeling of textile has attracted significant interest over the last decade. In the work conducted by Govindaraj et al a haptic system for virtual fabric handling

R. Nakatsu et al. (Eds.): ECS 2010, IFIP AICT 333, pp. 87–100, 2010.
© IFIP International Federation for Information Processing 2010

experience was developed [1]. The approach was limited to static modeling and used Kawabata machine to calculate the mechanical properties of textile. Another important project was HAPTEX [2, 3], in which a similar approach for development and validation of haptic model of fabric was developed.

In spite of extensive research, no generic system has yet been proposed. The majority of the haptic models developed in the previous work assume a 2D mesh model for textile which is not an accurate representation of the geometric configuration of the textile. In addition, they are based on empirical parameters obtained from textile samples using specialized instruments such as Kawabata system. The process is often time consuming and elaborate, consisting of manual measurement of physical and mechanical properties of the artifacts. The development of a generic approach for 3D haptic modeling of hand-woven textile artifacts is pursued in this work.

In the proposed approach, the textile pattern and structure are recognized by digital processing of the artifact still image. A fuzzy-rule based expert system is developed to perform the recognition process. The data obtained in this process is employed to automatically generate the 3D geometric model of the artifact in VRML. The mechanical properties of the artifact are estimated by processing the textile geometric characteristics and yarn properties in a neural network system. These mechanical properties are then deployed in the construction of the textile mechanical model. The mechanical model is superimposed over the 3D geometric model to construct the haptic model. The proposed system is validated using a number of artifact samples.

Overall, the work conduced in this study offers a novel 3D generic haptic modeling for textile artifacts. It can be deployed in museums providing an opportunity for the visitors to touch unique samples of hand-woven textile artifacts. The approach is cost-effective, reliable and reproducible, as the haptic modeling of these samples doesn't need time-consuming and costly laboratory conditions.

In the remainder of the paper, the image processing method and the fuzzy rule-base expert system deployed in the construction of the geometric model are described. The outcome is a 3D geometric model of the artifact in VRML that could be explored in a virtual reality world viewer. Similarly, the neural network model designed to estimate the mechanical characteristics of an artifact is presented. The approach is validated and conclusion is made.

2   Textile Pattern Recognition

A woven fabric has a complicated structure made of the cross combination of the wrap and weft yarns in a two-dimensional lattice structure. Textile weave pattern recognition has attracted many researchers since the mid-1980's. The problem field could be divided into crossed-points detection that deals with interlacing areas between wrap and weft yarns and crossed-states detection which determines which yarn is over the other in the interlacing areas.

Different approaches have been proposed to deal with both problems. The developed approaches, however, have proved to be inadequate to deal with the non-rigidity of the hand-woven artifacts. In this work, a new algorithm is developed to address such shortcomings [4]. An overview of the approach is provided in this section.

2.1 Crossed-Points Detection

The methods reported in the literature for crossed-points detection can be categorized into two groups:

- Employing Fourier filtering techniques to find periodic weave pattern in a woven fabric image by either identification of the peaks in the power spectrum image [5-7] or finding the peak points of the autocorrelation function of the gray level data in warp and weft directions [8].
- Identifying the peaks in accumulation gray level values in vertical and horizontal directions pixels [9, 10].

In this work, the second approach is deployed and a piecewise-linear algorithm is introduced to model the non-linearities in the structure of the fabric. The image features – representing the peaks of local accumulating gray level values for each vertical and horizontal image slice – are extracted. A fuzzy rule-base engine is then applied to process the image features and identify the structure of the artifact.

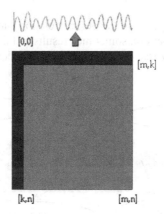

Fig. 1. Image slicing and accumulating gray level curve

The image matrix ω_{m*n} is sliced horizontally and vertically. The image slices SV_i in vertical and SH_i in horizontal directions are defined as elements of ω matrix which is represented by a '_' operator in (1) and (2), where k is the thickness of the image slice:

$$SV_i = \omega_{i*k,0} \_ \omega_{i*k,n} \_ \omega_{(i+1)*k,0} \_ \omega_{(i+1)*k,n} \tag{1}$$

$$\text{and } 0 \leq i \leq \left\lceil \frac{m}{k} \right\rceil - 1$$

$$SH_i = \omega_{0,i*k} \_ \omega_{m,i*k} \_ \omega_{0,(i+1)*k} \_ \omega_{m,(i+1)*k} \tag{2}$$

$$\text{and } 0 \leq i \leq \left\lceil \frac{n}{k} \right\rceil - 1$$

By considering the $\Omega_{x,y}$ the gray level conversion function of the pixel in position x and y, α_i a vector with m elements as the accumulating gray level values for the vertical slice i, SV_i could be calculated as:

$$\alpha_{i,j} = \sum_{z=0}^{k} \Omega(SV_i^{z,j}) \qquad \text{for } 1 \leq j \leq n \qquad (3)$$

And the same for β_i a vector with n elements as the accumulating gray level values for the horizontal slice i, SH_i:

$$\beta_{i,j} = \sum_{z=0}^{k} \Omega(SH_i^{j,z}) \qquad \text{for } 1 \leq j \leq m \qquad (4)$$

Finally, Feature point set μ_{vi} for the vertical slice i and μ_{hi} for the horizontal slice i are calculated as below:

$$\mu_{vi} = \{ p | p \in \min(\alpha_i) \} \qquad \text{for } 1 \leq i \leq m \qquad (5)$$

$$\mu_{hi} = \{ p | p \in \min(\beta_i) \} \qquad \text{for } 1 \leq i \leq n \qquad (6)$$

While ideally, the minimum peaks of the autocorrelation show the yarn border in that section, variation in artifact pattern, sometimes results in false peaks. Hence, a special filter is developed to identify real peaks in the yarn boarder. Figure 2 illustrates this filtering mechanism.

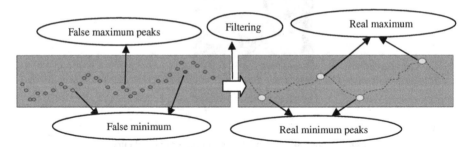

Fig. 2. Intelligent filtering mechanism for removing the false peaks and picking the real peaks

In addition, a mechanism is also required to locate the corresponding points in different slices belonging to one specific yarn boarder. At this stage, some peak points might be merged as one point or some might be identified as false peaks.

Accordingly, a fuzzy rule based algorithm is developed to perform the following actions:

1. Local Filtering: filtering the false maximum and minimum peaks and pick up real peaks in each slice.
2. Global Combination: Merging some close points as one point and removing false points based on the global knowledge of the whole artifact rather than only a slice.
3. Edge Detection: locating corresponding points in different slices which belong to a specific yarn boarder.

For this algorithm to work effectively, the maximum peaks of the autocorrelation function should be also calculated. It is expected that a max peak should be seen between two sequential minimum peaks which presents somewhere on top of the yarn where the light is maximum due to yarn convexity.

Figure 3 demonstrates the Global Combination mechanism. The distance is described by a distance fuzzy variable and merging of the points is carried out by the algorithm.

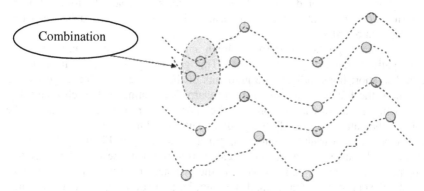

Fig. 3. Global combination mechanism

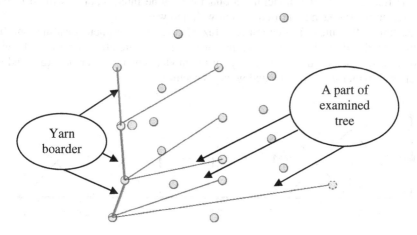

Fig. 4. Edge detection mechanism

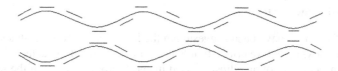

Fig. 5. Gradient pattern for yarn boarder

Figure 4 shows the edge detection mechanism which locates corresponding points in different slices belonging to a specific yarn boarder. This mechanism searches for the points as a backtracking algorithm in a tree structure. It starts from the bottom left minimum peak in the artifact and finds different paths of closest points based on their fuzzy distance. The mechanism continues by considering next points recursively. This process creates a virtual tree. The fuzzy algorithm selects a path in the tree from root to leaves with the best estimation as a yarn boarder. The selected points are removed from the feature point set and the mechanism continues from next bottom left point. The algorithm ensures that a maximum peak point curve is located between two neighboring yarn boarders.

The yarn boarder gradient pattern is known and could be used for predicting the yarn edge path in tree structure (Figure 4). This gradient prediction is illustrated in Figure 5. The short lines indicate the gradients of the edge curve. The narrow cross sections show the locations where weft and warp are floating over each other. The shape is changing due to friction forces and compression in these areas. Finding the next point in the path has to satisfy the gradient pattern and the fuzzy rules.

The distance fuzzy variable membership function is shown in Figure 6. The Fuzzification of the distance is carried out by calculating the distance of point p relative to all the points in slice i+1 and normalizing the distances between 0 to 1. The fuzzy set consists of very small, small, small-medium, large-medium, large and very large values.

In the final stage of the modeling, a quadratic spline interpolation is fitted to the yarn edge points for each identified yarn in weft and warp direction.

After tuning the rules, fuzzication & defuzzication, and parameters estimation, the system is validated for 21 samples and has proved to be quite effective. Manual comparison has shown around 85% accuracy for the model. The model errors are found in artifacts with patterns or complicated woven structures.

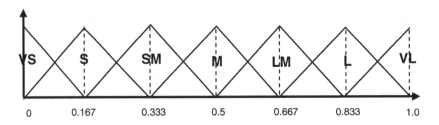

Fig. 6. The distance fuzzy variable membership function using for Fuzzification

2.2 Crossed-States Detection

A variety of methods have been suggested in the literature for crossed-states detection including employing texture orientation features in each one of the detected cells [11], normalized aspect ratio of an ellipse-shaped image at crossed points of the fabric [12], fuzzy c-means clustering [9, 10], and Fourier image analysis techniques [5, 7, 13-15]. The outcome of this stage is a weave pattern diagram showing the warp over weft or weft over warp in each cell of cross points.

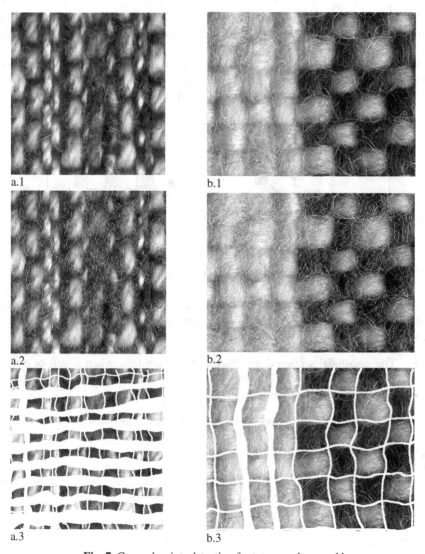

a.1

b.1

a.2

b.2

a.3

b.3

Fig. 7. Crossed-points detection for two samples a and b

In this study, the yarn edges-texture orientation features of each side of the cell are calculated for each detected cell. The derived features are then transformed to frequency domain by deploying Fast Fourier Transform. The Frequency spectrum is finally analyzed for crossed-states detection process. This method is novel and has not been explored in textile industry for this problem.

Figure 7 illustrates the image processing steps applied to two samples of hand woven textiles of (a) and (b). Indexes 1 to 3 represent the following stages:

- Index 1: The original scanned images of textiles.
- Index 2: Textile image with its vertical and horizontal feature points.
- Index 3: Fuzzy rules implication for finding the yarn edges.

A typical weave pattern diagram produced in crossed-states detection process is shown in Figure 8. Black cells are warp float areas and white ones are weft float areas.

The proposed method is verified by applying it to 21 artifact samples. The texture orientation method in frequency domain is evaluated with 87% accuracy compared with conventional methods with less than 70% accuracy.

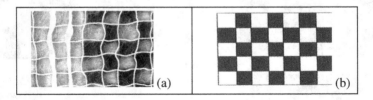

Fig. 8. Weave pattern diagram produced in crossed state detection

3   Textile 3D Geometric Model Generation

The textile structure and the measurements made of the weft and warp in pattern recognition process are deployed in developing the 3D geometric model of the fabric. The weft or warp yarn flow is modeled in two sections:

- The sinusoidal section that is used in transition flow when a weft or a wrap flows over or below the corresponding yarn
- The linear section that is used in constant flow

The weft and warp yarn cross-section is modeled as an ellipsoid with its dimensions set according to the pattern identified in the textile. Variation in the shape of the ellipsoid occurs due to internal, friction and compression forces between warp and weft yarns of the textile.

Figure 9 illustrates the linear flow section, sinusoidal flow section and yarn cross sections in both wrap and weft directions.

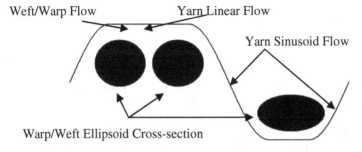

Fig. 9. Weft/Wrap flow in textile 3D geometric model

Defining weft and warp yarn diameters by d_{weft} and d_{warp}, respectively, the amplitude of weft and warp sinusoidal flow, A_{weft} and A_{warp} should satisfy (7):

$$A_{weft} + A_{warp} = \frac{d_{weft} + d_{warp}}{2} \tag{7}$$

A_{weft}/A_{warp} ratio is dependent on the weft and wrap yarns raw material, composition and dimension. It determines the tension and compressibility of yarn and can be estimated empirically.

The weft and warp sinusoidal flow curve in 3D Cartesian coordinate space could be formulated as follow:

$$z = \pm A_{weft} \; Sin \; \left(\frac{2\,\Pi\,x}{d_{weft} + d_{warp}}\right) \tag{8}$$

$$z = \mp A_{warp} \; Sin \; \left(\frac{2\,\Pi\,y}{d_{weft} + d_{warp}}\right) \tag{9}$$

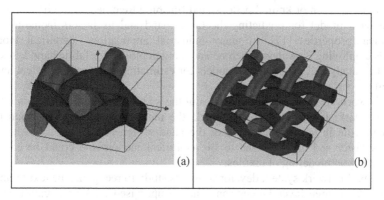

Fig. 10. 3D geometric model for: a) A plain artifact sample b) A twill artifact sample

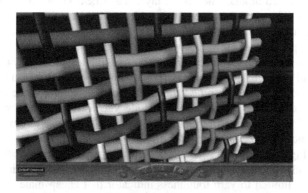

Fig. 11. An artifact VRML 3D geometric model in Virtual Reality Viewer

The flow of the center of weft and warp yarns in x and y directions are shown by (8) and (9). By adding the ellipsoid cross-section for each specific point in curves, the textile 3D geometric model is generated. This model is converted to VRML by a developed automatic VRML generator. The VRML geometric model is displayed as a virtual reality world that can be explored by user.

Figure 10 demonstrates the 3D geometric model for the two artifacts samples. Figure 11 shows an artifact VRML 3D geometric model in the virtual reality viewer. The textile texture also could be added to the model for a realistic representation of the sample in the virtual reality world.

4 Textile Mechanical Model Generation

The Fabric Hand of a cloth or garment is defined as the overall fabric quality perceived through operations such as touching, squeezing, or rubbing [16]. Many factors affect the Fabric Hand including flexibility, compressibility, elasticity, resilience, density, surface contour (roughness, smoothness), surface friction and thermal characteristics of the fabric. The properties of the textile raw material, yarn structure, planner structure (woven or knitted pattern) and finishing treatment could be employed in a mechanical model for predicting the fabric hand and its factors including textile mechanical properties [17]. In many industrial applications, empirical modeling methods employing Kawabata machine are being deployed for fabric hand assessment rather than analytical or empirical models for estimating the textile physical and mechanical properties.

In this work, the mechanical properties of the textiles are estimated via an artificial neural network. In this stage of the work, the mechanical properties, which play a significant role in tactile perception of the hand-woven textile, are calculated. This model is faster and cheaper than textile empirical models and could be easily deployed in haptic modeling of textiles.

The neural network system developed in this study to recognize the textile physical properties is a three layer Perceptron. The unsupervised back-propagation learning method is used for tuning the system weights for any specific problem. The first layer has 16 neurons for 16 inputs. The output layer has 3 neurons for 3 outputs. The hidden layer size is different for any specific problem. There are different ways available to estimate the size of the hidden layer. One of the famous empirical rules is the mean of input and output layer size. In this approach, different hidden layer sizes from 5 to 15 neurons are examined to find the minimum error in back-propagation training. The average of input and output layer size is 10 and hence a boundary around this point is selected. The hidden layer, learning ratio and primitive weights are estimated based on the training data. The system inputs include yarn raw materials, weft and warp dimensions and weft and warp structure. The outputs of the system include static friction, dynamic friction and compressibility.

In the training system, the raw materials are limited to natural materials – wool, linen, cotton and silk. The yarn dimension expressing the average diameter and the yarn structure is limited to yarn toughness indicator that encapsulates the yarn structure parameters and yarn degree of twist. Figure 12 demonstrates the system architecture for a specific weave pattern.

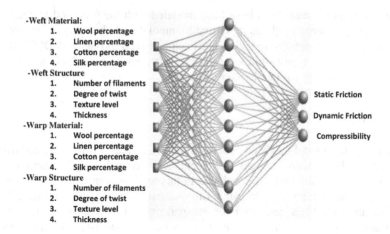

-Weft Material:
    1.   Wool percentage
    2.   Linen percentage
    3.   Cotton percentage
    4.   Silk percentage
-Weft Structure
    1.   Number of filaments
    2.   Degree of twist
    3.   Texture level
    4.   Thickness
-Warp Material:
    1.   Wool percentage
    2.   Linen percentage
    3.   Cotton percentage
    4.   Silk percentage
-Warp Structure
    1.   Number of filaments
    2.   Degree of twist
    3.   Texture level
    4.   Thickness

Static Friction

Dynamic Friction

Compressibility

Fig. 12. Neural Network system for textile mechanical & physical properties prediction

5 Haptic Model Generation

The haptic model is generated by superimposing the textile mechanical model over 3D geometric model. The implementation is achieved through Reachin computing platform. The Reachin API is a multi-sensory rendering engine that integrates visual and haptic rendering through the use of one single scene graph. It parses the graph and provides the 3D presentation of an object as well as providing tactile perception for the world. It is system and haptic device independent which makes it suitable for future applications with other haptic devices. Reachin API is based on the concept of the scene graph. A scene graph is a hierarchical data structure that describes a 3D scene. It holds the geometry of all objects in the scene and their relative positions, appearance attributes such as color, transparency, textures and surfaces and also light sources, viewing position and information about the scene. A scene graph provides a framework for managing objects in a scene, and makes it easy to express the relationship between those objects [18].

Fig. 13. The 6 DOF Phantom haptic device

Several hand-woven artifacts have been modeled with the proposed methodology. These models have been rendered in Virtual Manipulation Laboratory at University of Wollongong and the tactile interaction has been achieved through a 6 DOF Phantom haptic device. Figure 13 illustrates the 6 DOF Phantom device which has been employed in the laboratory for tactile interaction.

6 Validation

The 3D geometric model has been generated for 21 samples. From them, 13 twill and plain samples have been selected for mechanical/physical model generation. The haptic model generation method developed in this work is applied to all the samples. In addition, other haptic models using Bumpmapsurface and FrictionImageSurface from Reachin have been generated for comparison and validation. Several experiments were designed and implemented to examine the model validity and performance of the methodology.

In one of the experiments, 5 observers were selected. Each one was instructed to touch the 13 hand-woven artifact samples and the haptic models developed for them by using the Phantom haptic device. The observers were given 3-5 minutes to examine each real artifact and the corresponding haptic model. For accurate comparison, a pen with the same shape as haptic device pen was given to each candidate. The observers were asked to touch the real artifact with the pen and the haptic model with Phantom device. They would then give a score of 0 to 10 for each sample, with 0 indicating no similarity and 10 meaning complete similarity. The candidates were told to pause for 2-3 minutes between samples. The experiment took about 1.5 to 2 hours for each observer. They were then asked to repeat the experiment for Bumpmapsurface and FrictionImageSurface methods in the following day. The sequence of samples was changed in each set of experiments, eliminating the previous judgment on the result.

The average of similarity scorers gathered from five candidates for 13 samples are provided in Table 1 for each method.

Table 1. The subjective experiment result for 13 samples and 3 different methods

Sample number	1	2	3	4	5	6	7	8	9	10	11	12	13	The Method Average
FrictionImageSurface	3.6	4.2	2.6	6	5.2	4.8	6.2	4.4	3.2	3.6	4.2	5.4	6.4	**4.6**
BumpmapSurface	4.2	3.8	3.4	5.2	6.4	5.6	5.8	4.2	5.6	3.2	5.8	7.4	6.8	**5.2**
Proposed method	4.4	7.2	6.8	8.2	7	8.8	7.8	6.6	7.8	6.8	8.4	8.8	7.2	**7.4**

As shown in the table, the subjective assessment of the three methods has identified the highest similarity score for the method proposed in this work using the developed 3D geometric and physical models. The FrictionImageSurface method is the worst one. The proposed method shows an average similarity score of 74% which is about 60% lead over FrictionImageSurface method and around 40% improvements over BumpmapSurface.

In the second experiment, each observer was exposed to 3 artifact samples and the haptic model of one of the samples. The model was randomly chosen and the observers were not informed of the corresponding sample. The observers were then expected to identify the sample by examining both the model and the samples. Each candidate was given three minutes for each model. The experiment was repeated for FrictionImageSurface and BumpmapSurface haptic models as well as the model developed in this work. Fifteen haptic models were observed by each candidate, 5 in each group. Therefore 25 tests were carried out for each haptic group.

The overall results are provided in Table 2, illustrating the number and percentage of true identification for each haptic model.

Table 2. Number of True identification in 25 tests for each haptic group

	Number of True Identification (25 total)	True Identification Percentage
FrictionImageSurface	12	48%
BumpmapSurface	16	64%
Our method	21	84%

As highlighted in the table, identification based on the proposed method has again score the highest with true identification percentage of 84%. The true identification rates for FrictionImageSurface and BumpmapSurface are only 48% and 64% respectively. The result shows almost 75% and 31% improvements over FrictionImageSurface and BumpmapSurface respectively.

Both experiments prove the validity and efficiency of the proposed model with acceptable success rates.

7 Conclusion

The development of a generic approach for 3D haptic-rendered modeling of hand-woven textile artifacts was reported in this paper. The proposed methodology relies on processing of the still images of the artifact using computational intelligence as well as the knowledge of the artifact material and yarn structure. Effort was made to ensure that the developed mechanism was a faster and more reliable alternative for textile modeling compared to the costly and time consuming manual fabric hand assessment. The approach was also designed to build the haptic model of the textile based on an accurate 3D geometric model of the artifact rather than conventional 2D mesh structure used for graphical representation.

Future work will concentrate on pattern recognition and neural network enhancement as well as customizing the physical simulator and haptic render engine for hand-woven artifacts.

References

1. Govindaraj, M., et al.: Haptic simulation of fabric hand. Technical report, National Textile Research Annual Report and in Eurohaptics 2003 Conference (2003)
2. Mäkinen, M., et al.: Influence of Physical Parameters on Fabric Hand. In: Proceedings of the HAPTEX 2005 Workshop on Haptic and Tactile Perception of Deformable Objects, Hanover (2005)
3. Magnenat-Thalmann, N., Bonanni, U.: Haptics in virtual reality and multimedia. IEEE Multimedia 13(3), 6–11 (2006)
4. Shidanshidi, H., et al.: 3D geometric modelling of hand-woven textile. SPIE, San Jose (2008)
5. Xu, B.G.: Identifying fabric structures with Fast Fourier Transform techniques. Textile Research Journal 66(8), 496–506 (1996)
6. Lachkar, A., Gadi, T., Benslimane, R., D'Orazio, L.: Textile Woven Fabric Recognition using Fourier Image Analysis Techniques: Part I: A Fully Automatic Approach for Crossed-points Detection. J. Text. Inst. 94(1), 194–201 (2003)
7. Ravandi, S.A.H., Toriumi, K.: Fourier-Transform Analysis of Plain Weave Fabric Appearance. Textile Research Journal 65(11), 676–683 (1995)
8. Jeon, B.S., Bae, J.H., Suh, M.W.: Automatic recognition of woven fabric patterns by an artificial neural network. Textile Research Journal 73(7), 645–650 (2003)
9. Kuo, C.F.J., Shih, C.Y., Lee, J.Y.: Automatic recognition of fabric weave patterns by a fuzzy C-means clustering method. Textile Research Journal 74(2), 107–111 (2004)
10. Kuo, C.F.J., Shih, C.Y., Lee, J.Y.: Repeat pattern segmentation of printed fabrics by hough transform method. Textile Research Journal 75(11), 779–783 (2005)
11. Lachkar, A., Benslimane, R., D'Orazio, L., Martuscelli, E.: Textile Woven Fabric Recognition using Fourier Image Analysis Techniques: Part II - texture analysis for crossed-states detection. J. Text. Inst. 96(3), 179–183 (2005)
12. Kang, T.J., Kim, C.H., Oh, K.W.: Automatic recognition of fabric weave patterns by digital image analysis. Textile Research Journal 69(2), 77–83 (1999)
13. Campbell, J.G., Murtagh, F.: Automatic visual inspection of woven textiles using a two-stage defect detector. Optical Engineering 37(9), 2536–2542 (1998)
14. Kuo, C.F.J., Tsai, C.C.: Automatic recognition of fabric nature by using the approach of texture analysis. Textile Research Journal 76(5), 375–382 (2006)
15. Rallo, M., Escofet, J., Millan, M.S.: Weave-repeat identification by structural analysis of fabric images. Applied Optics 42(17), 3361–3372 (2003)
16. Hui, C.L.: Neural Network Prediction of Human Psychological Perceptions of Fabric Hand. Textile Research Journal (May 2004)
17. Hatch, L.K.: Textile Science. West Publishing Company, Minneapolis (1993)
18. AB, R.T., Reachin API 3.2 Programmer's Guide (1998-2003)

Pocket Gamelan: Realizations of a Microtonal Composition on a Linux Phone Using Open Source Music Synthesis Software

Greg Schiemer[1], Etienne Deleflie[1], and Eva Cheng[2]

[1] Faculty of Creative Arts, University of Wollongong, Wollongong, Australia
[2] School of Electrical Engineering, RMIT University, Melbourne, Australia
schiemer@uow.edu.au, ed386@uow.edu.au, eva.uow@gmail.com

Abstract. This paper discusses a new approach to computer music synthesis where music is composed specifically for performance using mobile handheld devices. Open source cross-platform computer music synthesis software initially developed for composing on desktop computers has been used to program a Linux phone. Work presented here allows mobile devices to draw on these resources and makes comparisons between the strengths of each program in a mobile phone environment. Motivation is driven by aspirations of the first author who seeks to further develop creative mobile music performance applications first developed in the 1980s using purpose-built hardware and later, using j2me phones. The paper will focus on two different musical implementations of his microtonal composition entitled Butterfly Dekany which was initially implemented in Csound and later programmed using Pure Data. Each implementation represents one of the two programming paradigms that have dominated computer music composition for desktop computers namely, music synthesis using scripting and GUI-based music synthesis. Implementation of the same work using two different open source languages offers a way to understand different approaches to composition as well providing a point of reference for evaluating the performance of mobile hardware.

Keywords: Linux, mobilephone, csound, pure data, chuck, synthesis toolkit.

1 Introduction

The processing capabilities of Linux phones offer the promise of a new playground for music synthesis suitable for the ongoing development of the Pocket Gamelan project in which music for performing ensembles was produced by the first author using j2me phones. Others have already taken the concept of the mobile phone performance ensemble much further initially using Symbian phones and later the iPhone. Open source operating systems and computer music programming resources have facilitated the development of a new genre of interactive musical performance; Mo-Pho performances combine the live synthesis capabilities of RISC processors with new tools for interaction using embedded peripherals [1, 2].

R. Nakatsu et al. (Eds.): ECS 2010, IFIP AICT 333, pp. 101–110, 2010.
© IFIP International Federation for Information Processing 2010

Fig. 1. (a) Neo phone (b) Neo phone development environment

Figure 1 (a) shows the Neo FreeRunner, or Neo, the phone of choice for this project; the phone supports a number of operating systems including OpenMoko and Android and offers similar hardware features as other open source phones. Not only is its software open source, the hardware schematics and CAD specifications for both printed circuit board and molded enclosure are also available open-source.

While a full discussion of the psycho-acoustic, compositional and theatrical reasons for the choice of the Neo are beyond the scope of this paper, the choice was influenced by a need to swing the phone to produce chorusing and Doppler shift which features in works produced to date for the Pocket Gamelan [3]. In short, Neo was chosen because it had a ready-made hole - a significant factor because this eliminated the need to manufacture special pouches for swinging phones.

2 Development Environment

The development environment allows users to create a prototype musical application on a desktop machine and run it on the Neo. It is for users already familiar with making music using one of the open source composition environments ported to the Neo.

It consists of a host machine connected to a client as shown in figure 1 (b). The host is an Acer Netbook running Ubuntu 8.10, and is connected via a USB network cable to the Neo client running Debian. A more detailed description of the preliminary technical work associated with setting up this development environment can be found elsewhere [4].

We modified the Neo to boot two systems: the original OpenMoko 2007.2 distribution (factory installed) from the internal flash memory, or Debian, which we stored on the microSD card; to boot into Debian the auxiliary and power buttons are held and pressed simultaneously.

USB networking on Debian is enabled by default and should always be running. This allows the Neo to communicate via an ssh terminal launched from the Acer. All commands on the Neo must be issued from the Acer terminal.

3 Butterfly Dekany

The work first used to test Csound [5] and Pure Data [6] on the Neo was a microtonal composition entitled Butterfly Dekany composed by the first author. This was an outgrowth of compositions created for j2me phones as part of the Pocket Gamelan project. The work was initially created using Csound for a performance in which a traditional Chinese zither called a Gu Zheng was accompanied by a single battery powered sound source. The first performance was presented at the UNESCO-sponsored GAUNG Music for the New Millenium Workshop in Bedulum, Bali on 29th April 2009. The performer was Eni Agustien.

'Butterfly' in the title refers to a visual characteristic of the Gu Zheng owned by the performer. The instrument has two sets of strings radiating in opposite directions from a central bridge; the bridge forms an axis like the wings of a butterfly radiating from its body on either side. 'Dekany' refers to name of a 10-note microtonal scale devised by contemporary tuning theorist Erv Wilson; this scale is one of a class of scales generated using Wilson's Combination Product Set method [7].

Another microtonal feature is chorusing, a bi-product of the processing algorithm developed for the work as well as the movement of the sound source with its resultant Doppler shift.

One of the features of the work is that sound projection relies on making effective use of the reverberant properties of room acoustics instead of artificial acoustic rein-forcement achieved using high levels of electronic amplification. Movement of the sound source and amplitude modulation produced by microtonal intervals and plays an important role in sound propagation.

3.1 Harmonic Organisation

One of the unique musical properties of scales generated using Wilson's method is that these scales produce groups of harmonically related intervals and chords even though, unlike traditional scales generated from harmonics, the fundamental is not present in the scale. In the case of the scale used for Butterfly Dekany, the set of five harmonics used to generate the combination product set are the harmonics: 1, 3, 7, 9 and 11 which are combined by forming a set of products of pairs of harmonics to produce the scale shown in table 1.

Table 1. Notes of the Dekany formed from product of harmonics 1, 3, 7, 9 and 11

```
; 1:    33/32    undecimal comma                     .3. . . .11
; 2:     9/8     major whole tone                   1. . . . .9.
; 3:    77/64                                        . . .7. .11
; 4:    21/16    narrow fourth                       .3. .7. .
; 5:    11/8     undecimal semi-augmented fourth    1. . . . . .11
; 6:     3/2     perfect fifth                      1.3. . . .
; 7:    99/64                                        . . . .9.11
; 8:    27/16    Pythagorean major sixth             .3. . .9.
; 9:     7/4     harmonic seventh                   1. . .7. .
; 10:   63/32    octave - septimal comma             . . .7.9.
```

This scale is in fact two interleaved pentatonic scales, one formed on the odd-numbered notes of the dekany, the other formed on the even notes. Even though the pentatonic scale is one of the most universal scales the harmonic relationship between the two pentatonic scales that occur in this dekany has no cultural precedent.

Butterfly Dekany consists of ten sections in which each section is built on one of the two pentatonic scales. The first - and every subsequent section - is built on notes of the odd-numbered pentatonic scale while the second is built on notes of the even-numbered pentatonic scale. Each half of the Gu Zheng is tuned respectively to the odd- and even-notes of the dekany.

3.2 Scripting Paradigm - Csound Implementation

The Csound score for Butterfly Dekany takes the form of layers of sustained notes that enter canonically. Each note consists of five oscillators four of which are pitch-shifted using dynamically changing envelopes in an adaptation of a chorusing algorithm created by Risset [8]. The adaptation involves pitch bends applied to each envelope to form microtonal intervals that occur on the natural harmonic series between harmonics 100, 99 and 98. The microtonal intervals 100/99, 99/98 and 50/49 (i.e. 100/98) are derived from the same set of harmonics used to generate the scale.

Each note produces audible beat fluctuation that slowly accelerates and decelerates over the duration of each note independently of other notes. One of the five oscillators remains on pitch for the duration of the note, while two are pitch shifted above the note at different rates and by different amounts and the remaining two are pitch shifted below the note. Figure 2 shows the Csound instrument created to do this.

```
instr 1
    ibend1   =        1.010101010    ; 100/99
    ibend2   =        1.010204082    ;  99/98
    ipitch   = p5
    itrans   = 0.01
    ifreq1   cps2pch ipitch, -4
    kfreq    =        ifreq

    kover    linseg  0, p3*0.05,  ampdb(p4), p3*0.95, 0, 0.05, 0

    k0       linen kover, 0.01,     p3, p3*0.9
    k1       linen kover, 0.02,     p3, p3*0.8
    k2       linen kover, 0.03,     p3, p3*0.7
    k3       linen kover, 0.04,     p3, p3*0.6
    k4       linen kover, 0.05,     p3, p3*0.5
    k5       linseg ifreq, p3*0.5, (ifreq)*ibend1,      p3*0.4, ifreq
    k6       linseg ifreq, p3*0.4, (ifreq)*ibend2,      p3*0.5, ifreq
    k7       linseg ifreq, p3*0.3, (ifreq)*(2-ibend1),  p3*0.6, ifreq
    k8       linseg ifreq, p3*0.2, (ifreq)*(2-ibend2),  p3*0.7, ifreq

    a0       oscil   k0,  kfreq,   100
    a1       oscil   k1,  k5,      100
    a2       oscil   k2,  k6,      100
    a3       oscil   k3,  k7,      100
    a4       oscil   k4,  k8,      100

    asigl    =        a0 + a1 + a4
    asigr    =        a0 + a2 + a3
             outs     asigl, asigr
             endin
```

Fig. 2. The Csound instrument

Figure 3 shows an extract from the Csound Score.

```
i 1      0      60      68      9.02    i 1     18      42      68      8.02
i 1      3      57      68      9.04    i 1     21      39      68      7.04
i 1      6      54      68      9.06    i 1     33      27      68      8.08
i 1      9      51      68      9.08
i 1     12      48      68      9.10
```

Fig. 3. The Csound score

3.3 GUI-Based Paradigm - Pure Data implementation

For the purpose of comparing the relative advantages of the two composition environments the Csound implementation for Butterfly Dekany was rewritten in Pure Data. The canonic entry of voices in Pure Data is implemented using additional instantiations of the instrument where abstractions represent parameter fields in the Csound score file as shown in Figure 4.

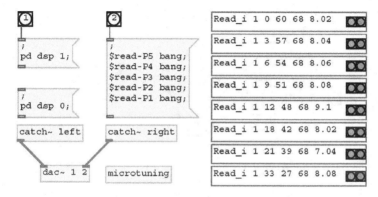

Fig. 4. Shows a Pd patch to read the score used in Butterfly Dekany. Each event is arranged in Csound score format with five parameter fields representing instrument number, start time and duration, level (decibels) and scale degree (octave and pitch class). Abstractions in PD correspond to parameter fields shown in Figure 3.

It has proved non-trivial to implement a composition that fitted easily into Csound in a different composition environment. Each line of Csound orchestra code behaves like an object that receives arguments or passes arguments to subsequent lines. Verifying the PD implementation of a process that fits comfortably within Csound sometimes made it necessary to determine the order in which signals are processed or to clarify an underlying concept. The functionality of each line and the flow of information became clearer once it was represented visually in a PD patch and this in turn has opened up new possibilities for live interaction.

One example of this is the left hand column of buttons shown in the Read_i window in Figure 4 above. The left button was introduced as a trigger to test an event out of sequence. This in turn has identified an entry point in the PD implementation where events may be actuated in real time.

Another example is the PD implementation of the envelope generator used to control the overall amplitude of each of the five audio oscillators. Figure 5 shows the PD implementation of the signal called kover which changes dynamically over the duration of each note. The changing output signal is passed to five independent envelope generators. The signal is first packed for transmission before being unpacked sample by sample. This ensures that each of the five envelope generators receive the same sample at the same time.

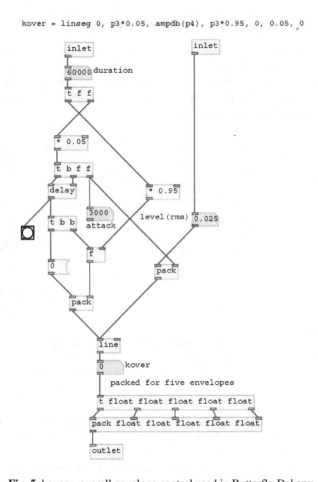

kover = linseg 0, p3*0.05, ampdb(p4), p3*0.95, 0, 0.05, 0

Fig. 5. kover – overall envelope control used in Butterfly Dekany

The transmission of signal from the output of kover to subsequent envelope generators clarified the visual representation of the configuration as represented in the sub-patch shown in Figure 6. This allowed signals read from the parameter fields of the score to be traced more easily on the Read_i parent canvas as shown in Figure 7.

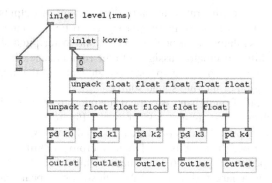

Fig. 6. kover distributed to envelope generators k0 to k5

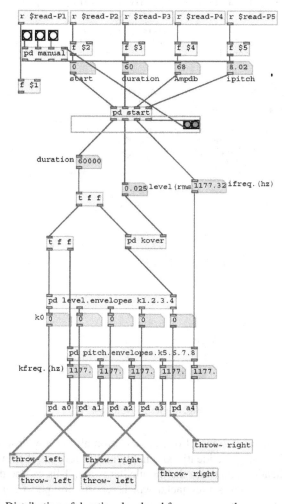

Fig. 7. Distribution of duration, level and frequency on the parent canvas

The parent canvas also illustrates the stereo assignment of outputs of each of the five oscillators; the fixed pitch oscillator is assigned to both channels while the left channel is assigned oscillators with one upper and one lower pitch shift with the remaining two pitch shifted oscillators assigned to the right channel. In a tethered stereo sound system the combination of the speaker assignment and the amplitude modulation produces a sensation of moving sound source.

The implementation of pitch bend is critical for microtonal chorusing. This is represented by the pitch envelope sub-patch k5 shown in Figure 8.

In k5 the microtonal pitch bend is pre-calculated and stored within sub-patch peakbend_A; the value in peakbend_A is the larger microtonal shift of 99/98 above the fixed pitch, while peakbend_a in k6 is a smaller shift of 100/99 above; similarly, peakbend_B in k7 is a larger shift of 99/98 below, while peakbend_b in k8 is a smaller shift of 100/99 below.

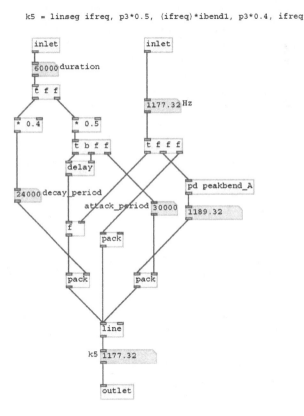

Fig. 8. Pitch envelope k5

Having two implementations of one composition allows any drop outs that might occur in the audio pipe to be identified quickly and to form a reliable estimate of the demands an application makes on the mobile hardware. This can be done by observing the output of the jack server jackd which reports dropped frames via the xrun message.

Clearly, the GUI that enabled the application to be prototyped in the desktop environment is no longer needed for launching the application on a mobile device. So the –nogui flag was enabled when the PD implementation of Butterfly Dekany was launched on the Linux phone.

The Csound implementation of the work can also be launched on the Linux phone. And while recent developments in Csound are more suited to real-time interaction than its earlier scripted versions, the real advantage of implementing Butterfly Dekany in PD will be that for future development of similar works there are already many new PD externals that allow real-time control to be refined in mobile devices. Earlier work for java phones by the first author can now not only be emulated in PD on a desktop computer but implemented to run directly on the Linux phone.

4 Conclusion

Several widely used computer music languages can now be used in conjunction with Linux phones. This brings together the resources of the open source community and a growing body of composers who use these resources for composing music. As these resources migrate to the mobile environment the GUI features of the desktop environment will become less important as other interfaces available in embedded hardware of mobile phones allow us to create instruments that respond to gestural input. We have already done preliminary work and successfully used the Neo hardware with other languages such as STK [9] and ChucK [10]. Plans for the future include a more substantial test of the comparative strengths and weaknesses of various languages using this hardware that would involve creating a single application that can be implemented in each language under test. In addition to a single test based on rendering audio, these tests will need to factor in the effect on processing bandwidth of onboard interface hardware such as accelerometers and wireless network interfaces. In time the Neo or indeed other Linux phones will acquire a community of users who will contribute to the ongoing development of mobile musical applications.

Acknowledgements

Eni Agustien, collaborator in the performance of Butterfly Dekany; Dr Serrano Sianturi and Dr Franki Raden Notosudirdjo, from The Sacred Bridge Foundation, organizers of GAUNG Music for the New Millenium, Bali; Australian Research Council for support for the Pocket Gamelan Project 2003-2005; Mark Havryliv from the University of Wollongong and Norikazu Mitani from IDMI, National University of Singapore for j2me development on the Pocket Gamelan between 2004 and 2008.

References

[1] Wang, G., Essl, G., Pentinnen, H.: MoPhO: Do Mobile Phones Dream of Electric Orchestras? In: Proceedings of the International Computer Music Conference, Belfast (August 2008)
[2] Essl, G., Rohs, M.: Mobile STK for Symbian OS. In: Proceedings of the International Computer Music Conference, New Orleans (November 2006)

[3] Schiemer, G.M., Havryliv, M.: Pocket gamelan: tuneable trajectories for flying sources in Mandala 3 and Mandala 4. In: 6th International Conference on New Interfaces for Musical Expression (NIME 2006), Paris, France, pp. 37–42 (2006)

[4] Schiemer, G., Chen, E.: Enabling Musical Applications On A Linux Phone. In: Proceedings of ACMC 2009, Improvise, The Australasian Computer Music Conference, Queensland University of Technology, July 2-4 (2009)

[5] Boulanger, R.: The Csound Book: Perspectives in Software Synthesis, Sound Design, Signal Processing and Programming. MIT Press, Cambridge (2000)

[6] Puckette, M.: Pure Data. In: Proceedings, International Computer Music Conference, International Computer Music Association, San Francisco, pp. 269–272 (1996)

[7] Wilson, E.: D'Alessandro Like a Hurricane. In: Xenharmonikôn, vol. 9, pp. 1–38 (1986)

[8] Risset, J.C.: 1969 Introductory Catalogue of Computer-Synthesised Sounds. Bell Telephone Labs., Murray Hill (1969)

[9] Scavone, G., Cook, P.: RtMIDI, Rtaudio, and a Synthesis Toolkit (STK) Update. In: Proceedings of the 2005 International Computer Music Conference, Barcelona, Spain (2005)

[10] Wang, G., Cook, P.: ChucK: a programming language for on-the-fly, real-time audio synthesis and multimedia. In: Proceedings of the 12th Annual ACM International Conference on Multimedia 2004, New York, NY, USA (2004)

Creating Memory:
Reading a Patching Language

Michael Barkl

Illawarra Institute, Wollongong NSW Australia

Abstract. Musical analysis from score, particularly of structural principles used by the composer, is an area fraught with potential errors caused by conjecture and interpretation. Analysis of music composed using a computer patching language may, alternatively, provide a far more reliable document of a composer's methods. This paper examines a small number of patches created using Miller Puckette's Pure Data (Pd), composed as part of a series of large scale electronic pieces.

Keywords: Music composition; electronic music; Pure Data; Pd.

1 Introduction

Some years ago I analysed a complex piece of instrumental music written by a well known 20th century Italian composer[1]. The chamber work, for flute, clarinet, violin, cello and piano, crammed with virtuosic fast notes, was known to be completely and systematically derived from a fragment of music taken from a single bar of a piano piece by an even more famous composer[2].

How did all those notes come from that small fragment?, I asked myself. If I could find out, the mysteries of musical development would become apparent to me, so I thought.

I had the recording and the musical score. The recording gave me the sound of the work; the notation showed me how those sounds were made. However, what was missing was what I desperately wanted: what organising principles did the composer use? How did all those notes, so exciting and beguiling, relate together as an artistic whole?

The analysis I eventually made answered these questions to my own satisfaction. However, the process took me four years, which is not a particularly efficient use of time for a nine-minute piece (an average of two and a quarter minutes of progress per year). At that rate my lifetime would be too short to scarcely begin investigating the number of pieces that interested me[3].

---

[1] Michael Barkl, Franco Donatoni's *Etwas ruhiger im Ausdruck* (1967), MM dissertation, University of New England, 1986.

[2] The first three beats of the eighth bar of the second of Arnold Schoenberg's *Five Piano Pieces* (Op 23, 1923).

[3] My next attempt was even less efficient: I spent eight years analysing a seven-minute piece. See, Michael Barkl, Vertigo: Riccardo Formosa's Composition Technique, PhD dissertation, Deakin University, 1994.

R. Nakatsu et al. (Eds.): ECS 2010, IFIP AICT 333, pp. 111–117, 2010.

Barely one year after I completed my analysis, a professor of musicology at the Sorbonne published his analysis of precisely the same work[4].

To be sure, there were some aspects of his analysis that were almost identical to mine. However, there were other conjectures and interpretations that were completely unrelated. Indeed, the differences were so startling that a comparison and discussion of the two analyses occupied almost half a recent doctoral dissertation from Cornell University[5].

My confidence in the power of analysis, even of systematic creative processes, was severely shaken. If only we could be more sure…

2 Patching Language as Evidence of Process

Some four or five years ago I began composing electronic music using the open source patching language Pure Data (Pd) developed by Miller Puckette.[6] The first thing that struck me about Pd's patching language was its ability to document compositional algorithms. It seemed to me that, with a little care, Pd patches would be easily readable, not so much as a finished or publishable "score", but as a documentation of a composer's sketches and evidence of process; that is, serving as a kind of descriptive analysis of the piece[7].

I completed a series of three large-scale electronic works, entitled *Music of Grace*, which used sine tones only[8]. Examples of patches from *The cat dances and the moon shines brightly*, the first work of the series, follow, which show some basic aspects of the principle in action. In Figure 1 data flows down the page from panel 1 to panel 5. The [bang] GUI signals that the previous section is complete as well as initiating the next section[9].

---

[4] Robert Piencikowski, "Sauf-conduit (Analyse d'*Etwas ruhiger im Ausdruck*)", *Entretemps*, 2 (November 1986), later published as "Salvacondotto. Analisi di *Etwas ruhiger im Ausdruck*", in *Donatoni*, ed. Enzo Restagno, Turin: Edizioni di Torino, 1990: 147-158.

[5] Yotam Haber, Aleatory and Serialism in Two Early Works of Franco Donatoni, DMA dissertation, Cornell University, 2004, published as *Aleatory and Serialism: Two Early Works of Franco Donatoni*, Köln: Lambert Academic Publishing, 2009.

[6] Software by Miller Puckette, http://crca.ucsd.edu/~msp/software.html

[7] Using sketches or examples from a musical score, with minimal annotations, as an analytical tool is well known. Schenker is perhaps the most obvious example of this. See Heinrich Schenker, "Vom Organischen der Sonatenform," in *Das Meisterwerk in der Musik*, Vol.II, Munich: Drei Masken, 1926; trans. W.Drabkin as "On Organicism in Sonata Form," in *The Masterwork in Music*, Vol.II, Cambridge University Press, 1996.

[8] Michael Barkl, Composition: Pure data as a Meta-Compositional Instrument, DCA dissertation, University of Wollongong, 2009, published by Köln: Lambert Academic Publishing, 2009.

[9] GUI boxes are rendered [GUI], object boxes are rendered [object], message boxes are rendered [message(and comments are rendered "comment".

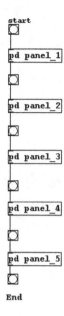

Fig. 1. *The cat dances* Panels 1-5

Figure 2 shows what is inside the [pd panel_1] sub-patch. Again, data flow is down the page and shows that panel 1 comprises two subsections.

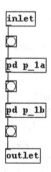

Fig. 2. *The cat dances* Subsections 1a and 1b within Panel 1

Figure 3 shows what is inside the [pd p_1a] sub-patch. Here the data flow is more complex, with feedback to [pd high_control_1-22].

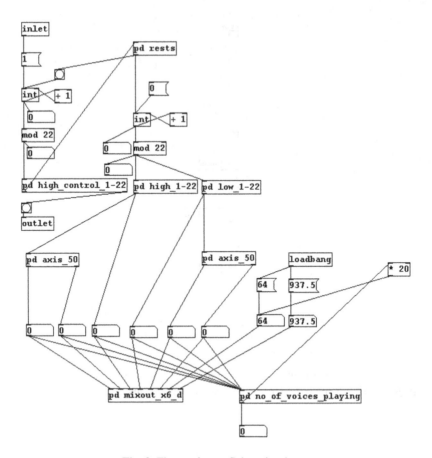

Fig. 3. *The cat dances* Subsection 1a

Opening further sub-patches, such as [pd high_control_1-22], [pd rests], [pd axis_50], [pd high_1-22], [pd low_1-22], [pd mixout_x6_d] and [pd no_of_voices_playing], would delve deeper into the structure down to the level of elemental operations[10].

The fifth and final panel of the piece has fewer layers of embedded objects and is thus easier to describe. It applies procedures that control duration, add trills, and direct two musical lines into contrary motion.

A [bang) from the [inlet] begins each side of the patch simultaneously, the left controlling the descending line and the right controlling the ascending line. To discuss the left hand side of the patch first, the [bang) initiates the [int 1][+ 1] counter which advances [pd high_1-22] via [mod 22]. Every output from [pd high_1-22] bangs [pd 0_1_out] in order to alternate the duration of the notes: short (3700 ms) or long (15000 ms).

At the same time, the output from [pd high_1-22] is sent to the far left hand side of the patch, where the values from [pd high_1-22] are "forced" into an ascending series,

---

[10] Indeed, this particular piece comprises 50 different patches; the series of three pieces comprises 1025 different patches in total.

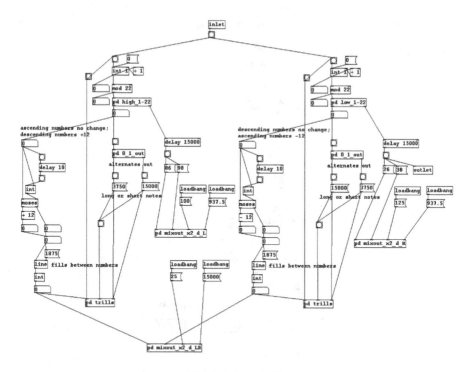

Fig. 4. [pd panel_5]

and then the difference "filled" with integers. This is accomplished by comparing the "new" value with the previous value: every value is slightly delayed by the [delay 10][int] combination of objects in order to seed [moses]. The new value is thereby "compared" with the previous value: if the new value is equal or higher it is sent from the right outlet of [moses]; if it is lower it is sent from the left outlet and 12 is added to it. The [line] object fills the difference between the values over a period of 1875 ms, and these are converted to integers by [int] before being sent to [pd mixout_x2_d] for performance, and to [pd trills] (Figure 5) for the addition of decoration. The output of [pd trills] is sent back to the top of the patch to advance the counter.

The left [inlet] of [pd trills], labelled "Pitch in", receives the values from the [line][int] combination of objects and sends them to two [float]s, adding a value of 2 to the second one. The second and third [inlet]s control the length of the notes by seeding [delay 15000] and then banging it. The second inlet turns on the [toggle) and the output of [delay 15000] turns it off while simultaneously sending a [bang) to the [outlet] to advance the patch as a whole. The [toggle) turns [metro 937.5] on and off, which begins [select 0 1] alternately banging the two [float]s, creating the trill effect.

The right hand side of the [pd panel_5] patch operates in exactly the same way as the left side, except that the values are taken from [pd low_1-22], and the line is "forced" to descend via [- 12].

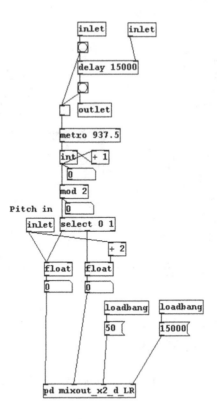

Fig. 5. [pd trills]

The final chord to end the piece is played once the two [pd trills] have banged [pd high_1-22] and [pd low_1-22] enough times for them to have completed their cycle. A bang is sent from the right hand outlet of these objects which, after a delay of 15000 ms, bangs [86(and [98(, routed to stereo left, and [26(and [38(, routed to stereo right, for the final chord.

3 Conclusion

The principal motivation for laying out the patches in a clear somewhat linear way has been to clarify my own understanding of the compositional processes taking place in my work by finding a suitable way in which to document them. Indeed, there are many cases in my own previous work where I simply cannot recall the composition process or method.

Nonetheless, visually examining a complex dynamic patch some time after its construction can be challenging, not only to imagine all its events dynamically changing, but to imagine how the outcome of the patch interacts with other patches operating concurrently. Additionally, when describing the patches in this paper, it became clear that even being able to follow the functional operation of a patch or group of patches is not the same thing as discerning the musical effect or musical meaning of the composition or even parts of the composition.   For this, additional commentary at the "interpretive" level (as distinct from the "descriptive" level) will always be necessary. Nonetheless, it was shown that it is possible for a composition in Pd to explicitly show its own construction and interrelation of compositional elements, providing a kind of descriptive analysis of the work.

However, the importance of this particular way of using the patching language lies in the potential or capacity for artistic development, improvement and refinement. That is, I, a composer, am much more likely to develop consistently if I am not struggling to remember the last thing I did.   For me, therefore, the value of the documentation of composition process is one of memory and recall, irrespective of the genre in which I happen to work.   Additionally, it is conceivable that the documentation of the creative process might, some day, be of value to the interested listener, musicologist or even composition student.

References

1. Barkl, M.: Franco Donatoni's Etwas ruhiger im Ausdruck. MM dissertation. University of New England (1986)
2. Barkl, M.: Vertigo: Riccardo Formosa's Composition Technique. PhD dissertation, Deakin University (1994)
3. Barkl, M.: Composition: Pure data as a Meta-Compositional Instrument. Lambert Academic Publishing, Köln (2009)
4. Haber, Y.: Aleatory and Serialism: Two Early Works of Franco Donatoni. Lambert Academic Publishing, Köln (2009)
5. Piencikowski, R.: Salvacondotto. Analisi di Etwas ruhiger im Ausdruck. In: Restagno, E. (ed.) Donatoni, pp. 147–158. Edizioni di Torino, Turin (1990)
6. Puckette, M.: Software, http://crca.ucsd.edu/~msp/software.html
7. Schenker, H.: On Organicism in Sonata Form. In: Drabkin, W. (trans.) (ed.) The Masterwork in Music, vol. II. Cambridge University Press, Cambridge (1996)

The Promise of Fuzzy Logic in Generalised Music Composition

Wendy Suiter

University of Wollongong,
NSW, Australia
ws999@uow.edu.au

Abstract. The paper outlines the rationale for using Fuzzy Logic, and Granular Computing, to emulate compositional decision making processes. Significant features of this Fuzzy Logic framework are that ambiguity in the music is maintained, while allowing the evolution of unfolding processes which reflects the temporal nature of music as performed. Granular Computing and Fuzzy Logic have been designed for physical and IT engineering applications to automate complex tasks. Fuzzy Logic is not only useful as an analytical concept, but also, can be generally applied to the production of music itself through a Fuzzy Logic control system. As artificial intelligence design and computing power both improve, it may well become possible to perform this work by digital means. My present research will contribute to this development through the identification of the significant compositional elements and their connective grammar. Once, these have been determined, then automated ways to compose music can be developed.

Keywords: Fuzzy Logic, Granular Computing, Music Composition, Algorithmic Music.

1 Introduction

If you were composing a piece of music from scratch, how would you decide what to do? Naturally, you would first consider the general requirements for the piece. Of course there are not only technical constraints, like how long is the piece to be, and what technology is available for the performance, but there are also contextual considerations such as the location of, and the reason for, the performance.

Yet once these initial conditions have been clarified, there are many more decisions waiting to be made. What about the first sound event: its pitch? It's duration? It's amplitude? What about the next sound event: its pitch? It's duration? It's amplitude? What about every other event that falls between this and the final one? How would you decide what to do?

Composers are faced with making these decisions every time they work. To reduce the number of micro-level decisions needed, my goal is to find a set of elements and rules, which will ultimately enable me to construct an algorithmic compositional system which can produce expressive music if so desired. Typical analysis of conventional music throws little light on these questions [13].

R. Nakatsu et al. (Eds.): ECS 2010, IFIP AICT 333, pp. 118–127, 2010.

My present goal is to produce a theoretical model of music that is applicable across all genres of music, including both acoustic music and computer music. This is substantially different from other theories which, typically, can only be applied to one style of music. For instance, Forte's work applying classical set theory to music analysis is limited to atonal music [6]. He specifically states that his work is not applicable to serial music, which, interestingly, is the more algorithmic compositional technique of the two.

Fuzzy Logic principles seem to be the most useful way of describing completely, both the elements, and their interactions, which contribute to the aesthetic outcomes of music. This is supported by the application of Efstathiou's decision making paradigm [4] to the research itself, which will be discussed in more detail later in the paper.

2 Literature Review

Very little work has been done in the application of Fuzzy Logic to music composition, although there are several papers which outline the need for this work. Two composers have mentioned the conceptual incorporation of Fuzzy Logic in automated musical decision making, without any justification for the specific inclusion of FL as a methodology in the models. Yet several others have developed specific musical applications such as chord generators, but they have not engaged with modelling complete systems from an aesthetic perspective.

In the first of the two papers mention the conceptual use of Fuzzy Logic in music composition is Whalley's paper presented to the 2002 International Computer Music Conference [14]. In this paper Whalley provides a brief overview of literature on emotion as musical narrative, semiotics of music in relation to automated composition systems. This review shows that there is a need for this type of work, without providing any rationale for the potential inclusion of Fuzzy Logic methodology.

Milicevic has published a series of papers exploring the reception of computer music, each reframing the same idea as new philosophical frameworks become available. One of his papers uses some elements of Fuzzy Logic as the means to advance his argument [9]. Milicevic argues that computer music composers need to consider the human brain mechanisms of the audience when composing their music, as this will result in a more positive reception of their music. He proposes the development of an automated Fuzzy Logic system which could analyse each piece of music for its patterning, which would then enable the composer to determine whether the music would engender a positive reception.

Several composers have incorporated Fuzzy Logic into specific creative work. Cadiz produces continuous a-rhythmic compositions through the control of several sound synthesis parameters [2]. That is, the musical work unfolds as the synthesised timbres change. Other programmers have also made modules which work in various programming languages to generate single musical elements using Fuzzy Logic engines. Elsea [5], has developed a chord generating mechanism, while Sorensen and Brown [12] have developed a Fuzzy Logic module for their jMusic program which operates on volume levels. While this work can potentially be developed into complex algorithms for a large range of musical elements, they have not engaged here with the concept of modelling complete musical systems from an aesthetic perspective.

3 Efstathiou's Decision Making Paradigm

Janet Efstathiou's paper on rule-based multi-attribute decision making [4] sets out a decision making process/paradigm that is immediately comprehensible, espouses ethics of including the decision maker(s) in the entire process, and is entirely human oriented. Indeed in simple cases, computers and numerical calculations (whether based on fuzzy logic or not) may not be necessary, because the computation can be done entirely in natural language, "...with pencil, paper and common sense." [4]

There are two parts to Efstathiou's decision-making paradigm. The first part deals with how to find an appropriate methodology to calculate potential solutions for a specific problem given the environment in which the question is being posed. This is done by asking a series of meta-questions [4]. The second part deals with developing a preference ordering for the various proposed outcomes to the specific multi-attribute problem. This takes place by the decision makers ranking each possible solution against the complete range of attributes to be addressed in the solution. The process she suggests is based on Fuzzy Logic using natural language, taking place in an iterative learning environment.

The paradigm seems very similar to Adaptive Resonance Theory which was developed in the AI context of machine learning. As a result, ART is very engineering oriented with much technical writing. As ART has become an accepted form of machine learning for robotics, it would seem that the date of Efstathiou's model is not relevant. Efstathiou [4] recognises the relationship between her model and robotics in her conclusion, making the distinction between machines and human decision making. As Fuzzy ART had not been developed at the time of her article this distinction was important. However, the development of Fuzzy ART [3] [7] has produced a type of machine learning which is very close to Efstathiou's paradigm. Fuzzy ART, typically, seems to be concerned with machine learning and system control of automated processes.

What is essentially useful about Efstathiou's model is its orientation towards human decision making, means that the mental and intuitive requirements of humans are considered at every step.

3.1 Part 1: Finding the Solution Methodology

Applying the notion of meta-questions from the first part of Efstathiou's model leads through an iterative process of refining and clarifying the best methodology to use for any specific decision making problem. Her methodological model [4] is based on the proposition that it is not practical for all possible problem solving methods to be tested. The question then becomes one of deciding which methodology will provide the best possible solutions for any given problem.

The iterative process Efstathiou proposes, teases out the essential attributes, in relation to the problem, that the solution method must hold. Thus if the solution method addresses all the significant issues surrounding the original question, then the solution to a specific problem provided by the selected problem solving method will provide a satisfactory and useful answer. The iterative process, when applied to this research question, results in the choice of Granular Computing and Fuzzy Logic.

The process of establishing a useful methodology is worked through below. In working through the process I have relabelled some of her steps to provide a more clearly defined pathway.

Question (Q0) derived from an underlying research topic: Is it possible to compose process music which is expressive?

Meta Question (MQ1) arises from the original question (Q0) on the basis that it is not possible to test most possible methodologies for their usefulness, how is a good solution method chosen from all the possible methods?

MQ1 is answered here by MA1: The solution must be a method which can become the compositional technique when it is fully developed.

MQ2 follows from MA1 on the basis that given there may be multiple frameworks which can do this, how do I choose which technique to use to resolve this question? MQ2 is answered here by MA2: The solution method must be a clearly defined rule based procedure, that is an algorithmic process, which is logical and transparently meaningful, while reflecting the essential qualities of music itself.

MQ3 follows from MQ2 on the basis that given there may be multiple frameworks which can do this, how do I choose which technique to use to resolve this question? MQ2 is clarified here by MQ3: What will ensure that these essential qualities will be reflected in the solution method?

MQ3 is answered by MA3: The solution must be an algorithmic problem solving model which is capable of handling imprecision and vagueness, while permitting both time and context dependent, multi-attribute decision making, while remaining transparent and inherently meaningful.

MA4 follows from MQ3 on the basis that it is not possible to test most possible solutions, how is a good solution chosen from all the possible solutions? MA4 here is: A good solution method is Granular Computing (derived from principles of fuzzy logic) based on natural language.

3.2 Part 11: Using the Solution Methodology to Solve the Problem

The second part of her model is concerned with using the solution finding methodology discovered through the meta-question process to find a range of possible solutions, and a method for assessing the most optimal solution for the given problem. The evaluation method involves obtaining a "preference ordering" of the attributes which must be addressed by the specific solution to this particular problem. This preference ordering is derived through a set of natural language IF/THEN rules.

Each IF/THEN rule compares a single element from each of two attributes by comparing two antecedents to produce a consequent mapping into an 'evaluation space' (my term) which will contain several fuzzy sets such as Poor, OK, Very Good. Each IF/THEN rule results in an individual evaluation outcome for this specific problem. (For example: IF... the dynamic level is 'very soft' ...AND...the pitch is 'very low'...THEN ...this option is POOR.) But the determined level of the consequent assessment will depend on the particular problem-solving context in which the decision is being made, so that in some circumstances, such as when evaluating 'music for relaxation', this rule may be changed to produce a consequent evaluation of VERY GOOD.

Then the elements of each alternative solution are simultaneously fed through the set of rules to provide the evaluation set for that solution, which, in total, will give the overall quality of that alternative.

Each one of the alternative solutions can then be given a "preference ordering" according to the resulting quality of the evaluation set for that alternative solution.

4 Fuzzy Logic and the Specific Properties of Music

The production of musical art involves consideration of its intrinsic qualities. It is Time dependent; an Abstract art form; it includes a combination of emotional and intellectual qualities in varying degree; and it's terminology is imprecise. Discussion about music, music theory and analysis, including its techniques, its description, critiques, and instructions to performers are very often described in words. Common musical notation is an attempt at precision, but even some elements of notation are vaguely defined. While words themselves have relative meaning, there is no absolute meaning of 'loud' or 'cantabile' or < or ⌢. Fuzzy Logic has been formulated specifically to deal with the imprecision and 'vagueness' which is present when using natural language descriptors.

A significant feature of music is that the aesthetic outcome is often more than the sum of its technical elements. Indeed, what is the role of timbre, attack, duration, decay, articulation, spatialisation, register, texture, voicing, entries and timing, rhythm, tempo or meter? What does musical form, structure, or process contribute? In fact, it is often the means and details of the interactions between the distinct elements which significantly influence the effectiveness of the whole work. This means music is, technically, a non-linear system. "Non linear systems are systems that cannot be mathematically described as the sum of their components." This behaviour can be observed across a variety of disciplines including biology and economics as well as physics. [10]. Fuzzy Logic is good for modelling non-linear systems as little prior knowledge of the original system is required [7]. This is a significant reason for using Fuzzy Logic as the principle with which to build this theory of music.

It may be noted here that in practice musical features such as amplitude and register, flow in differing time scales. Hence my interest in pursuing granulation of time as a significant feature. The application of Fuzzy Logic through Granular Computing, which allows different attributes to be granulated in different sized chunks, will ultimately be a useful method [11][15.].

5 Application of the Principles of Fuzzy Logic

5.1 Inputs to the Fuzzy Logic System

One of the features of using Fuzzy Logic modelling is the possibility of using either expert or non-experts to provide inputs into the Fuzzy Logic system. These inputs include both identifying the elements which are significant to the situation, and the ways in which these elements interact with each other to produce outcomes.

Different types of systems have been built using expert and non-expert inputs. For example Fuzzy ART systems learn through repeated experience [3], while Fuzzy

Logic inference engines, for example [8], operate on the basis of rules derived from the experience of experts in the field. At this point as a composer of many years standing and some academic achievement, I claim to be sufficiently expert to provide a provisional set of elements for this prototype model. This model will be refined over time using more complex works. Thus its development will, incorporate both input types.

5.2 How Fuzzy Logic Works

The most striking thing is the ability of Fuzzy Logic to contain imprecise, or 'vague' concepts. Here is a brief explanation of how Fuzzy Logic works with imprecision. The first relevant concept is that of the 'universe of discourse' for a musical attribute, for example 'register', which measures the relative pitch or frequency range of sound events. The universe of discourse for 'register' includes all possible registers. Within this universe of registers, there exist any number of sets applicable to 'register'. It should be noted here that the 'universe of discourse' does not have to be completely covered by defined sets in order for the logic to work.

However, each defined set contains elements which are closely related to each other. The sets are labelled with words. For examples some possible 'register' sets could be labelled, or speaking more technically, the attribute 'register' could be given a 'term set' of 'high', 'upper mid', 'lower mid', 'low', and 'deep'. Yet even within these registral locations there may still be ambiguity about what should be contained by these possible sets, for example 'upper mid' and 'upper'. In particular, the useful thing about fuzzy logic is its inclusivity. Variables do not have to take only binary (true/false) values, but everything can simultaneously be partially true.

Typical musical analysis would classify specific sound events, or even phrases, as being in only one set or another, however when using Fuzzy Logic can be classified in several or all categories.

Secondly, typical analytical decisions about how to classify a note, a chord, a sound, a section, or even a whole work are justified on the basis of the relations of some musical elements, while ignoring those that don't fit. The ambiguous harmonies in the Prelude to *Tristan und Isolde*, are a well known example. In instances like this, the useful thing about fuzzy logic is its inclusivity. Variables do not have to take only binary (true/false) values, but everything can simultaneously be partially true.

The basic proposition of Fuzzy Logic is that any object belongs to all possible sets, but with varying degrees of membership. Consequently, each object, in Fuzzy Logic, acquires several properties - the sets to which it is assigned, and also the 'degree' with which it is thought to belong to each set.

Recall that each universe of discourse refers to only one musical attribute, while the term sets refer to the range of values that specific attribute may take. For example, the attribute 'amplitude' may be given a 'term set' of three elements: Loud, Moderate and Soft.

The relevance of each elemental fuzzy set to each musical configuration is recorded through the allocation of membership values for that configuration to each of the elemental fuzzy sets. Membership values will be greater than zero only for those elemental sets which are relevant to a particular musical configuration. So, if the musical configuration does not seem to fit into a specific set to any degree, then the value of its membership for that set is zero. For example, it is possible that the register of a specific bar of music could be assigned to two sets: 'upper' with a membership value of 0.4; and 'upper-mid' with a membership value of 0.8, which reflects my evaluation that at this point the music is more in the middle range than in the upper range, yet it does still contain some upper registral characteristics.

Although the actual membership values are determined on the basis of my expertise, rather than on some predetermined quantitative measure, there is a meta-rule at play here. Namely, that in places where a particular musical occurrence is ambiguous or 'vague' it will be classed in as many sets as it may possibly suit. One of the features of using Fuzzy Logic is that no features are lost, as the classification process allows for ambiguity, which in itself may be a significant feature of some music. Another aspect is that all details are maintained for future use, including those which which may yet prove to be significant, are not destroyed by early choices. It is my contention that expression in music is derived from the interplay of constituent elements over time.

Then, looking to the future purpose of this methodology, the feature of Fuzzy Logic which makes it practical and useable is the change in perspective from individual object to the fuzzy set as a whole. Since objects have been classified with a degree of membership of each set, then each set includes information regarding membership values of the objects within it. In this sense, each set then contains its own individual 'membership function' for its objects. These membership functions can then be used to represent each set in 'fuzzy' mathematics, according to strict logical principles applied through a mathematically precise and rigorous Fuzzy Logic inference engine. It is this procedure which will enable Fuzzy Logic to become a practical and useable control mechanism.

5.3 Terminology

The terminology I am developing has been generalised away from traditional analytical terms which originate from notational foundations. My terminology covers the chief characteristics by which sound itself is shaped and processed through compositional decision making. Terms, such as 'articulation: discrete', which describe the elemental details of the music, have been used to generalise characteristics across both acoustic and computer music domains. Thus the term 'sound events' is used instead of 'note' so that the palette of sounds available in computer music, which are likely to be unpitched, and a-rhythmic, can be accommodated. It is likely, however, that further refinement of both terminology and model will take place as more music is analysed using these principles.

The development of appropriate 'Term Sets' is a requirement of Fuzzy Logic, while the development of an appropriate connective 'Grammar' is an additional major implication of Granular Computing for the eventual Fuzzy Logic control mechanism.

5.4 The Benefits of Fuzzy Logic Processing

Granular Computing is a useful methodology because it can be used as an algorithmic compositional technique. It is a coherent conceptual and algorithmic method for the representation and processing of information [11]. Granular Computing, based on

Fuzzy Logic techniques, provides the mechanism for the relatively new technique of 'computing with words' [15]. These methodologies are used to construct intelligent systems which can respond efficiently to variable contexts and data inputs. This has a number of benefits as the use of natural language grammar and linguistic variables, such as "deafening" rather than a numerical "120dB", means that its logic is transparent and meaningful [4]. Although some elements of musical notation are vaguely defined, others are very specific, for example metronome markings . Granular Computing allows both vague and crisp elements to be combined.

Granulation is a process of compressing data by grouping objects because they may be indistinguishable, for example by masking; have similar properties; are closely located; or have similar functions. This clumping process may be crisp or fuzzy, physical or virtual, and may produce dense or sparse results. Fuzzy granulation is particularly useful in environments of imprecision, uncertainty and partial truth. This method permits the subjective aggregation of vague information. This leads to Granular Computing, where the data sets, or information granules, are labelled with words from natural language [23].

Time itself, is an important variable to be subjected to granulation [17]. This is immediately relevant to music which is a temporal art. Indeed, time is used in different ways in different elements of the music. Most musical attributes from small rhythmic details to larger formal structures, depend on various time scales.

Fuzzy Logic models can be used in a non-numerate way resulting in a methodology that is extremely user-friendly. Even though natural language descriptors may only provide ordinal information (that is the elements can be ranked in order, from lowest to highest preference) this may be enough for the problem to be solved [4]. While, if necessary, fuzzy sets can be developed from these descriptors, with membership functions, to provide a mathematical basis for calculating solutions.

6 Future Work

This proposal to use Fuzzy Logic to model and compose a musical work has already highlighted some important issues which may require detailed investigation in order to allow my research to progress to a useful and functional conclusion in the form of a compositional method.

These issues include the further refinement of a appropriate elemental sets and terminology, as well as their interaction through connective grammar, to allow implementation through a Fuzzy Logic control system.

Another issue to be addressed is the granulation of Time, since different musical elements change at different rates, thus different time scales are likely to be relevant. In fact a significant part of the work to be done, is to examine various musics to obtain some generalised time domain results, and to formulate terms for modelling different interactions between elements.

At this point my work is being conducted manually. Although ny present research will contribute to the development of digital tools, however, the first step is to identify the significant compositional elements. Once, these have been determined, then automated ways to compose music can be developed.

The final issue is the development an appropriate perspective on a complete musical work as a self-determining system. The use of Fuzzy Logic implies that little prior knowledge of the whole system is required [7], however there may be other aspects of systems approach that could be usefully considered. There are models of control systems for terminating and non-terminating systems. Are these relevant to this work, now or in the future?

7 Conclusion

The requirements set out by Babbitt [1], that any musical theory be logical, coherent, useful, and intelligible are also met by Fuzzy Logic Principles. This is amplified when, as discussed earlier, Efstathiou's model of decision making is applied to the underlying question.

It is important that the modelling methodology allows for all these attributes while itself being rule bound, with evolutionary decision making, thus providing for variation in the elements and their combination over time. These are significant reasons for using Fuzzy Logic and Granular Computing as the principles on which to build this theory of music. Other reasons come from diverse quarters, together building a compelling argument for exploring this as a fruitful line of research. And finally, my initial investigations show that very little applied work has been done specifically in this area.

What distinguishes my work is the use of Fuzzy Logic principles, which allows for the incorporation of ambiguity, to assess at several levels, the construction of a broad range of Western music through two lenses simultaneously. Firstly, the detailed elemental perspective, that is the construction of the individual sound events in each piece of music. Secondly, the time domain perspective, that is how all these elements, and their variations, change and combine over time. Composers already do this kind of multidimensional thinking as an intrinsic part of their work. What differs from composer to composer and style to style, is the amount of, and which details in one or other of the dimensions they concern themselves with, the remainder being left to compositional algorithms.

Clearly, music is an excellent domain in which to apply Fuzzy Logic. In summary, a compositional method based on Fuzzy Logic principles can meet all these requirements, This is because each musical work can be conceptualised as a system, based on initial constraints and ongoing decisions made by the composer, between variables that are sometimes related and sometimes treated independently.

References

1. Babbitt, M.: The Structure and Function of Music Theory 1. College Music Symposium: Journal of the College Music Society 5, 49–60 (Fall 1965)
2. Cadiz, R.F.: Compositional Control of Computer Music by Fuzzy Logic, Ph.D. thesis, Northwestern University (2006)
3. Carpenter, G.A., Grossberg, S., et al.: Fuzzy ART: Fast Stable Learning and Categorisation of Analog Patterns by an Adaptive Resonance System. Neural Networks 4, 759–771 (1991a)

4. Efstathiou, J.: Practical Multi-Attribute Decision Making and Fuzzy Set Theory. Studies in Management Sciences 20, 307–320 (1984)
5. Elsea, P.: Fuzzy Logic and Musical Decisions, ftp://arts.ucsc.edu/pub/ems/FUZZY/Fuzzy_logic_and_Music.pdf
6. Forte, A.: The Structure of Atonal Music. Yale University Press, New Haven (1973)
7. Kosko, B.: Fuzzy Thinking: The New Science of Fuzzy Logic. Flamingo, London (1994)
8. Mamdani, E.H., Ostergaard, J.J., et al.: Use of Fuzzy Logic for Implementing Rule Based Control of Industrial Processes. Studies in Management Sciences 20, 429–445 (1984)
9. Milicevic, M.: Positive Emotion Learning through Music Listening, http://myweb.lmu.edu/mmilicevic/NEWpers/_PAPERS/papers.html
10. Monash University's Complexity Virtual Lab, http://vlab.infotech.monash.edu.au/simulations/non-linear/
11. Pedrycz, W.: Granular Computing-The Emerging Paradigm. Journal of Uncertain Systems 1(1), 38–61 (2007)
12. Sorensen, A., Brown, A.: jMusic: Music Composition in Java, http://jmusic.ci.qut.edu.au/index.html
13. Suiter, W.: Text Manipulation: Voice with Audio or Acoustic Augmentation. MCA-Res thesis, Faculty of Creative Arts, University of Wollongong (2007)
14. Whalley, I.: Towards a Closed System Automated Composition Engine: Linking 'Kansei' and Musical Language Recombinicity. In: ICMC 2002, Goteborg, Sweden, pp. 200–203 (2002)
15. Zadeh, L.A.: Some reflections on soft computing, granular computing and their roles in the conception, design and utilization of information/intelligent systems. Soft Computing 2, 23–25 (1998)

Structuralism, Attitude and the Computer: Questioning the Notion of "Cultural Computing"

Warren Burt

Faculty of Creative Arts, University of Wollongong

Abstract. The terms "cultural computing" and "entertainment computing" can be disturbing if looked at from the artists' point of view. Computing has always been part of the culture of the time, and this was especially true in the decades surrounding the birth of computing, when the structuralist paradigm was dominant in many areas of human endeavour. Perhaps what distinguishes, or should distinguish, "cultural" computing from other types of computing is its attitude: one of playfulness and light-hearted cleverness. This premise is discussed mainly from a musical point-of-view – examples from the computer music literature, including works by the author, are discussed in this context.

Keywords: Structuralism, post-structuralism, algorithmic composition, inherent structures, emergent structures, John Cage, Iannis Xenakis, Herbert Brun, Lejaren Hiller, Kenneth Gaburo, process composition, computer-aided composition.

1 Dealing with the Terms

When I first saw the terms "cultural computing" and "entertainment computing," I was a bit troubled. "Entertainment computing" seemed obvious, at first. It described computing that was used in the service of the entertainment industry. Industrial strength sound editing systems for the film industry and computer games immediately came to mind. But as an artist, this disturbed me a bit. My job as an artist is to continually change models of culture and peoples' ideas about them. (That is, if we believe philosophers and art critics such as Donald Brook.[1]) So much of what immediately came to mind with "entertainment computing" simply suggested old paradigms, whether it was the mathematical elegance of something like Tetris or the rock-em sock-em action of any shoot-em-up; or the same-old same-old narrative structures of Hollywood cinema – even when those narrative structures were articulated by state-of-the-art computer graphics, such as in James Cameron's recent "Avatar."[2]

Then it occurred to me that "entertainment computing" could also describe the pleasure one gets from crafting a particularly elegant bit of code. Here the computing itself was "entertaining." Another idea that came to mind was systems which deliver entertainment over the web, such as YouTube and the streaming radio services. One

---

[1] Brook, Donald, "The Social Role of Art" Experimental Art Foundation, Adelaide (1977); Brook, Donald, "The Awful Truth About What Art Is" Artlink Australia, Adelaide (2008).
[2] Cameron, James, "Avatar" 20th Century Fox (2009).

R. Nakatsu et al. (Eds.): ECS 2010, IFIP AICT 333, pp. 128–136, 2010.
© IFIP International Federation for Information Processing 2010

friend, in fact, told me (via email, of course) a couple of years ago, that he scarcely watched TV anymore. Most of his audio-visual experiencing was done through You-Tube and other web video services. Finally, I thought of social networking sites such as Facebook, Twitter, Linked-In and the like. Surely these were being used by many people as a source of entertainment. The code that underlay all these uses could be described as utilitarian programming designed to serve the needs of people in entertaining activities. That seemed one good definition of "entertainment computing."

The term "cultural computing" seemed more serious to me, and more worth investigating. On one level, it seemed to imply that the term was invented by someone for whom "computing" was their primary activity, and they drew a distinction between "computing" and "culture." I envisioned a programmer who wrote banking software who instead, wanted to be writing game software, or poetry writing software. A distinction was being made here between computing used for business, and computing used for having fun.

As understandable as this interpretation is, it seems to me that it misses the point. For computing IS a cultural activity. In fact, in terms of the general society, computing is now central to the culture. Hardly any activities, whether business or entertainment oriented, whether artistic or financial, do not involve the use of a computer in some way. Further, the activities of computer scientists are as susceptible t o study by anthropologists and cultural theorists as are any other human endeavors.

Finally, it occurred to me that computing did not evolve in a vacuum. It began in the late 1940s and early 1950s in parallel with, and in interaction with (even if subconsciously) ideas from the larger culture. It is no accident that the computer, that structural machine par excellence, evolved in the way it did, at the same time as ideas of structuralism were prevalent in anthropology, psychology, mathematics, music, literature, etc. And in fact, once the first "proof of concept" projects were finished (such as the CSIRAC music project[3]), and it was clear that the computer could be used in the production of "culture" (in the most traditional sense of the term), the first uses of the computer for music, experiments by Lejaren Hiller[4] and Iannis Xenakis[5] were indeed informed by the ideas of structuralism that pervaded the arts and sciences at that time. And the structuralism which was a part of mathematics, anthropology, linguistics, psychology, and the arts at that time was very much part of the mindset that produced the first programs and programming languages.

My own relation with the computer is a utilitarian one. I am primarily a composer of music, animated graphics, and sound poetry. The computer is one very important tool among many that I use to create my work. The work comes first, however: the computer is a tool, and one that I am not obligated to use. I can, for example, also whistle. I might also point out that even though I started my artistic career in the mid-late 1960s, it was not until the very late 1970s / early 1980s that I fully embraced the computer as a creative medium. Before that, I could see the potential of the computer, but working with them was just too expensive, required access to guarded insti-

---

[3] Doornbusch, Paul, "The Music of CSIRAC, Australia's first Computer Music" Common Ground Publishing, Altona, Vic. (2005).

[4] Hiller Lejaren, and Isascson, Leonard, "Experimental Music: Composition with an Electronic Computer" McGraw Hill, New York (1959).

[5] Xenakis, Iannis, "Formalized Music: Thought and Mathematics in Composition" Pendragon Press 2nd edition, Stuyvesant, NY (2001).

tutional facilities, and was just too hard. It was only when computers became inexpensive enough that I could afford to own my own (most of my career as an artist having been spent outside of institutions), that I really began to get my hands dirty with them. Before that, for example, I was just as happy to build and design my own digital circuitry for use in my music and performance art projects.

So for me, the computer has become, as said above, just another art-making tool. However, I acknowledge this thought by composer, percussionist and writer Gino Robair: "I am reminded on a daily basis that we are creating music on general-purpose business machines, which we cleverly subvert for our creative purposes." So it's a tool, but one developed primarily for other purposes than mine. Robair's thought seems to suggest to me that he, too, would subscribe to there being a difference between "cultural" uses of computing, and other uses[6].

As an artist, I am very interested in the uniquely inherent possibilities of each medium I use. I'm continually asking myself – for each new tool I come across - what are the compositional implications of this tool? What can it do that no other tool can? Are there any artistic possibilities I can see in this tool that are unique? I am also interested in not just how I can affect my tools, but how they affect me. On a note which is either light-hearted or ominous – and I'm not sure which – when I was discussing this paper with my wife, the multi-media artist Catherine Schieve, she said "Cultural computing? Have you noticed in the past year, that as you've spent more and more time on the email, you're beginning to talk like email?" She pointed out that in my day-to-day speech, I was using phrasing and structures that seemed like they were derived from email – "talking in blocks" she called it. I was quite embarrassed by this – I believe my response to her was a worried, "Oh, dear......." On later reflection, she said that she thought that "cultural computing" was what the engineers at Google and other high tech companies had been doing for years – engineering the culture by creating structures for computer use (cloud computing being only one of the most recent). I replied that I thought that social networking sites were another example of this - an area where people were creating their own cultures using computer tools.

2 Structuralism as a General Cultural Condition

In the mid-20th-century, the idea of structuralism took hold in many intellectual fields. The idea was that underneath the surface of "a thing" were inherent structures which, to some extent, produced the surface that was observed. In anthropology Claude Levi-Strauss proposed these ideas; in psychology, Jacques Lacan; in mathematics, Nicholas Bourbaki's work is paradigmatic.[7] In music a number of people worked with ideas such as these. Although it might be argued that Arnold Schoenberg's use of his "method of composing with 12 tones related only to one another" in the 1920s-40s was more expressive than structural, by the time working with his method was expanded into that many-faceted phenomena known as "serialism" in the 1950s and 60s

---

[6] Robair, Gino, "Robair Report" http://blog.emusician.com/robairreport/2010/02/11/longterm-investing/ - access 12 Feb, 2010.

[7] Aczel, Amir: "The Artist and the Mathematician: The Story of Nicholas Bourbaki, The Genius Mathematician Who Never Existed" High Stakes Publishing, London (2006).

(and indeed, in many different guises, up to the present) it was definitely a part of the structuralist sensibility.   Nor was serialism the only manifestation of structuralism in music.   Composers critical of serialism, such as John Cage and Iannis Xenakis, wrote a number of pieces in the 1950s in which the generative structure they invented for a particular piece produced the surface of the music that was listened to.   And they did this, for the most part, without the use of a computer.   (Neither of them began using computers in a serious way until the 1960s.)   Their work at this time stands as a fascinating example of "computing without computers" that is, they worked out their scores and processes by hand, but their work was of such a systematic nature that they could have carried it out with the aid of a computer.

An example of this is Cage's tape collage, "Williams Mix,"[8] from 1952, which was computerized by Cage's colleague Larry Austin in the mid-1990s, several years after Cage's death.   Austin's program has the potential of generating an infinite number of different versions of Cage's original collage.   Austin's composition "Williams Re-Mixed" consists of a number of variations composed with this program.[9]   At about the same time, I reconstructed the process Cage used (using a computer) to compose his "Two" for flute and piano (1987).[10]   Using John Dunn's algorithmic composing environment "Kinetic Music Machine"[11], I composed a piece called "(There Will Never Be Another) Two," for microtonal flute and piano samples, in which the textures introduced in the Cage piece were extended into the realm of sampled timbres and microtonality.[12]   So Cage's "manual" composing methods were indeed susceptible to encapsulation in computer programs.

A number of other composers were involved in different aspects of this structuralist enterprise.   The German-American composer and philosopher Herbert Brun's "Sawdust" series of electronic music pieces, for example, are examples of sound structures which emerge from the properties built into Brun's automated combining of a set of rules.   That is, the actual waveforms – the timbres – are assembled from a set of automated rules that Brun specified.[13] [14]   Xenakis also explored such a rule-based generating of emergent timbres in his Gendyn series of computer programs[15]. These programs are distinctive in computer music because most of the work to that date in timbre research involved having the ability to precisely specify what each component of a musical timbre would be.   The idea that one would write a program to produce timbres, the details of which one could not predict, was quite different from mainstream musical interest in timbre.   As Herbert Brun said, "This is not just a different aesthetic attitude, it is a political difference as well."[16]

[8]   Cage, John, "Williams Mix" C F Peters, New York (1952).

[9]   Austin, Larry, "Williams Re-Mixed" EMF Music, Albany, NY (2001).

[10]   Cage, John, "Two" C F Peters, New York (1987).

[11]   Dunn, John, "Kinetic Music Machine" http://algoart.com accessed Feb 13, 2010.

[12]   Burt, Warren, "(There Will Never Be Another) Two" Scarlet Aardvark, Melbourne (1996).

[13]   Brun, Herbert, "Sawdust, Computer Music Project" EMF Media EM112, Albany NY (1999).

[14]   Brun, Herbert, "A Manual for Sawdust" http://grace.evergreen.edu/~arunc/brun/sawdust/ accessed Feb 13, 2010.

[15]   Hoffman, Peter, "The New GENDYN Program" Computer Music Journal, Vol. 24, No. 2 (July 2000).

[16]   Brun Herbert: Selected Articles http://grace.evergreen.edu/~arunc/brun accessed Feb 13, 2010.

Another example of structuralism in music is the work of the Los Angeles based microtonal music theorist Ervin Wilson. In fact, Wilson's seminal papers on musical tuning consist of nothing but diagrams of his structures, with no explanation[17]. He claims this is because he doesn't want to dictate to people how his ideas should be realized. He has also said that this cryptic means of presentation is a means of making sure that only people who are dedicated to the ideas are able to use them. When a musician realizes one of his structures into sound, whether it was me making a long-tone drone, or Marcus Hobbs making a pulse-pounding techno piece, he seemed equally happy. Maybe Wilson just happens to like both drones and techno, but I do get the feeling that for him, the structure is the main interesting part, with the realizations being simple manifestations of one form or another of the structure.

One of the most interesting of contemporary composers, and one whose life exemplified the turn away from structuralism that happened in the last third of the 20th century, was Kenneth Gaburo. His early 1950s work in what he termed "compositional linguistics" – the making of sound structures derived from both musical and linguistic ideas, was as much based on the structural linguistics of Jakobson and Chomsky as on ideas of musical serialism. By the late 70s, he had turned decisively from structural ideas into a more radical consideration of the human body. His later work used a process he called "scatter," in which unconscious and subconscious bodily processes, often accomplished under sensory deprivation conditions, were used to generate a set of stimuli, which were then used to generate a piece of music. Some of these involved unorthodox approaches to the use of digital devices, and some didn't. However, notice that he was still engaged in searching for an emergent structure, one that grew out of a carefully specified set of initial conditions. It's just that the materials here were not machine-based (even when technology was used), but body based. Another example of the remnants of structuralist thinking in his work can be seen in this excerpt from his 1970 essay, "The Beauty of Irrelevant Music." "If the world-at-large never awakens to the incredible structures which some have given it, but could never *demand* that it accept, the beauty will never-the-less, remain."[18] Notice that what is given to the world are *structures*. We are all still heirs to the legacy of structuralist thinking. But Gaburo's position was, I believe, that the body was central to art making. And it is a position that I would still support, two decades later. Despite various Extropian and Transhumanist fantasies, I think the fundamental stuff of what we are IS our bodies – and the more we learn about computers, and artificial intelligence, and the body, and its embodied intelligence, the farther we realize we are from making a machine that is either a reasonable approximation of the body, or a reasonable "vessel" in which a body-based consciousness could comfortably exist[19].

In computer science, there are a number of fields which also share this interest in emergent structures. In their own very different ways, the ideas of neural networks, cellular automata, and genetic algorithms all propose that the functioning of very simple networks of rules can produce results with very complex surfaces in ways that are somewhat analogous to the functioning of biological life forms. The early

---

[17] Wilson, Ervin: "Wilson Archives" http://www.anaphoria.com accessed Feb 13, 2010.

[18] Gaburo, Kenneth, "The Beauty of Irrelevant Music" Lingua Press, La Jolla, Ca (1970) now distributed by Frog Peak Music, www.frogpeak.org

[19] http://www.extropy.org/ accessed Feb 13, 2010.

structuralists proposed that there were underlying structures which produced various kinds of behavior. But more recent investigations of emergent properties seem to take this one step further, in that structures are being intentionally developed in order to explore the kinds of behaviors that result.

However, in the past 30 years or so, ideas of structuralism have taken quite a battering. In Aubin's essay on the work of the Bourbaki group of mathematicians, he writes about mathematics, but the thoughts expressed quite easily apply to music, psychology, visual arts, and any number of other fields. "Surveying the mathematics of the 1970s, Christian Houzel, soon to be the elected president of the Societe mathematique de France, revealed to the public that "the age of Bourbaki and fundamental structures is over." While the previous period was one that had witnessed the development of powerful new theoretical tools of great generality, he noted, the 1970s were characterized rather by a tendency to revive an old interest in more concrete problems. Houzel did not venture an explanation for this reversal. "I cannot say," he simply wrote, "to what extent this [tendency] is conditioned by the internal dynamics of the development of mathematics, or by ideological currents like the degradation of science's superior image in public opinion and scientists' questioning of the social status of their practice."[20]

This turning away from the importance of structural ideas, or a turning away from the idea that the observation and study of emergent properties might be a fascinating thing in itself, has been replaced, in some peoples' minds, by a renewed fascination with the qualities of surface. In this view, it's the surface of a work of art (or work from other intellectual areas) that creates interest. Structure may be all well and good, but if the work is not attractive in some way, it will fail. In the arts, this has produced a lot of writing under the banner of post-modernism; in psychology, there has been a re-emergence of interest in the reactions and the emotions of the individual; in music, a renewed interest in the traditionally attractive qualities of timbre, harmony and rhythm, or the sociologically "easy" forms of popular music and culture. One early example of this was the work of the California minimalist sculptors of the 1960s. While their New York counterparts used plain, often rough materials, according to Peter Schjeldahl[21], the West Coast sculptors, such as James Turrell and Larry Bell, fused a concern for structuralist rigor with the use of beautiful surface materials. "Finish Fetish" was a term that was applied to this work. Another example of this would be the computer music that came out of Stanford University in the 1970s, from composers such as John Chowning and William Schottstaedt, which was notable for the clean, elegant and sensuous qualities of the sounds used.

At its worst, this surface oriented new sensibility simply produced work which was overly familiar, weak and indulgent – it was simply an expression of the worst aspects of the immediately expressive ego that had been put aside during the structuralist experiment. But in the best works of this type, the toughness of structural thinking was combined with a concern for the sensuous appeal of elegant sonic (and other) surfaces.

---

[20] David Aubin, "The Withering Immortality of Nicolas Bourbaki: A Cultural Connector at the Confluence of Mathematics." *Science in Context*, 10 (1997), p. 297-342.

[21] Schjeldahl, Peter, "Way Out West", New Yorker Jan 25, 2010, p. 76-77.

A friend tells me, and I haven't followed this up or found references for it, but mentioning the idea should be sufficient for purposes of this discussion, that there are some perception scientists who are now claiming that, for human perception, there is nothing BUT surface, that all ideas of sub-surface structure are illusions, or at best, fanciful after-the-fact constructions. That those who are investigating structure - "that which cannot be seen immediately" – are in fact, investigating "nothing." If so, the work of the Bourbaki mathematicians, who produced 12 volumes of writing investigating deep mathematical structures – that is – "nothing" – and attributed them to a non-existent author, Nicholas Bourbaki, has a certain pleasing elegance and symmetry about it, at least to my mind.

McLuhan points out[22] that the first duty of any new media is to reproduce the old. Consider Greg Schiemer's work with mobile phones as a continuation and complexification of his earlier work with portable analog oscillators, the UFOs, as an example of this.[23] However, the quest for works of art or forms of art which uniquely come out of the inherent characteristics of their media is an ongoing one. Once we have new tools, we can figure out what might be uniquely made with them. If this quest can be combined with a consideration for the sensuous qualities of the expressive medium (sound in the case of music, metal in the case of (some) sculpture), that is, with a concern for the properties of the materials being used, then perhaps works which combine the best of structuralism with the best of the contemporary quest for sensuously engaging materials can be made.

Another thing that might be considered here is attitude. Perhaps one of the essential aspects of "cultural computing" might be revealed by considering the difference in attitude between, say, making or using a piece of accounting software, and making or using a piece of music software. Although I don't accept that the accounting software (or accountancy) is any less "cultural" than the music software (or making music), I do acknowledge that both fields have somewhat different attitudes towards creativity. I recall that an old accountant of mine once wisecracked "The only creative accountants are in jails." According to him, the free wheeling sense of fantasy that was valued in music creation was definitely a quality that was not wanted in accountancy.

As an example of what I mean by "attitude," I offer a recent piece of mine "Finnegans Wake versus the World's Longest Prime."[24] This is a piece of computer music in two channels. In the left channel is some bell-like music which is produced by interpreting the digits of the world's longest prime number (as of December 2009) as pitch, duration, and loudness specifications for an ongoing bell-sound texture. In the right half of the stereo sound space is a sampled Irish folk band, playing a demented, microtonal version of Irish folk music. This is produced by taking the letters, one at a time, of James Joyce's *Finnegans Wake*, and using those (modulo 26 of course, since we're dealing with the English alphabet) as pitch, duration and loudness instructions for four sampled Irish folk instruments. The two musics – the bells and the folk band

---

[22] McLuhan, Marshall, "Understanding Media: The Extensions of Man" Gingko Press (2003).

[23] Schiemer, G and Havryliv, M, Pocket Gamelan: a Pure Data interface for Mobile phones, in Proceedings of NIME 05 New Interfaces for Musical Expression, Media & Graphics Interdisciplinary Centre, Vancouver, 156-159.

[24] Burt, Warren "Finnegans Wake Versus The Worlds Longest Prime" Scarlet Aardvark, Wollongong (2009).

DO sound different – although how much of that difference is due to my algorithm and timbre programming, and how much is due to the inherent difference in structure between the prime number digits and the *Wake* is perhaps a question best left to musicologists. (I mean, let's be serious, folks. What could be more ludicrous than making music by sonifying materials like prime numbers and the letters of *Finnegans Wake?*)

But the playful and irreverent handling of materials typified by this piece is an example of "attitude" that I think should be a clear part of at least some efforts in cultural computing. And as a further example of the conceptual playfulness of this piece – both the *Wake* and the digits of the world's longest prime number are, of course, enormous data sets. I figured that if played for its full length, the piece would be several months in duration at least. But I decided to give people only 5 minutes of it. Not only am I playful and irreverent with my materials, I'm teasing people with them as well.

I think that when we begin to emphasize attitudes to our technology that are not reverent or earnest, but playful and light-hearted, when we start treating language as a toy as well as a tool, that is when we might begin to assemble something that is truly "cultural," in the sense of being distinct from the earnestness of business and science oriented computing, and thus have a different attitude and a different context for computing; something that might indeed be a gift to the larger "culture."

3 A Question

Has computer science come into its (to use flawed terms) post-modern, post-structural period yet? To be sure, there are many artists *using* the technology in this way. Consider any of the many pieces made in the past few years which feature sampling of random sounds stored on the net, or a number of web-based improvisation ensembles, in which composers spread all over the planet improvise with a set of hardware or software instruments in a remote location as but two examples of this. I was involved in one such performance in March 2009. Performers in Belgium, Portugal, Mexico and Australia improvised using a scripting language which controlled a set of computer-controlled acoustic musical instruments in the concert hall of the Logos Foundation in Gent, Belgium.[25] And in mathematics, it could be said that the non-linear mathematics of fractals, chaos and the like might be considered as a kind of post-structural mathematics – as distinguished from the elegant linear-logic structures that fascinated the Bourbaki group.

But seeing as how early computer programming and business applications from the 1940s-1960s seem to be so closely related to the structuralist nature of work in other fields, I wonder if there are any developments in computer science today which parallel contemporary developments in music, art, psychology, etc. Or could it be that the nature of the tool itself – digital logic – precludes the participation of the computing community in experiments such as these. (I mean, how post-modern can a NAND gate be? And while we're at it, take my XOR gate, please! (nyuk nyuk nyuk)) I speculate – it might only be when one is dealing above the level of digital logic that one can talk about non-linear, post-structural, post-modern, (call it what you like) uses of the computer. This is a speculation from an outsider. I await responses from the members of the computer science community with interest.

---

[25] http://logosfoundation.org/mnm/index.php accessed 13 Feb 2010.

References

1. Brook, D.: The Social Role of Art. Experimental Art Foundation, Adelaide (1977); Brook, D.: The Awful Truth About What Art Is, Artlink Australia, Adeliade (2008)
2. Cameron, J.: Avatar, 20th Century Fox (2009)
3. Doornbusch, P.: The Music of CSIRAC, Australia's first Computer Music. Common Ground Publishing, Altona (2005)
4. Lejaren, H., Isascson, L.: Experimental Music: Composition with an Electronic Computer. McGraw Hill, New York (1959)
5. Xenakis, I.: Formalized Music: Thought and Mathematics in Composition, 2nd edn. Pendragon Press, Stuyvesant (2001)
6. Robair, G.: Robair Report, http://blog.emusician.com/robairreport/2010/02/11/longterm-investing/ (access February 12, 2010)
7. Aczel, A.: The Artist and the Mathematician: The Story of Nicholas Bourbaki, The Genius Mathematician Who Never Existed. High Stakes Publishing, London (2006)
8. Cage, J.: Williams Mix. C.F. Peters, New York (1952)
9. Austin, L.: Williams Re-Mixed, EMF Music, Albany, NY (2001)
10. Cage, J.: Two. C.F. Peters, New York (1987)
11. Dunn, J.: Kinetic Music Machine, http://algoart.com (accessed February 13, 2010)
12. Burt, W.: (There Will Never Be Another) Two. Scarlet Aardvark, Melbourne (1996)
13. Brun, H.: Sawdust, Computer Music Project. EMF Media EM112, Albany NY (1999)
14. Brun, H.: A Manual for Sawdust, http://grace.evergreen.edu/~arunc/brun/sawdust/ (accessed February 13, 2010)
15. Hoffman, P.: The New GENDYN Program. Computer Music Journal 24(2) (July 2000)
16. Herbert, B.: Selected Articles, http://grace.evergreen.edu/~arunc/brun (accessed February 13, 2010)
17. Wilson, E.: Wilson Archives, http://www.anaphoria.com (accessed February 13, 2010)
18. Gaburo, K.: The Beauty of Irrelevant Music. Lingua Press, La Jolla (1970), Now distributed by Frog Peak Music, http://www.frogpeak.org
19. http://www.extropy.org/ (accessed February 13, 2010)
20. Aubin, D.: The Withering Immortality of Nicolas Bourbaki: A Cultural Connector at the Confluence of Mathematics. Science in Context 10, 297–342 (1997)
21. Schjeldahl, P.: Way Out West, New Yorker, January 25, pp. 76–77 (2010)
22. McLuhan, M.: Understanding Media: The Extensions of Man. Gingko Press (2003)
23. Schiemer, G., Havryliv, M.: Pocket Gamelan: a Pure Data interface for Mobile phones. In: Proceedings of NIME 2005 New Interfaces for Musical Expression, Media & Graphics Interdisciplinary Centre, Vancouver, pp. 156–159 (2005)
24. Burt, W.: Finnegans Wake Versus The Worlds Longest Prime. Scarlet Aardvark, Wollongong (2009)
25. http://logosfoundation.org/mnm/index.php (accessed February 13, 2010)

Looking for Culture in Video Games: Three Conceptual Approaches

James K. Scarborough[*]

Department of Communication, Stanford University,
McClatchy Hall, 450 Serra Mall, Stanford, CA 94305, USA
joseppi@stanford.edu

Abstract. As the popularity of computer games has increased markedly in recent years, many researchers have become concerned with the potential effects on gamers. However, by looking past the outward appearance of popular games that may be perceived as violent by some, we can begin to see dramatic cultural indicators as well as many other academically interesting phenomena emerging. Social psychologists and effects researchers must begin delving deeper into this rapidly expanding genre of popular media. Herein, I propose three possible approaches to the study of video games as cultural events rather than a common medium that influences participants in a simple way.

Keywords: Video game, culture, play, media effects, social influence, psychology, research methods.

1 The Culture of Modern Media

In the beginning there was radio. And it was good. We gathered on Saturday nights to listen to stories, news, and music. Radio brought us together in a way that only government and religion had done before then. Not only was the entire family sitting around the monophonic radio receiver box at the same time, the entire nation was present. Together we shared experiences that quickly became cultural events with their own rules, norms, and traditions. Don't be late or you'll miss the best part of the program, 8 o'clock sharp! Yet we craved interesting imagery and visual stimulation. We wanted to see what was happening.

Then there was television. TV in all its audio-visual glory: black and white maybe but to us as vivid as real life. We *were* the family living in suburban America, with two kids and a family car. Again, we quickly established our scheduled traditions and program preferences. If little Johnny didn't finish his homework he wasn't going to be allowed to participate in the ritual which, of course, was socially unacceptable among his school friends. However, whether we were cheering our favorite sports team on to victory or we were hootin' and hollerin' with the Lone Ranger and Tonto, we longed to be part of the action. We became so intimate with the characters of our favorite soap operas that we just wanted to reach out and tell them how we felt about

---

[*] Corresponding author.

R. Nakatsu et al. (Eds.): ECS 2010, IFIP AICT 333, pp. 137–148, 2010.
© IFIP International Federation for Information Processing 2010

their recent actions or comfort them in their time of need. But television couldn't hear us. Television only told and never listened.

So came the Internet, the Web, web 2.0, and we were heard. A new form of news, entertainment, and information gathering was at our very fingertips. We found others, nay *many* others who were also fans of old-time radio programs like The Shadow. Not only did they share their thoughts and insights about the program but recordings of the programs were made available for us to enjoy all over again. We regained the nearly lost sense of community that the potential personalization of the Internet almost destroyed. Once again, we belonged. We quickly came to know the rules, norms, and traditions of our newfound communities or risked being flamed and marked as a newbie. But alas, as major businesses, educational institutions, and masses of social groups came together, the form of their community was merely text and images. So much data yet so few tools to receive, compose, and transmit. Visual and auditory, yes, interactive maybe, but "real-time" still a long way off; nowhere near as good as being there.

1.1 Video Games as Modern Media

Arguably, video games are the only media able to meet the interaction needs of humans. Video games are audibly involving with amazing sound-tracks and sophisticated audible queues, visually exciting with ever-improving graphics and realism rivaling any other virtual reality technology. They are stimulatingly interactive with advanced artificial intelligence and intellectual challenges for even the most creative imagination, and inescapably real-time; turn away for one second and things can go seriously wrong for your avatar.

Even though video games are one of the most complex and sophisticated forms of modern media, the question remains: why study games? The fact that there are now more than 13 million World of Warcraft subscribers (a larger population than Sweden, Hungary, Cuba, or Greece) is interesting but seems more of value as a marketing statistic than cultural phenomenon. However, with the rapid advance and massive user populations of social/entertainment video games, clear indicators of emergent culture are starting to appear [cf. 6, 7, 15].

1.2 A Few Important Distinctions

At this point it is important to identify the taxonomy of video games. A great distinction exists between Pong and Pac-Man not to mention the modern Massively Multiplayer Online Game (MMOG for short) and the many other types of games, simulations, and virtual environments. Figure 1 shows an updated list of video game

• Arcade Style Action	• First Person Shooter (FPS)
• Action Adventure	• Adventure
• Construction and Management Simulation	• Life Simulation
• Role-playing	• Strategy
• Real-Time Strategy (RTS)	• Vehicle Simulation
• Other notable genres: Music, Party, Puzzle, Sports	

Fig. 1. Modern Video Game Genres

Achiever – Focus on achievement and material gain
Explorer – Focus on exploration and geographical knowledge
Socializer – Focus on socialization and making friends
Killer – Focus on engaging and dominating other players

Fig. 2.1. The Bartle Test of Gamer Psychology - Four Categories of Player

| • Friend | • Griefer | • Hacker | • Networker |
| • Opportunist | • Planner | • Politician | • Scientist |

Fig. 2.2. Updated list of eight Gamer Categories

genres, originally and brilliantly conceived by Cris Crawford back in 1982 at the inception of the modern video game industry. One additional type of application that should be included in the list is the Multi-User Virtual Environment (MUVE). Since they typically lack any interactive game content or AI, MUVEs can not be strictly described as video games thus they are omitted from the list.

In addition, it is imperative to distinguish between several types of video gamer players. Figure 2.1 shows the four categories of computer gamer as first conceived by Richard Bartle in his Test of Gamer Psychology [4]. Figure 2.2 shows an updated list of categories based on feedback since Bartle's original Test was released. The Bartle Test has been taken by well over 500,000 gamers and works something like the Meyers-Briggs Personality Type Indicator. The answers to a series of questions lead to a type indicator result that describes the player's preferences and to some degree motivations. While the Bartle Test applies primarily to MMOG players, it identifies the myriad of game player personalities that contribute to the complexities of social interaction within game worlds.

2   The Culture of Video Games

In identifying, investigating, and interpreting video games as culture there are a great variety of ways to approach the research [7, 15]. Herein I will begin with just a few simple examples. We might consider video games as cultural events similar to sporting activities. With this approach we would need to stratify competitive game events by level of competition starting with casual local and regional competitions (a.k.a. LAN parties) and extending to major national events like the Korean Starcraft Championships that take place in giant stadium environments. Next we might attempt to assess the impact of the rapidly increasing number of computer gamers and the powerful sub-culture's influence on markets and cultures outside their traditions [6]. This approach would require a solid detailed knowledge of economics as well as a deep understanding of actual game mechanics that could potentially impact external forces. Finally, we might consider an ethnographic approach to video game players and the social institutions that are vital to coordinating complex interactions and events at the highest levels in MMOGs [15]. Any of these approaches as well as a variety of quantitative methods could be leveraged to yield very interesting research studies.

2.1 Distinguishing Game from Play

Before moving on to further details of the possible research frameworks, it will be beneficial to distinguish between *game* and *play*, a difference that is quite present in most all video games. This contrast differentiates the concepts of playing for fun and playing to win. Making this distinction also clarifies the divergence between video game genres as well as types of video gamers. Understanding this diversity will help explain the significance of different levels of video game competition, will assist in identifying the cultural impact of video games, and will support the existence and implications of social institutions and emergent culture in virtual worlds.

Most cultures have easily accessible examples of games. International sports are one example of game with which most of us are quite familiar. Take, for instance, the example of soccer or 'futbol'. Soccer is played in nearly every civilized country in the modern world. All you need is a ball, some friends, and a place to play. However, soccer is also the most popular competitive international sport in the modern world. While little children may play soccer in the street for fun with few consequences, serious athletes approach professional soccer as though each game was an epic battle for life or death between their team and "the enemy" or opposing team. There is no concept of *play* in professional sports. Teams are run as businesses, players are assets (or liabilities), and fans treat each win and loss as a personal victory or defeat in the quest for their team's greatness and a shot at a championship ring or trophy.

Similarly, the concept of play can be exercised both within and without the presence of a game. While children, of course, play sports they also play with blocks, play Cowboys and Indians, and play House. Games usually have distinct goals and outcomes (i.e. winning and losing or a final score) and games typically have a start and an end while play requires none of these things. Play might be defined simply as engagement in an activity with few or no consequences. With this definition of play it becomes clear that even Little League Baseball or Pop Warner Football games are not strictly for play.

One reason this distinction is relevant for studying video games is that popular belief suggests video games are purely for entertainment or distraction. This is certainly not the case when it comes to the more sophisticated games like MMOGs [13]. While there are many gamers who play MMOGs exclusively for entertainment, the vast majority of players who spend significant amounts of time with their avatars (20 hours per week) [16] have long since made fun a secondary pursuit. These players have far more diverse motivations. Gaining levels, building virtual wealth [6], establishing and maintaining social relationships [17], gaining knowledge of game mechanics and social norms, engaging in compelling narrative, building a reputation, and working toward common goals and objectives with friends and 'guildmates' are all far more typical motivations than simply playing for fun [17]. The reality of massive multiplayer games is that it is the minority who play for fun, the rest approach the activity more like professional athletes looking for better and faster ways to "win." This is also true, to a lesser extent, of nearly all competitive video games.

Among high school gamers, anecdotal evidence suggests that a person's entire social reputation can be based on their ability to dominate other players in the most popular FPS games. Entire social enclaves are formed and might also be dissolved over the group's collective ability to consistently defeat other players within the game world. The most surprising aspect of this phenomenon is that the social groups that are formed ignore other common social norms and boundaries such as age, race, and even gender. If a player has the ability to contribute to the team's overall success then they will quickly be initiated and absorbed into the group for fear that an opposing team will recruit that player first.

This approach to competitive team building is paralleled, again, by major league sports [12]. Lewis suggests that traditional methods of valuing baseball players such as batting average or stolen bases, distinctly individual measures, are less effective than more modern statistical methods of valuation such as on-base percentage and slugging percentage which are more aligned with team performance than strictly individual statistics (i.e., Sabermetrics). Admittedly, the methods employed by most competitive video gamers are not quite as sophisticated as those described by Lewis. Yet their approach to team building by finding undervalued players goes against the more traditional method of finding the best individual players and recruiting them with teamwork as an afterthought.

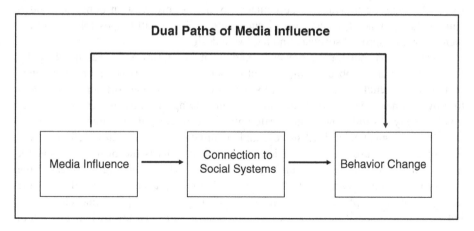

Fig. 3. Bandura's Dual Paths of Media Influence Model

3 Implications for Research

With these important distinctions in mind, it is now possible to move deeper into the task of finding the true nature of culture in video games. James Carey suggests that one way to go beyond the simple effects model of media is to change our approach from one of media consumption (the transportation model of media) to one of media as ritual [5]. This approach allows us to leverage the distinctions of media uses and gratifications [14] rather than rely on a naïve hypodermic model approach wherein media is studied as though it were a novel medication. By individuating players by type, a la Bartle, rather than aggregating all video game players as a group we can also begin to better understand the persuasive effects of gaming and involvement in gaming communities through more sophisticated means such as Bandura's Dual Path of Media Influence Model (see Figure 3). Using these methodologies to study both video gamers and the social institutions that drive high-end gaming, it becomes possible to move beyond the stigma that typically accompanies the study of video games. Researchers can now utilize the appropriate tools to study video games in a far more sophisticated way rather than the shallow superficial structure that is frequently engaged in existing research.

As video games are played in many different countries it will also be possible to differentiate the impact of games within geographically separate populations. There are two distinct issues at stake. First, there are the differences various cultures may have regarding types of games played. Clear differences in genre preference may help researchers to better understand the uses and gratifications of interactive media within that culture or may point to varying motivations for play. Second, it will be of interest to identify the variability in external impact of gaming on different cultures. While gamers in western countries may experience a high degree of social interaction playing certain types of games it is likely that gamers from other regions separated by language and cultural differences will have sharply contrasting experiences. Identifying these differences will ultimately lead to a much better understanding of racial issues that may be unwittingly perpetuated by the largely western dominated video game industry. Once the underlying issues are revealed it will be possible to address them through improved software and hardware design.

Geertz claims that the best way to understand a culture is to get involved by means of naturalistic observation [9]. Subsequently, researchers should rely on interpretation and 'thick description' to report findings. This framework allows research to provide a narrative of events and identify underlying meaning that even the actors involved may not fully understand. Attempting to arrive at a deeper understanding of a culture through standardized surveys and quantitative measures may well mislead a researcher and cause false conclusions to be made. This is the primary reason for many of the current myths surrounding video games. By aggregating members of the video game community and not differentiating between players who spend their time primarily in single-player games and those who spend their play time closely involved in active social institutions, resulting relationships can not realistically claim validity.

With this in mind, studies of game players must be differentiated by game genre as well as by player type and cultural affiliation. Even then, a variety of methodologies as well as a number of different research tools must be used to discover the deeper meaning of involvement in game communities [7, 15]. The complexities and intricacies of MMOGs alone would warrant this not to mention the idiosyncrasies of mediated social relationships. When discussing doing research in the most popular MMOG to date, World of Warcraft, Corneliussen and Rettberg echo this sentiment by saying, "in order to understand World of Warcraft we must study it both as a game and as a cultural site requiring the application of multiple disciplines' analytical tools, concepts, and methods so that we may fully comprehend this phenomenon."

4 Three Conceptual Approaches

4.1 Simple Pastime or National Sport?

In China they play table tennis, in America football, baseball, or basketball. In Korea they play Starcraft. In fact, there are several "professional" competitive Starcraft teams in Korea that boast major corporate sponsors, player's annual incomes that rival any American professional athlete, and multiple television channels providing complete tournament coverage.

> The computer game StarCraft has an active professional competition circuit, particularly in South Korea. The two major game channels in South Korea, Ongamenet and MBCGame, each run a Starleague, viewed by millions of fans. Starting in about 2002, pro-gamers started to become organized into teams, sponsored by large South Korean companies like Samsung, SK Telecom and KTF. StarCraft is also the most popular computer game competition during the annual World Cyber Games thanks to its Korean fan-base, and it is overall one of the world's largest computer and video game competitions in terms of prize money, global coverage and participants. -Wikipedia

The real-time strategy video game Starcraft is not a new game. It was published in 1998 as "just another RTS" in a long line of successful games. However, the RTS player community did not accept this premise. As with many other aspects of the computer game industry, the players decided to take control of the game and change the rules [11].

Many publishers now provide players with an engine for generating game content. In the case of Starcraft, the generation engine allowed players to not only create new game maps but it allowed them to modify the fundamental rules of the game. With this new ability, players became level designers and co-authors of the game. Due to

Fig. 4. An e-sports stadium where professional Starcraft games are played

the popularity of the Starcraft map editor, the game publisher followed up with another more powerful system with the release of the game Warcraft III, arguably the most advanced RTS game ever made. Players generated new versions of game maps, new rule sets, and eventually a new game almost entirely different than the original Warcraft III known as Defense of the Ancients or DotA (pronounced Doe-ta). This series of events started a new trend in game publication that put players in control of the growth and transformation of new games. While this transition occurred over several years it altered the video game industry forever.

The competitions involving these games are played in stadium-sized venues and draw exceptionally large crowds as well as international press coverage (see Figure 4). This provides an excellent opportunity for study. Starcraft champions are considered national heroes in Korea the same way that professional athletes are treated in America. Another aspect of this phenomenon is how amateur Starcraft players are influenced by professional players. A small local competition can quickly be transformed into an international cultural event with the presence of a few professional players and the power of digital press coverage. Closer examination of this could reveal many interesting indications of how the new digital generation influences existing Korean culture and perhaps how the Korean gaming culture exerts influence on the rest of the world.

4.2 Virtual Dollars to Real Dollars

In 2005, Edward Castronova authored one of the earliest books that investigated video games' influence on the world outside the game [6]. While he mainly focused on economics he also explored some aspects of computer game player culture. The main theory put forward and backed up by solid data is that virtual economies found inside game worlds have a measurable influence on the real economy. This effect is due to two factors.

The first factor is the sheer number of players that are involved in games like World of Warcraft. In early 2009 over 13 million players subscribed to World of Warcraft. At around $15 per month each, this number alone is economically significant totaling $2.3 billion spent per year for a single game, not to mention the $30 or $40 initial cost per game license [8]. Granted, some number of subscribers may receive discounts and perhaps even earn free play time by volunteering to be a "guide" and helping other players from time to time with technical issues. Regardless, there is no arguing this dollar amount is respectable for any single software business.

The money spent by players to play the game is not the most interesting factor. Even more interestingly, the players or residents of virtual worlds including Second Life and World of Warcraft have begun spending large sums of money to acquire in-game virtual assets. Castronova followed the e-bay market sales of virtual game assets for a period of time. He established that, "The commerce flow generated by people buying and selling money and other virtual items (that is, magic wands, spaceships, armor) amounts to at least $30 million annually in the United States, and $100 million globally" [6]. While this may seem like a relatively small amount, the total has continued to grow rapidly over the years and while there is no more recent data on the trend, it is surely much higher today. Figure 5 shows a recent snap-shot of the actual exchange rates of Second Life's Linden dollars to real US dollars. Again, while the

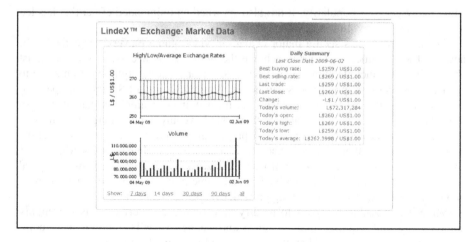

Fig. 5. Real market exchange rate data for Second Life's Linden dollars

exchange rate is not tremendous, the fact that a number of people assign real value to virtual items and currency gives those virtual items real value. As the popularity of MMOGs continues to increase, as all indicators suggest it will, the significance of this virtual to real exchange rate will become a sizeable market force.

In addition to the market influence of virtual worlds, Castronova also began exploring the real influence that virtual institutions such as player guilds can exert on real world social interaction. Beyond the anecdotal evidence of virtual relationships leading to real marriage, in-game groups have extended their interactions to the real world in the form of player meetings, fan faires, and conventions. These player summits often include game designers and corporate public relations. One of the objects in these circumstances is to hold meaningful discussions both among players and between players and game designers in an attempt to improve game mechanics and rules. Many game publishers are now taking fan faires very seriously and providing sponsorship and organization to enhance the players' out-of-game experience with the hopes it will positively affect their in-game experience as well.

4.3   Players vs. Designers

One of the most interesting trends in modern video games is the tendency of players to reverse their traditional role as consumers of the media. In the past, a game designer would create a game and the player would play it. This has been true for decades since the earliest video games like Pong and Venture (mainframe text game). Things have changed dramatically over the past decade. In order to increase the lifespan of their products as well as to meet the demands of an increasingly sophisticated player audience, many game designers now include "level editors" as a standard feature of their game. Level editors allow players to become designers by providing the ability to design custom game maps, deviant rule sets, and extended game play with increased complexity and difficulty. The original intention of level editors has indeed worked out to the designer's benefit helping games like Starcraft and Warcraft III enjoy many years of popularity. It has also spawned an unintended effect that has led to something of a revolution in video gaming.

The past decade has seen a major change in video game players' expectations of newly released games. In order to achieve the pinnacle of success, new games must absolutely either include some type of level editor or must be highly customizable to cater to various users' preferences and needs. While RTS and FPS games are particularly subject to this recent requirement, the most pointed example is that of modern MMOGs. All current MMOGs, at least those that have any hope of long-term success, feature a sophisticated API (application programming interface). These APIs allow users to customize their user interface in a staggering number of ways. Figure 6.1 shows the default World of Warcraft user interface while Figure 6.2 shows a typical user modification for a player involved in end-game play that demands each member of a team know exactly what is going on with every other team member.

While it is possible for users to modify their own user interface, this is a highly complex task and requires some technical knowledge. It has become far more common for player groups to publish their tested modifications for the entire player community to use. This trend has resulted in another change in the game that is somewhat more worrisome. As players progress through the game and reach the upper levels, other players' expectations increasingly include the use of certain modifications. In fact, if a player does not have a minimal set of UI modifications installed they are frequently not allowed to join a group. This can be a serious issue if the formation of a group is necessary to achieve certain required tasks. As teams approach the most exclusive advanced content available only to the highest level players, additional requirements of specific equipment (weapons, armor, exclusive abilities, etc.) are also imposed. This exclusionary behavior closely resembles classism and is a source of frequent frustration for newer players.

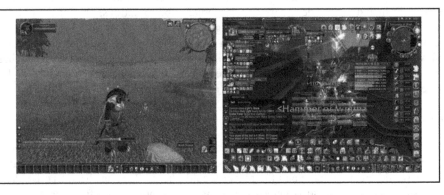

Fig. 6.1. Default WoW UI   **Fig. 6.2.** Modified WoW UI for team play

Elitism is a rampant problem in many MMOGs extending well beyond UI and equipment requirements. Certain combinations of avatar race and class can be highly discriminated against. For example, in World of Warcraft if you choose to be a Dwarf, a race that tends to be clumsy but very strong, and you choose to play a Rogue, a class that requires a great deal of stealth and dexterity, while being a perfectly valid race class combination the typical result is a high degree of ridicule by fellow players. Beyond this simple example there have been claims that the overall race design in WoW parallels post-colonialism [7]. The design choice to make Alliance races "familiar" (white Western races) versus Horde races made to be "foreign" (African, Jamaican, Native American, etc.) has caused a tremendous imbalance in the player base highly favoring the Alliance. This design decision makes salient Stuart Hall's concept of ideology and the inherent risks associated with intentional representation of social formations [10].

5 Conclusions

Video games have come a long way since Pong. From a simple diversion in entertainment to a dominant media market, video games have developed into a unique phenomenon that promises continued surprises and unparalleled opportunities for insight into the human psyche. As the direction of game development has been indelibly changed by the players, the player community has transformed into a distinct culture. In this transition, for instance, the distinction between an MMOG and a generic MUVE (multi-user virtual environment) has become blurred. These two very distinct genres have merged through a series of player dominated transitions reducing what was once a clear difference to a simple difference in content and AI. Now *all* games are, like only the MUVE was previously, virtual blank slates for players to fill with rules, norms, and traditions.

All members of the entertainment computing community must begin to understand the widespread and subtle cultural impact of what they do. Game players as well as developers of game software and those who produce the associated hardware required to play them need to have an understanding of the international scope of the issues surrounding video games. Rather than perpetuating racial stereotypes and prejudiced norms, both players and designers of game systems might use their newfound influence to begin breaking down barriers that have caused geographically separated cultures to remain distinct. It has now become possible through this subtle influence to begin laying the groundwork of the long anticipated "Utopia" of cyberspace as described so eloquently by Barlow in *A Declaration of the Independence of Cyberspace* [3]:

> We are creating a world that all may enter without privilege or prejudice accorded by race, economic power, military force, or station of birth.
>
> We are creating a world where anyone, anywhere may express his or her beliefs, no matter how singular, without fear of being coerced into silence or conformity.
>
> John Perry Barlow, 1996

In the tradition of Critical Theory, it is now time to re-examine video games, the player communities, and their impact on the world outside the game. Stuart Hall advocates a return of the repressed in media studies [10]. I can not imagine a community more repressed than video gamers. By forsaking the traditional wisdom that, "video games rot your brain" and looking beyond the surface of appearances, we find that not only is there real culture happening under our proverbial noses, but we may also find that the attitudes, beliefs, and behaviors of the "new generation" of video gamers could very well have tremendous impact on social, political, and economic issues far beyond the boundaries of their synthetic worlds [6].

References

1. Bailenson, J.N., Blascovich, J.: Avatars. In: Encyclopedia of Human-Computer Interaction, pp. 64–68. Berkshire Publishing Group (2004)
2. Bandura, A.: Social Cognitive Theory of Mass Communication, pp. 121–154. Bryant & Zillmann (2002)
3. Barlow, J.P.: A Declaration of the Independence of Cyberspace (1996), https://projects.eff.org/~barlow/Declaration-Final.html
4. Bartle, R.: Hearts, Clubs, Diamonds, Spades: Players Who suit MUDs (1996), http://www.mud.co.uk/richard/hcds.htm
5. Carey, J.W.: Communication As Culture, rev. edn. Routledge, New York (2009)
6. Castronova, E.: Synthetic Worlds. University of Chicago Press, Chicago (2005)
7. Corneliussen, H.G., Rettberg, J.W.: Digital Culture, Play, and Identity: A World of Warcraft Reader. MIT Press, Cambridge (2008)
8. Ducheneaut, N., Yee, N., Nickell, E., Moore, R.J.: Alone together? exploring the social dynamics of massively multiplayer online games. In: Proceedings of the SIGCHI Conference on Human Factors in Computing Systems, Montréal, Québec, Canada, April 22-27 (2006)
9. Geertz, C.: The Interpretation of Cultures. Basic Books, New York (1973)
10. Hall, S.: The Rediscovery of Ideology: The Return of the 'Repressed' in Media Studies, Michael Gurevitch et al., Culture, Society and Media, pp. 56-90. Metheun, London (1982)
11. Johnson, D.: StarCraft Fan Craft: Game Mods, Ownership, and Totally Incomplete Conversions. In: The Velvet Light Trap - Number 64, pp. 50–63 (Fall 2009)
12. Lewis, M.: Moneyball: The Art of Winning an Unfair Game. W. W. & Company, Inc., Norton (2003)
13. Reeves, B., Malone, T.W., O'Driscoll, T.: Leadership's Online Labs. Harvard Business Review (2008)
14. Rubin, A.M.: The uses-and-gratifications perspective of media effects. In: Bryant & Zillmann, pp. 525–548 (2002)
15. Taylor, T.L.: Play Between Worlds: Exploring Online Game Culture. MIT Press, Cambridge (2006)
16. Yee, N.: The demographics, motivations, and derived experiences of users of massively multi-user online graphical environments. Presence: Teleoper. Virtual Environ. 15(3), 309–329 (2006)
17. Yee, N.: The psychology of MMORPGs: Emotional investment, motivations, relationship formation, and problematic usage. In: Schroeder, R., Axelsson, A. (eds.) Avatars at Work and Play: Collaboration and Interaction in Shared Virtual Environments. Springer, London (2006)

Supporting Multiple Perspectives on 3D Museum Artefacts through Interoperable Annotations

Jane Hunter and Chih-hao Yu

School of ITEE, The University of Queensland,
St Lucia, Queensland, Australia 4072
j.hunter@uq.edu.au, chih.yu@uqconnect.edu.au

Abstract. Increasing numbers of museums and cultural institutions are using 3D laser scanning techniques to preserve cultural artefacts as 3D digital models, that are then accessible to curators, scholars and the general public via Web interfaces to online galleries. Museums are finding the cost of providing metadata for such collections prohibitive and are keen to explore how they might exploit Web 2.0 social tagging and annotation services to capture community knowledge and enrich the contextual metadata associated with their collections. Although there exist some annotation services for 3D objects, they are designed for specific disciplines, not Web-based or depend on proprietary software and formats. The majority also only support the attachment of annotations to whole objects – not points, 3D surface regions or 3D segments. This paper describes the 3DSA (3D Semantic Annotation) system developed at the University of Queensland that enables users to attach annotations to 3D digital artefacts. The 3DSA system is based on a common interoperable annotation model (the Open Annotations Collaboration (OAC) model) and uses ontology-based tags to support further semantic annotation and reasoning. This common approach enables annotations to be re-used, migrated and shared – across annotation clients and across different 3D and 2.5D digital representations of the one cultural artifact. Such interoperability is essential if cultural institutions are to easily harness knowledge from a broad range of users, including curators, students and remote Indigenous communities, with different client capabilities.

Keywords: 3D annotations, tags, semantics, interoperability, ontologies.

1 Introduction and Objectives

Advances in 3D data acquisition, processing and visualization technologies are providing museums and cultural institutions with new methods for preserving cultural heritage and making it more accessible to scholars, traditional owners and the public, via online search interfaces. Increasing numbers of museums are using 3D scanning techniques to overcome the limitations of 2D data representations and to improve access to high quality surrogates of fragile and valuable artefacts via the Internet [1-4]. The trend is increasingly towards the use of 3D laser scanners to capture precise 3D digital models that can be accurately analysed, measured and compared. However there are a number of challenges that come with building online collections of 3D

R. Nakatsu et al. (Eds.): ECS 2010, IFIP AICT 333, pp. 149–159, 2010.
© IFIP International Federation for Information Processing 2010

museum objects, making them accessible to different types of users and enabling their classification and the attachment of community knowledge through tags and annotations.

Firstly, the file size of the 3D digital objects is often problematic for many users who are unable to quickly and easily download and render the objects due to limited bandwidth, CPU, graphics cards or the need for specific 3D rendering software. Secondly, as the size of online collections of 3D artefacts grows, the ability to enable search and browsing across these distributed repositories becomes more difficult. Museums are finding the cost of providing metadata and rich contextual information for their collections prohibitive and are keen to explore how they might exploit social tagging and annotation services [5]. High quality tags and annotations – attached to both the complete object as well as to specific segments or features – have the potential to significantly improve the relevance of retrieved search results. Although there already exist some annotation services for 3D objects, they are designed for specific disciplines or depend on proprietary software and formats. The majority also only support the attachment of annotations to the whole objects – not to 3D points, surface regions, 3D parts or segments (e.g., the handle on a pot).

Hence the aims of the work described here are to develop services to support the following:

- Workflows for streamlining the generation of multiple alternative digital representations (high resolution, medium resolution and low resolution) of each 3D museum object in high-quality, standardized and widely used formats;
- Web-based, easy-to-use, 3D tagging/annotation tools that support the attachment of annotations to points, surface regions or 3D segments (i.e., meaningful parts or features) on a 3D model. The difficulty lies in specifying the particular feature of interest via simple drawing, selection and segmentation tools. For example, drawing the boundary of a 3D surface feature or a 3D segment can be very difficult and time consuming.
- Tagging and annotation tools that enable annotations/tags to be automatically attached to, migrated between and displayed, for different digital versions (high, medium, low resolutions) of each museum artifact;
- Semantic annotation tools – that use machine-understandable tags drawn from an ontology. Our aim is to use the CIDOC-CRM [7] ontology, which has been designed specifically for the museum community, but to extend it with discipline-specific sub-ontologies (e.g., Indigenous Carvings). Ontology-based annotations are valuable because, in addition to supporting validation and quality control, they allow reasoning about the annotated resources, enabling it to become part of the larger Semantic Web;
- A common model for attaching annotations to 3D artefacts regardless of their format. Such a model also enables re-use and display of annotations across different annotation clients. Our aim is to evaluate the Open Annotations Collaboration (OAC) model for supporting the migration of annotations between multiple versions of a 3D object and using different annotation clients.

2 Related Work

Most prior work in the field of 3D annotations has focused on the annotation of discipline-specific objects – for example, architectural and engineering CAD drawings [7,8], 3D crystallography models [26] and 3D scenes [27]. All of these systems enable users to attach annotations to 3D models and to browse annotations added by others, asynchronously. However they are all limited to the discipline-specific format of the target objects. Adobe Acrobat 3D also provides a 3D JavaScript API that allows annotation of 3D CAD models or U3 objects stored in PDF using a proprietary SDK. However the documentation is lengthy and attaching annotations is a programmatic exercise [23]. A survey of existing systems failed to reveal any interoperable, collaborative, Web-based annotation systems for 3D models of museum artefacts, that enable descriptive text or semantic tags to be attached (either to the whole object or a point or region on the object) – and then saved to enable later, asynchronous searching, browsing and response, by other users.

Projects such as SCULPTEUR [9], the Princeton 3D search engine [10] and Columbia Shape Search [15] use a combination of machine learning (to extract colour, pattern and shape) and application semantics (who, what, where, when etc.) to automatically cluster 3D objects. However these projects fail to take advantage of community-generated tags and annotations drawn from ontology-directed folksonomies. Hunter et al [14, 15, 16] have previously applied semantic inferencing rules to enable the automated high-level semantic annotation of 2D images from low-level automatically-extracted features – and demonstrated improvements in concept-based search performance. Hunter et. al. have also developed annotation tools for 3D museum artefacts, based on the Annotea model [13]. But this previous work has only enabled the attachment of tags and comments to 3D points and/or views of the complete object.

Other relevant prior work is in the area of segmentation of 3D models [22, 28] and the attachment of semantic annotations to segments [29, 30]. Previous segmentation approaches have involved mesh segmentation approaches and manual or user-guided approaches [12, 31]. The ShapeAnnotator [22] focuses on automatic segmentation to separate a 3D object into different segments. The ShapeAnnotator is not Web-based and does not enable users to annotate whatever region they select – only pre-identified segments. It also does not display textures for 3D models, which makes unattractive to cultural institutions. Our aim is to adopt an approach similar to Ji et al [12] to perform the automated segmentation and to apply and evaluate it within the context of a specific collection of 3D museum artefacts.

As far as we are aware, there are currently no open-source tools that: enable Web-based semantic annotation of 3D museum objects; that use ontology-based semantic tags; or that enable easy tagging of points, surface regions or 3D parts on a 3D digital object. Finally we are unaware of any system that enables the easy migration of tags/annotations between different digital versions of the one 3D object – a critical requirement if museums are going to engage with users from a range of different communities and with access to variable computer capabilities.

2.1   The Open Annotations Collaboration (OAC) Data Model

The lack of robust interoperable tools for annotating across heterogeneous repositories of digital content and difficulties sharing or migrating annotation records between users and clients – are hindering the exploitation of digital resources by many scholars. Hence the Open Annotations Collaboration (OAC) was established to facilitate the emergence of a Web and Resource-centric interoperable annotation environment that allows leveraging annotations across the boundaries of annotation clients, annotation servers, and content collections. To this end, an annotation interoperability specification consisting of an Annotation Data Model (Fig. 1) has been developed. Fundamental principles that were adopted by the OAC include:

- The core entities of an annotation (*Annotation, Content, Target*) are independent Web resources that are URI-addressable and hence discoverable and re-usable;
- The Annotation *Target* (the object being annotated) and the Annotation *Content* (the body of the annotation) can each be any media type;
- Annotation Targets and Content are frequently segments of Web resources;
- The Content of a single annotation may apply to multiple Targets or multiple annotation Contents may apply to a single Target;
- Annotations can themselves be the Target of further Annotations.

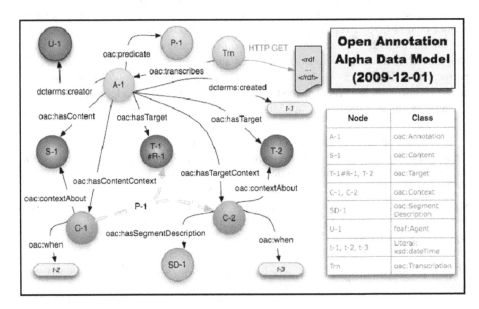

Fig. 1. The Alpha OAC Data Model [6]

   The case study in which different users from different backgrounds (curators, scholars, students, public) annotate and tag a museum object (represented in different digital formats) – and then share and aggregate those annotations - is an ideal case study for evaluating the OAC model. Fig. 2 below illustrates how the OAC is relevant to the 3DSA application through a simple example in which user "jane" attaches the

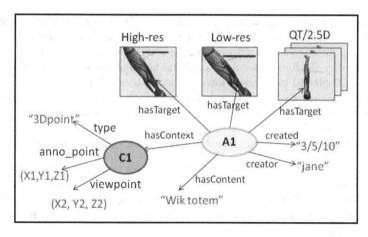

Fig. 2. Instance of the OAC model within the 3DSA application

textual annotation "Wik totem" to a point on a 3D object. This annotation is automatically migrated across the three digital representations of this object.

3 Case Study

To evaluate the proposed annotation services, we are currently using Indigenous wooden ceremonial sculptures from the Wik peoples of Western Cape York. This collection of wooden, ochre-painted sculptures is held in the UQ Anthropology Museum. Indigenous artists from Cape York are interested in emulating and extending the techniques used by artists from these earlier periods. They would like to be able to access high resolution 3D versions of the sculptures without having to travel to Brisbane for long periods. In addition, the UQ Art Museum is developing an exhibition around these sculptures, to open in 2010. The aim of this project is to work with the UQ Anthropology Museum curators, Indigenous artists from Cape York and the UQ Art Museum to develop a virtual collection of 3D models which can be used for remote access, collaborative annotation, knowledge sharing, exhibition development and the evaluation of this project's outcomes.

4 Implementation

4.1 Generating the 3D Models

The first phase of the project involves scanning each artefact using a Konica Minólta Vivid9i non-contact 3D laser scanner and generating the different 3D digital models using GeoMagic software. Each museum artefact is initially scanned into a VRML format, stored in Collada format using Autodesk Maya and converted into O3D format (Google's 3D scene graph API)) using Google's converter. The 2.5D file (FlashVR format) is generated by capturing a series of images from the O3D file. At this stage, the project has generated a sample set of Indigenous artefacts for evaluation purposes. More artefacts from a variety of backgrounds and materials, will be scanned in the future to more fully evaluate the search and indexing features.

A high quality 3D digital model for a cultural heritage artefact contains 50-200 MB of data and 20-50,000 polygons. However, many users don't have the bandwidth, computational power or graphics cards capable of downloading and rendering such objects in a timely fashion – or enabling real-time interaction (panning, rotating, zooming) with the 3D models. In order to support users with limited computation power or bandwidth, we generate four different representations of each artefact:

- Archival quality 3D model (Raw 3D data): for storage purposes only, not accessible online.
- High quality 3D model for users who have standard CPU and internet speed.
- Low quality 3D model - compressed version for users with limited CPU, graphics card or slow internet.
- 2.5D VR object - non-3D version, suitable for users who do not have a graphical processor and with a very slow internet connection.

4.2 System Design and Implementation

Using the 3D objects generated via the scanning and conversion process described above, we have developed a Web interface to a gallery of objects. Users can search and browse the gallery of 3D objects via thumbnails, a tag cloud and keyword search. The 3DSA annotation prototype (shown in Fig. 4) is also accessible via a link from the project website's 3D gallery[1]. A high-level view of the system architecture is shown below in Fig. 3.

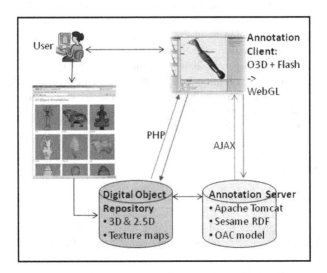

Fig. 3. Screen-shot of the Web-based 3D Annotation prototype 3DSA

---

[1] http://www.itee.uq.edu.au/~eresearch/projects/3dsa

The Annotation prototype was developed using a combination of Web 2.0 technologies and third party services including:

- 3D viewer – Google's O3D scene graph API, provides a browser plug-in with a shader-based, low-level graphics API and a high level Javascript library. O3D is flexible, extensible [17], cross-compatible, open source and Google's proposal as an open Web standard for 3D [18].
- 2.5 VR object viewer – this was developed using Adobe Flex, a free, open source framework for building web applications using ActionScript 3.0.
- Annotation storage – is implemented using AJAX and Danno, an HTTP-based repository that provides APIs for creating, updating, deleting and querying annotations and replies, and for bulk upload and harvesting of annotations [19].
- User interface – this was developed using AJAX, PHP and jQuery, a JavaScript Library that simplifies HTML document traversing, event handling, animating, and Ajax interactions for rapid web development [20].

Fig. 4 shows a screen shot of the prototype in use. On the left hand side, are the different versions of the artefact being annotated – users choose the most appropriate for their environment. In the center is the display panel showing the currently selected 3D object and attached annotations. On the right hand side is the annotation search and browse panel. Clicking on the "New Annotation" button displays a new panel that enables users to enter the contextType of the annotation (object, point, region, segment), the Type of annotation (tag, comment, query, feedback) and the body of the annotation. The creator and date/time information is also captured. The complete details/metadata for a chosen annotation are displayed in the bottom centre panel.

After the user enters the annotation data, they can specify the context/point on the object to which it is attached. (Region and Segment annotations are still under development). After saving the annotation, the system then determines if there are other representations of this artifact available. If there are, then the annotation context is

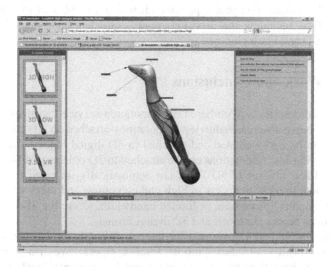

Fig. 4. Screen shot of the 3DSA Annotation Prototype

re-calculated to automatically migrate the annotation to the other formats (e.g., from 3D high-res to 2.5D Flash). For example transferring a 3D coordinate (X, Y, Z) to 2D coordinate (X, Y), the formula below is implemented [24]:

$$P(X,Y,Z) = LP(X,Y,Z) \times WM \times VM \times PM$$

$P(X,Y,Z) =$ *Point that had been projected on to a 2D screen.*
$LP(X,Y,Z) =$ *Local position of the object.*
$WM = World\ matrix.;\ VM = View\ matrix.;\ PM = Projection\ matrix.$

5   Discussion

Feedback from museum curators on the 3DSA system has been extremely positive. They are very excited about the added dimensions and details that 3D scanning can offer but they realize that there are a number of barriers preventing wide-spread adoption of 3D digital formats in online museum collections, including: the time it takes to generate the 3D objects, the size of the files, the time to download and render the files and the graphical and computational power required to support real-time rendering and interactive panning, zooming and rotating. In this paper we firstly describe workflows to streamline the generation of multiple 3D/2.5D digital representations of museum artefacts to satisfy the anticipated range of users and users' computer capabilities, whilst still maximizing quality and minimizing effort. We have then demonstrated a prototype to enable the attachment of community-generated tags and annotations to 3D digital objects. We have also demonstrated how the Open Annotations Collaboration Model can be extended and applied to support interoperability of annotations across clients, across target objects in different digital formats and their attachment to segments (points, regions, 3D parts) of 3D/2.5D digital objects. The complex algorithms for mapping annotations between objects of different resolution have been comprehensively tested and have demonstrated high performance – both speed and accuracy. User evaluations of the annotation prototype have identified a number of improvements to the user interface, including the need for greater consistency in annotation displays between the O3D and Flash plug-ins.

6   Future Work and Conclusions

In this paper we describe a Web-based 3D annotation service that does not entail a steep learning curve to create/edit/view annotations attached to 3D digital objects. Annotations can be easily created and attached to 3D digital objects via the O3D or Flash browser plug-ins. Annotations can be attached to 3D objects in different formats (high-res, med-res, low-res (2.5D)) and are automatically migrated between them. This enables both users with access to high-end computers and users with slow computational or graphical processors or limited bandwidth, to use the 3DSA tool and to share annotations across platforms and 3D digital formats.

Future aims include adding support for the new WebGL format that will be supported by major browsers (Safari, Chrome, Firefox, Opera). We also plan to explore how users attach annotations to surface regions and 3D segments. In addition, we plan to allow tags to be extracted from folksonomies and/or the CIDOC/CRM ontology (ontology-directed folksonomies), to support faceted search. As such, this project differs from projects such as SCULPTEUR, the Princeton 3D search engine and Columbia Shape Search, in which indexing is entirely based on machine learning and semantics but fails to take advantage of folksonomic tags. By combining both user-generated tags and automatic feature extraction, we will significantly enhance the discovery of 3D cultural artefacts and associated content. The outcome will be an online digital repository/gallery of 3D cultural heritage artefacts enriched with both manually-generated and automatically-generated metadata to enable fast accurate search and retrieval of 3D objects by both museum experts and the general public.

Finally, we have begun experimenting with the QR codes [33] to enable museum visitors to retrieve community-generated annotations via their iPhones. QR codes (small printable tags) can be generated from the 3DSA web pages, and attached to the physical museum artefacts in the exhibition. This enables museum visitors with the QR code app on their iPhone, to retrieve the related 3DSA web page that displays the 3D digital version with aggregated annotations. This is a very exciting development with significant potential that will also require further testing and evaluation.

To conclude, the 3DSA system represents a highly innovative approach to cultural heritage that combines the best of Web 2.0, Semantic Web and mobile technologies to maximize the preservation, capture, dissemination and re-use of knowledge about cultural heritage.

Acknowledgments. The work described in this paper has been funded by Microsoft Research Asia through the e-Heritage program and through a University of Queensland Major Equipment and Infrastructure (MEI) grant. The Open Annotations Collaboration component has been funded by the Andrew W. Mellon Foundation.

References

1. Hunter, J., Schroeter, R., Koopman, B., Henderson, M.: Using the semantic grid to build bridges between museums and indigenous communities. In: Proceedings of the GGF11-Semantic Grid Applications Workshop, June 10, pp. 46–61 (2004)
2. 3D digital preservation of cultural heritages, ikeuchi Lab: University of Tokyo, http://www.cvl.iis.u-tokyo.ac.jp/gallery_e/
3. Rowe, J., Razdan, A.: A prototype digital library for 3D collections: Tools to capture, model, analyze, and query complex 3D data. In: Bearman, D., Trant, J. (eds.) Museums and the Web 2003, Archives & Museum Informatics, Toronto, pp. 147–158 (2003)
4. Isler, V., Wilson, B., Bajcsy, R.: Building a 3D Virtual Museum of Native American Baskets. In: Proceedings of the Third International Symposium on 3D Data Processing, Visualization, and Transmission (3dpvt 2006), 3DPVT, June 14-16, pp. 954–961. IEEE Computer Society, Washington (2006)
5. Chun, S., Cherry, R., Hiwiller, D., Trant, J., Wyman, B.: Steve.museum: An Ongoing Experiment in Social Tagging, Folksonomy, and Museums. In: Museums and the Web 2006 (2006)
6. CIDOC Conceptual Reference Model, ICOM, http://cidoc.ics.forth.gr/

7. Jung, T., Do, E.Y., Gross, M.D.: Immersive Redlining and Annotation of 3D Design Models on the Web. In: 8th International Conference on Computer Aided. Architectural Design Futures, Kluwer, Dordrecht (1999)
8. Jung, T., Gross, M.D., Do, E.Y.: Annotating and sketching on 3D web models. In: Proceedings of the 7th International Conference on Intelligent User Interfaces, IUI 2002, San Francisco, California, USA, January 13-16. ACM, New York (2002)
9. Addis, et al.: New Ways to Search, Navigate and Use Multimedia Museum Collections over the Web. In: Trant, J., Bearman, D. (eds.) Proceedings of Museums and the Web 2005, March 31, Archives & Museum Informatics, Toronto (2005)
10. Princeton 3D model search engine. Princeton Shape Retrieval and Analysis Group, http://shape.cs.princeton.edu/search.html
11. Goldfeder, C., Allen, P.: Autotagging to Improve Text Search for 3D Models. In: IEEE Joint Conference on Digital Libraries (JCDL), Pittsburgh (July 2008)
12. Ji, Z., Liu, L., Chen, Z., Wang, G.: Easy mesh cutting. Computer Graphics Forum 25(3), 283–292 (2006)
13. Schroeter, R., Hunter, J., Guerin, J., Khan, I., Henderson, M.: A Synchronous Multimedia Annotation System for Secure Collaboratories. In: e-Science 2006, Amsterdam, Netherlands, December 4-6 (2006)
14. Hollink, L., Little, S., Hunter, J.: Evaluating The Application of Semantic Inferencing Rules to Image Annotation. In: Third International Conference on Knowledge Capture, KCAP 2005, Banff, Canada, October 2-5 (2005)
15. Hunter, J., Little, S.: A Framework to enable the Semantic Inferencing and Querying of Multimedia Content. International Journal of Web Engineering and Technology (IJWET) Special Issue on the Semantic Web 2(2/3) (2005)
16. Little, S., Hunter, J.: Rules-By-Example - A Novel Approach to Semantic Indexing and Querying of Images. In: McIlraith, S.A., Plexousakis, D., van Harmelen, F. (eds.) ISWC 2004. LNCS, vol. 3298, pp. 534–548. Springer, Heidelberg (2004)
17. Papakipos, M.: Introducing O3D (April 20, 2009), http://o3d.blogspot.com/2009/04/toward-open-web-standard-for-3d.html
18. Google O3D official website FAQ, http://code.google.com/p/o3d/wiki/FAQs
19. Danno/ Dannotate Overview, http://metadata.net/sites/danno/index.html
20. jQuery Official Website, http://jquery.com/
21. Vector Math for 3D Computer Graphics, Fourth Revision (July 2009), http://chortle.ccsu.edu/VectorLessons/vectorIndex.html
22. Attene, M., Robbiano, F., Spagnuolo, M., Falcidieno, B.: Semantic Annotation of 3D Surface Meshes based on Feature Characterization, Genova, CNR, Italy
23. Adobe Acrobat 3D Annotation Tutorial, July 27 (2005), http://www.adobe.com/devnet/acrobat/pdfs/3DAnnotations.pdf
24. Koci, R.: Computer Graphics Unveiled – World, View and Projection Matrix Unveilded, http://robertokoci.com/world-view-and-projection-matrix-unveiled/
25. Laurila, P.: Geometry Culling un 3D Englines, September 10 (2000), http://www.gamedev.net/reference/articles/article1212.asp
26. Hunter, J., Henderson, M., Khan, I.: Collaborative Annotation of 3D Crystallographic Models. J. Chem. Inf. Model. 47(6) (2007), http://pubs.acs.org/cgi-bin/article.cgi/jcisd8/2007/47/i06/pdf/ci700173y.pdf

27. Kadobayashi, R., et al.: 3D Model Annotation from Multiple Viewpoints for Croquet. In: Proceedings of the Fourth International Conference on Creating, Connecting and Collaborating through Computing, C5 2006 (2006)
28. Shamir, A.: A survey on mesh segmentation techniques. Computer Graphics Forum (2008)
29. De Floriani, L., Papaleo, L., Carissimi, N.: A Java3D framework for inspecting and segmenting 3D models. In: Proceedings of the 13th International Symposium on 3D Web Technology, Web3D 2008, Los Angeles, California, August 9-10, pp. 67–74. ACM, New York (2008), http://doi.acm.org/10.1145/1394209.1394225
30. Attene, M., Robbiano, F., Spagnuolo, M., Falcidieno, B.: Part-based Annotation of Virtual 3D Shapes. In: Proceedings of Cyberworlds 2007, Spec. Sess. on NASAGEM Workshop, pp. 427–436. IEEE Computer Society Press, Los Alamitos (2007)
31. Funkhouser, T., et al.: Modeling by example. ACM Transactions on Graphics 23(3), 652–663 (2004)
32. The Open Annotation Collaboration Alpha Data Model, http://www.openannotation.org/documents/OAC-Model_UseCases-alpha.pdf
33. Tales of Things, http://www.talesofthings.com/

Interactivity in Games: The Player's Engagement

Stéphane Natkin

CEDRIC CNAM 292 rue St Martin 75141 Paris Cedex 03, France
stephane.natkin@cnam.fr

Abstract. Is the core of a video game a story or a gameplay system? Out of this scholastic debate we try to show in this paper that the main difference between games and other types of media is the player's engagement. We consider two radically different games, an interactive fiction designed by the student's of ENJMIN, "Fear Window" and a formal probabilistic game based on the finite drunkard's walk process "Drinking around Crocodiles". We try to show that, in both cases, the core of the game design and, as a consequence, the aesthetic of the game is the way to let the player feel his responsibility in the progress of the game.

Keywords. Videogames, Gameplay, Narration, Rules, Engagement.

1 Introduction

When, in 2001, a group of people started to create the pedagogical contents and the spirit of the graduate school of games, ENJMIN (http://www.enjmin.fr), I had to write some document to explain what was the differences between this formation and, for example, a graduate degree on digital arts or on cinema? A way to answer to this question is another question: what is the difference between computer games and movie or other form of linear storytelling media?

This leads to the well known opposition between narratology and ludology:. This debate can be considered as a theoretical subject: from the narratology point of view, games are novel forms of narrative; from the ludology point of view games should be understood as formal systems of rules [1].

But the same debate arises from Game Design practices. For example David Cage, the creator of *Omikron: The Nomad Soul* (1999) and *Fahrenheit* (2005) designs his game mainly as interactive stories. In the opposite Will Wright, the creator of *Simcity, Sims* and *Spore* has a much more sandbox point of view:

"Other games, the games that tend to be more creative, have a much larger solution space, so you can potentially solve this problem in a way that nobody else has. If you're building a solution, how large that solution space is gives the player a much stronger feeling of empathy. If they know that what they've done is unique to them, they tend to care for it a lot more. I think that's the direction I tend to come from." [2]

Eric Viennot, the creator of *In Memoriam*, has another way to think the relationship between the gameplay and the story:

R. Nakatsu et al. (Eds.): ECS 2010, IFIP AICT 333, pp. 160–168, 2010.
© IFIP International Federation for Information Processing 2010

« Is the story that inspires the gameplay or the opposite? Many students, journalist or even gamers use to ask me this question. In my case both have to work together. If the principle of game often starts from an idea of gameplay, it will certainly evolve with the story... Reciprocally some ideas coming from the scenario leads to new gameplay principles... Both have to be tightly related..."

http://ericviennot.blogs.liberation.fr/ericviennot/2008/11/loeuf-ou-la-pou.html#more

In this paper we will consider this subject from another point of view: the player's engagement. We consider two radically different games, an interactive fiction designed by the student's of ENJMIN, *Fear Window* and a formal probabilistic game based on the finite drunkard's walk process, *Drinking around Crocodiles*. We try to show that, in both cases, the core of the game design and, as a consequence, the aesthetic of the game is the way to let the player feel his responsibility in the progress of the game.

2 Aesthetic of Games

Probably everybody agree that the main difference between games and other types of media is interactivity. But what is the meaning of interactivity in games? We start from Jesper Juul's [3] definition of game:

"A game is a rule-based formal system with a variable and quantifiable outcome, where different outcomes are assigned different values, the player exerts effort in order to influence the outcome, the player feels attached to the outcome, and the consequences of the activity are optional and negotiable."

From the player's engagement importance point of view, the fact that the player exerts effort in order to influence the outcome, and feels attached to the outcome is the core point.

To point out the important components of a game, it is necessary to coin a definition that leaves aside the game's dynamics structure and focuses on video games from the player's point of view.

Robin Hunicke describes a game using a Mechanics, Dynamics and Aesthetics (MDA) framework [4]. Mechanics are the tools we use to build a game (e.g. physics engines, path finding algorithm...), Dynamics describes the way the Mechanic's components behave in response to the player, and Aesthetics is the desirable emotional responses evoked to the player. Of course, the design goal is the Aesthetics, that is to say the player's emotions.

Umberto Eco's book *The Open Work* is a fundamental research about interactive art's aesthetics [5]. Umberto Eco states that when we face a piece of art, we are interpreting it, seeking patterns, looking for information. Depending on our culture and knowledge, we will find something to grab on within the stimulating field of the piece of art. But then we will go further, and find another interpretation and feel lost for short moment, while shaping our new pattern. Moreover, when a piece of art is interactive, the aesthetic value comes both from the tension resolution and from the fact that this resolution is a consequence of our choice. Assuming that a video game is an open work we can propose a similar analysis. Every time the player faces an obstacle, he gets lost. Then he has to find and choose a pattern, to press the right buttons, and takes pleasure both from resolving a tension as a consequence of his choice. Thus, we can draw from Umberto Eco's work that in video games, challenge is fundamental because it creates tension situations that the player must solve through meaningful choices. This leads to the famous point of view of Sid Meier "A [good] game is a series of interesting choices". Thus, a definition of a game from the Aesthetic point of view and centered on challenges could be:

"The aesthetics of a game is created by tension / resolution cycles, where the resolution of a cycle are felt by the player as some consequence of his choices.'

This definition doesn't take into account every aspect of game aesthetic but is focused on the player's personal engagement. In the next sections we consider two examples to show how the engagement of the player can be the consequence of quite different design choices.

3 Fear Window

Fear Window is a first year project of the ENJMIN Master It was developed in 2007 by four students: Pascal Allançon, (Game Design), David Hart (Programming), Alexandre Marie (Art Direction) and Xavier Montels (Sound Design).

"It is an interactive experience where the act of taking a life is non-trivial, opposite to what happens in most videogames. This game was not meant to be "fun", and such it wasn't designed to reward or punish the player. This experience puts you in the place of a sniper stalking the windows of a big city apartment. It's the end of the day, and you're waiting for your target to arrive... It is a digital "huis-clos" with theatrical intentions that pays tribute to Alfred Hitchcock's 1955 masterpiece, *Rear Window*. You're "stuck" at the window and can only fire once. This project wants to show murder as a horrible, yet touching act to the player. The shot is hard to shoot, not technically (you have just one button to press), but in a humane way. The player should have to force himself to pull the trigger, struggling against himself. The team focused on creating an immersive, captivating experience, which appeals to the player's empathy. We also tried to raise questions about the way violence is portrayed in most media, video games, but also in movies and television. The other aspect we wanted to speak about was the notion of role-play, trying to see to what lengths can a player stray from the designer's original intention, even refusing to play the game for moral or emotional reasons. Other games have flirted with this idea, *Shadow of the Colossus* being one of the best examples of the player's struggle between duty and will.

One of the objectives of Fear Window is to get the player to think about what he has just done. We are going to show to him the target's wife and daughter before he arrives to his apartment. When he does, he will almost never be alone, making it hard for the player not to kill him in front of his family. To enhance this feeling of unease and doubt is the fact that the player knows nothing of his target's identity and personality, nothing about "himself", the shooter, nor anything about the person who gave you the target. He will only know his orders to kill someone. This should lead the player to wonder whether it is right to shoot, taking a life he knows nothing about with the push of a button." [5]

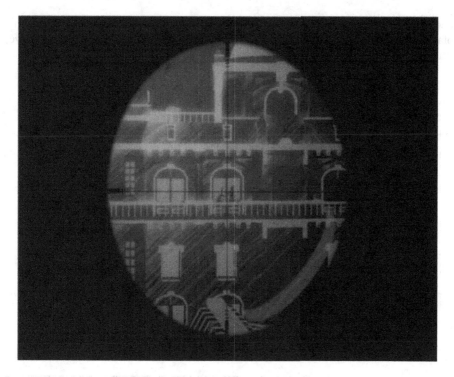

Fig. 1. Looking through the aim in Fear Window

Fear window is built as an interactive movie. When the game start, a voice phone call tells you the following:

"This afternoon, the owner of an apartment in Paris will be informed of a very important secret. In any case this secret must not be disclosed. We have manage you a sniper position, you are in charge to kill this person and any other people who may be aware of the secret"

Then the game starts: you are looking trough the aim of a gun and you hear all the things happening in the apartment in front of you. You can only do four things: move your aim, zoom in or out and fire.

You discover the wife and the child of the man you are expecting though the windows of the apartment like Chinese shadows. Some every day events happen: the little girl was slightly injured in a garden. The woman is angry against her husband who should be already back home as it is the little girl's birthday... At a given time the man comes back, has discussion with his wife, stay a little with his daughter and then get a phone call on the terrace outside the apartment...

The scenario is built such as you may think at several times that somebody knows the terrible secret: before the husband's arrival the woman receive a mysterious phone call, a delivery boy lives a parcel, the little girl open the parcel...

Each time you are implicitly urged, from a classical game point of view, to shoot somebody. In the opposite the dialog is constructed to create some empathy with the family. You are faced with an interesting choice based on the conflict of your first person shooter practice and your feeling of guilty to kill innocent people. This player's choice design is based on classical narrative principles: a dramaturgy curve, actor's management, dialogs construction...

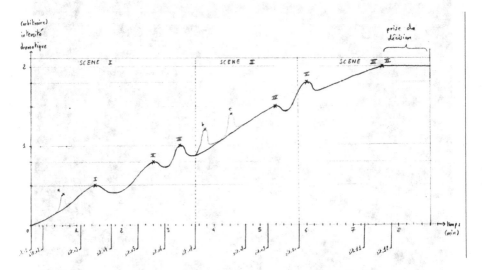

Fig. 2. Fear Window: The dramaturgy tension curve

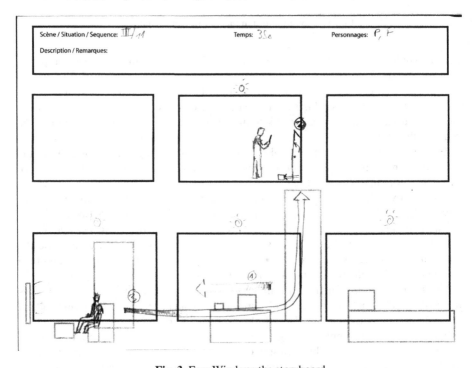

Fig. 3. Fear Window: the storyboard

From this analysis we can state the three following consequences:

- Fear Window is not exactly a game according to Juul's definition, but it has the core aesthetic feature of this new media: the player's engagement.
- Interesting choices does not necessarily mean pleasant or funny.
- It is possible to engage the player's in an interesting choice using narrative techniques

4 Drinking around Crocodiles

Let's now consider the following formal definition of a game:

```
Pick a random number N such as 0<N<P
Player choose either I:=Head (H) or I:=Tail (T)
k:= N
While k>0 and k<P do
Player runs a coin
If outcome =I k:=k+1 else k:=k-1
Endo
If k=0 player wins, if k=P player looses
```

Of course this game is not really interesting, it is just a complex version of Head or Tail but, as it is derived from a well known stochastic process called the finite drunkard's walk (finite discrete time birth and death process with two absorbing states [6]), we can use the historical anecdote and restate the game in a more narrative form:

You are a drunker leaving in Crocodile City. Your home is on a road at a certain distance (P steps) from the Crocodile River. One night, you wake up somewhere (position N) between your house and the Crocodile River. As you have drink a lot, and not only water, you walk randomly step by step. At each step either you get closer to your house (one step right) or closer to the river (one step left). The game ends when either you are back into your bed or you have felt in the river and been eaten by crocodiles.

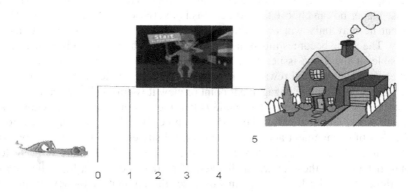

Fig. 4. Drinking with Crocodiles

Of course this is a little better: the designer can use some funny graphics and the sound of a clock for crocodiles like in the Disney movie *Peter Pan*. But even with this little story, it is difficult for the player to be really involved in the choice between Head or Tail.

So let's change slightly the rules:

```
Player chooses a number N such as 0<N<P
k:= N
While k>0 and k<P do
        Player runs a coin
        If outcome =H k:=k+1 else k:=k-1
Endo
If k=0 Player lose N
If k=P Player wins k-N
```

Now the player does not have to decide between Head or Tail, which is for a balanced coin a fake choice, but he chooses his initial position. In crocodile's style the game can written as follow:

```
Player chooses an initial position N on the road
While he is still alive (position>0) and not at home
(position<P)
        Player runs the dice
        If outcome =H walk one step on the right else walk
        one step on the left
End while
If the Player is in the river eaten by crocodiles he
loses N billions of dollars
If the player is back into his bed he wins P-N billions
of dollars
```

The difference between the two games seems to be small, but now the player can have a strategy. If he is a risky player and he can start near the Crocodile River (N=1). He may fall quickly but if he is lucky he can win P-1 billons dollars. On the opposite, if he is a wise player he can choose to start near his home (N=P-1). He has less chance to be eaten but he may only win one billion dollars. He can also choose an intermediate strategy. The game becomes much more interesting for the player feels, at least partly, responsible of the game issue. This feeling is mainly subjective as, whatever is his initial choice, his expected reward is null (see [6] for the whole mathematical analysis of the game), but from the engagement point of view it is drastically different.

The main problem with this last game is that there is only one initial choice, after the game works automatically like a slot machine. But there is many ways to add the feelings of engagement and to choose personal strategies in this game. For example the game can ask at each step if the player wants to drink more or want to be teetotal. If he drinks the rule are unchanged. If he does not drink, he walks one step in the direction of the house. But, in this case, the amount of money he may win decreases.

```
Player chooses an initial position N on the road
While he is in life (position>0) and not at home (position<P)
     Player chooses either
     to drink once more (run the dice)
               If outcome =H walk one step on the right
               else walk one step on the left
               end if
     Or to be teetotal
               walk one step on the right
               N:=N+1
End while
If the Player is dead he loses N
If the player is at home he wins P-N
```

5 Conclusion

In this paper we have tried to show that the main originality of a game as a media is the player's engagement trough a fine tuning of interactivity. Main level design techniques, like the player difficulty curves [7], rely on the same principle: the player must be able overcome game challenges with the feeling that he the main author of his victories. In the two examples given here there is no apprenticeship mechanism. One is a simple interactive narration, the other a minimalist random game. But in both cases the game is built in a way to give to the player the feeling of engagement. Another significant example is a game like Guitar Hero. From a gameplay point of view, the game can be played without sound using any device with colored buttons, which transform this game into a psychomotor test. There is no story in a classical sense. To be interested the player must dress up himself as Van Halen or Stevie Ray Vaughan and feel as a Guitar Hero. So, whatever technique is used, the originality of video games as a media is the player's engagement. This is, from our point of view, a way to define interactivity in games.

Acknowledgment. Section 2 of this paper is mainly taken from [7].

References

[1] Aarseth, E.J.: Cybertext: Perspectives on Ergodic Literature. Johns Hopkins University Press, Baltimore (1997), ISBN 0-8018-5579-9; [Allancon 2007] Allançon, P.: Fear windows: Concept, ENJMIN students project description, Angoulême (2007)

[2] Pearce, Sims, BattleBots, Cellular Automata God and Go , A Conversation with Will Wright by Celia Pearce, Game studies 2(1) (July 2002),
http://www.gamestudies.org/0102/pearce/

[3] Juul, J.: Half-Real: Video Games between Real Rules and Fictional Worlds. The MIT Press, Cambridge (November 2005)

[4] Hunicke, R.: The case for dynamic difficulty adjustment in games. In: Advances in Computer Entertainment Technology, pp. 429–433 (2005)

[5] Eco, U.: The Open Work. Harvard University Press, Cambridge (1989)

[6] Kemeny, J.G., Snell, J.L., Knapp, A.W.: Denumerable Markov Chains. Springer, Heidelberg (1976)

[7] Aponte, M.V., Levieux, G., Natkin, S.: Scaling the Level of Difficulty in Single Player Video Games. In: Natkin, S., Dupire, J. (eds.) Entertainment Computing – ICEC 2009. LNCS, vol. 5709, pp. 24–35. Springer, Heidelberg (2009)

[8] Howard, R.A.: Dynamic Probabilistic Systems Vol I Markov models. John Wiley and Sons, New York (1971)

[9] Bogost, I.: Unit Operations: an Approach to Videogame Criticism. MIT Press, Cambridge (2006), ISBN 978-0-262-02599-7

[10] Natkin, S.: Video Games and Interactive Media: A Glimpse at New Digital Entertainment. AK Peters Ltd. (2006)

Co-production and Co-creation: Creative Practice in Social Inclusion

Atau Tanaka[1], Lalya Gaye[1], and Ranald Richardson[2]

[1] Culture Lab
[2] Centre for Urban Regional Development Studies
Newcastle University
NE1 7RU Newcastle upon Tyne, United Kingdom
{atau.tanaka,lalya.gaye,ranald.richardson}@ncl.ac.uk

Abstract. We apply techniques drawn from interactive media art in fieldwork for social inclusion. Advanced mobile media and grassroots DIY techniques are used to bring creative practice with digital media into community based outreach work. We use these techniques in a participatory context that encourages the co-production of cultural output. We triangulate across artistic practice, technology engineering, and the social sciences to leverage methods from digital media art practice in contexts that result in social innovation.

Keywords: interactive music, social inclusion, social innovation, co-production of knowledge, triangulation.

1 Introduction

Interactive media arts practice has developed in the last quarter century from a highly specialized field that required high-end machines, to an increasingly democratized field of practice carried out on everyday technology. This history and progression of technology, aesthetic, and practice, can be retraced in the history of the festival Ars Electronica, and is chronicled in books such as [1, 2]. Media art can be characterized as creative artistic practice that makes use of digital technologies in mixed media settings including visual and sound media in interactive situations that invite varying degrees of spectator interaction.

Artists have responded to developments in technology in critical and embracing ways. Two important developments in the last twenty years include the rapid miniaturization and accompanying democratization of technology, and the arrival of wide public use of the Internet. The former is seen in the increasing power of laptop computers and mobile devices to perform numerical calculations and signal processing for graphics or audio rendering – tasks that earlier in the history of the field required mainframe computers. The availability of this calculation power on portable computers changes the cultural contexts in which media art is practiced – it can leave the studio and large arts center and be situated in public space and in the wild. Increased availability also brings with it lowered barriers of access, broadening both the range

R. Nakatsu et al. (Eds.): ECS 2010, IFIP AICT 333, pp. 169–178, 2010.

of artists practicing media art, and the ways in which works of media art are able to invite audience participation.

In parallel with the democratization of technology came the widespread take up of Internet technologies in all aspects of daily life. This has resulted in artists using the Internet as a new form of communication and distribution for their work. It has also spawned new art forms and artistic movements, notably that of net.art [3], artwork conceived for and delivered to a standard web browser.

We can characterize media art of having 4 distinct characteristics

1. Interaction
2. Sensor input
3. Malleable Media
4. DIY ethos

In the work described here, we draw upon techniques and methods from one specific area of media art practice, that of interactive music. Computer music is the field that emerged from the invention of digital audio in the 1950's [4, 5]. It elaborates techniques of sound synthesis, computer-aided musical composition, and representation that today are at the heart of the CD audio standard, generative game soundtracks, and perceptual coding techniques like MP3. One branch of computer music that is directly concerned with human-computer interaction is that of New Interfaces for Musical Expression (NIME). NIME began as a workshop at CHI 2001 [6] and has since evolved to sustain an annual international conference. As its nature implies, NIME is the discipline concerned with interaction in music. It is a field specialized in creating interactive music systems that use sensors and networks. Its activities can be described as those of instrument building, or *lutherie*. The typical context of a NIME system is to build a system for concert performance. A NIME system is conceived by an instrument builder, contextualized by a composer, to be used by a musician who is able to attain a profound level of interaction with the system through his/her virtuosity. As a field of practice, NIME has been specialist oriented. Recently, however, the increasing use of sensing technologies in consumer electronics, typified by the Nintendo Wii-mote controller with its accelerometers, have meant that interactive music practice has the potential to become more widespread.

2   Social Inclusion

Inclusion, in the social sciences, is most often described to counter the effects of social exclusion. Social exclusion is a complex process of alienation from mainstream society, detaching groups and individuals from relations and institutions and preventing full participation in the normal advancement of the society in which they live [7].

Poor health, disability, family breakdown, poverty and unemployment are just some of the reasons why people of all ages may become marginalized from society. These multiple symptoms prevent individuals or groups in benefitting from the economic, social, and political life around them. These effects are often self-reinforcing and self-perpetuating.

2.1 Digital Inclusion

Digital technologies represent, at once a possible solution to social exclusion, and a feature of mainstream society that makes inclusion all the more difficult to attain. The digital divide is the separation between those in society with access to information technologies and those without [8, 9]. Transforming information and communications technologies (ICT) from an exclusionary aspect to a society to an inclusionary force typically focus on questions of lowering barriers to access [10, 11].

Currently, the potential benefits of the information society are not being realized by all members of society; it is recognized that digital exclusion mirrors many aspects of the more general social exclusion described above. That is, not just poverty, but the mutually reinforcing consequences of citizens enduring unemployment, discrimination, poor housing, crime, bad heath and family breakdown.

Social innovation is broadly defined as forms strategies and actions that have direct benefit in civil society in education, community development, workplace conditions, and health [12]. Here it is relevant as a way to conceptualize the potential benefit of technology and creative practice on the socioeconomic empowerment of young people.

2.2 Social Inclusion through the Digital Economy

The 'Social Inclusion through the Digital Economy' (SiDE) research hub [13] is a project funded by the UK Research Council Digital Economy Programme that applies developments in ICT to social benefit. It aims to actively explore the transformative potentials of new technologies for individuals and communities at risk of or suffering from social exclusion. For that purpose, it addresses four fields where digital technologies may deliver major social benefits:

1. Assistive technologies in domestic environments
2. Accessibility of ICT to broader age groups
3. Inclusive Transport Services
4. The Creative Industries

SiDE's contention is that it is necessary to work with end-users in a sustained way, to understand their situation, environment and needs. Our multidisciplinary teams of researchers have access to large user groups affected by social exclusion, including a group of 3000 volunteers, containing people from a range of age groups and with a variety of social backgrounds and forms of exclusion. SiDE is also centered on the formation of communities of practice of social inclusion stakeholders, which include academics, practitioners, technology producers and those who are, or who feel themselves to be, excluded from parts of society. In establishing such a community, SiDE seeks not just to create products and applications to assist users in ameliorating social disadvantage, but to establish inclusionary processes to help excluded people participate in society. In this process, SiDE seeks to broaden the horizons, capacities and understanding of all partners and contribute to formulating future policy on a socially inclusive digital society.

3   Creative practice and Co-creation

The Creative Media Group represents one of the four strands of research within the SiDE project, the Creative Industries. It works specifically with creative arts practices and young people in methodologies of co-creation to combat effects of marginalization. This paper describes the work of the Creative Media group deploying digital technologies in fieldwork with marginalized youth, in collaboration with regional youth work organizations.

Creative practice encapsulates process and methods from the creative arts, in our case using interactive media technologies. The research hypothesis here is:

- Creative media arts practice represents forms of deep interaction with digital technologies not encountered in typical end-user usage of ICT
- That this deeper view of digital media as accessible and malleable create opportunities for democratizing the creative process itself
- In order to realize this vision, that arts skills can be transferred to a general public for broader benefit and impact

Creative skills serve three purposes in the context of this project: 1) as skills that make young people entering the workforce more competitive, 2) as critical cerebral activity to develop and maintain mental acuity, 3) as compelling cultural activity to engage disaffected youth.

Co-production is a broad term encompassing fields of activity ranging from cultural production to knowledge and skills, to business applications. Here we introduce the generalities of how the term is used in these respective fields, and from that establish a transdisciplinary, synthetic view that we apply as a means to bridge creative media art practice and community based work in social inclusion.

Co-production in the cultural sector typically refers to the collaboration of two organizational entities in the realization of a new artwork. It thus refers to the consolidation of means as a way to facilitate the production of ambitious, large-scale work that could not be supported by one venue.

The use of terms co-creation and co-production in the field of human computer interaction research typically refer to the inclusion of non-designers or non-engineers in an interaction design or technology development cycle [14]. Methods that implement dynamics of co-production in interaction design include User Centered Design (UCD), and Participatory Design (PD) [15]. These methods include the end user in the design process through techniques of structured brainstorming and ethnographically inspired forms of qualitative data collection, with the goal to better understand the actual people who will use the systems being designed.

Co-production of knowledge is used in both a social science as well as business development context to refer to ways, be they exploitative or altruistic, where two parties in a hierarchical relationship, often of establishment and individual, arrive at forms of mutual understanding [16]. In scientific knowledge production, coproduction of knowledge was codified as Mode 2 as a form of transdiscplinary, level field form of information sharing for scientific advancement [17]. We draw upon the social science literature where inclusive knowledge production contexts are used to facilitate social innovation. Co-production facilitated by digital technologies has been covered in [18, 19].

We were interested to apply the end user orientation of user centered design from HCI and the democratic ideals of coproduction of knowledge for social innovation to conceive of new processes of creative practice. This is most closely associated with developments in the Do It Yourself (DIY) movement. We call this participatory art practice and draw upon political texts of the 1960's to inform this [20, 21].

4 Triangulation across Disciplines

Triangulation is one approach to cross disciplinary research. It fulfills three interdisciplinary goals: the social science goal of understanding the needs and desires of users in a real-world setting, the engineering goal of field- testing the technology, and the design goal of inspiring users and researchers to think about new technologies [22]. By forming a perspective from related disciplines, it has the potential to provide a deeper understanding of a design problem. We establish a process of exchange between arts practice, technology engineering, and social science to build advanced creative technologies while confirming everyday usage of existing technologies and by doing so put in place parallel streams that intertwine and balance usability with musicality. We call upon the notion of *triangulation* to leverage the complementarities of music research and user centered design to create inclusive creative situations that can be studied through the lens of social science.

5 Methods: A Music Scenario

We engage with cultural sector partners with established outreach activities to identify and access groups of young people from difficult neighbourhoods, where school success rates or employment are low. We planned workshops where interactive technology is deployed in acts of creative practice. The general workshop plan was conceived to have several phases:

1. Acclimatisation – getting to know the group, asking them what kinds of music they like, having them come up to the front and showing the group websites of their favorite music
2. Basic Sampling – introducing audio editing software to show how music can be used not just to copy and share, but as the source material for basic content editing: cutting, pasting, looping
3. Advanced Tools – we then introduce advanced computer music composition tools we will develop in the project. This software democratizes heretofore specialist production techniques so that will run on accessible hardware including mobile phones
4. User Sampler Instrument – samples edited and saved during phase 2 will be loaded into the software introduced in phase 3 to allow the user to create their own sound sample playback instrument, being able to scratch, scrub, trigger, and pitch shift sounds through various interaction modalities such as the touchscreens and tilt-sensors of mobile phones
5. Publishing – once each user has created and saved a remix of music they listen to, it will be uploaded the SiDE website that allows exchange of media files

6. Peer Commentary – we plan to use the peer critique dynamic to allow users to comment on each other's work. This sensitizes them to use creative practice as a medium through which to give constructive criticism, as a means to teach by example positive communication as opposed to anti-social slander.
7. Virtual Music Economy – Once a body of work is created by the user group, it becomes a catalogue of creative cultural output that represents that community. We could imagine a virtual economy of credits and tokens for "purchase" and "exchange" of the contents created by the users.

6   Results

Based on this research work plan, we conducted a pilot study with our first partner, Generator Music. Generator is a leading regional and national agency for the development of popular music. Among other things, Generator provides a variety of programs for regional music business development, industry skill-building, and for the support for emerging and aspiring young musicians. One of the programs covered by Generator is an Urban Music Training (UMT) program for aspiring young musicians (from DJs to instrumentalists and vocalists) which supports them in creating, recording and performing their own music, as well as helps them organize and promote events and provides them with professional level training for entering the music industry. Generator tends to target youth from difficult neighborhoods who would benefit the most from engaging in such a program. Young people enrolled in the program represent a wide diversity of ethnic and educational backgrounds and ages. Generator encourages musical innovation and supports high-quality professional level endresults that the young people can take pride in and potentially enter the music business. UMT thus displays an aim to nurture the young people's self-esteem and open up professional opportunities. One of the UMT classes called UMT: BEATS is targeted towards DJs and urban music producers and runs twice a week after school hours over a period of 12 weeks. Another one called UMT: PLAY is focused on instrument playing in band formations, and runs each year for a week, full-time. Each program ends with a public performance in settings of professional standard.

Our collaboration with Generator consisted of contributing to the UMT program by exposing young people to interactive music technologies, as well as designing participatory activities aimed towards technology-supported creative engagement in physical and community space. The first part of the process in working with UMT was an approach phase consisting of reciprocal visits, demos and focused discussions that have lead to potential workshop ideas. This was followed by a short planning phase that resulted in a proposal for a 'Remix Your Instrument' pilot workshop, which we delivered shortly thereafter. The workshop took place during UMT: PLAY and aimed to build on the young people's existing musical skills. At the same time, it aimed to open a new world of possibilities and musical innovation to them and make a connection between urban electronic music and the physicality of instrument playing. Split into groups, the young people got to experiment with augmenting music instruments with sensors (pressure, light intensity, bend, movement etc) that modified the sounds that they produced. We used open-source, easily programmable hardware and software that we packaged in simple and approachable modules, in order to let the young people quickly learn how to use them while giving them a have chance to modify them themselves. Young people in each group collaborated to make music: playing instruments, using the sensor they were provided with, and modifying sound effects. Some even used their own mobile phones, voices and other resources at hand in the process. This workshop was successful in getting the young people excited and engaged in playing with innovative interactive music technology. One group was even eager to continue playing with the technology after the workshop and kept its module for the rest of week.

The next activities will take place over a longer period of time, within the UMT: BEATS training program. They will consist of three workshops centered on the use of mobile phones and MP3 players; technologies that young people are fairly familiar with and enjoy using [23]. These 'Remix Your 'Hood' (neighborhood) workshops will make use of RJDJ [24], an off-the-shelf free reactive music application that remixes ambient sounds into music in real time, in a way related to e.g. [25], typically through headphones. This enables one to see their own environment with new eyes, engage with it, and be creative with it in context. Various so-called 'scenes' (sound processing options) are available in RJDJ, together with the possibility to record the resulting music and share it online. Here as well, there is a DIY dimension to the technology: it is built on top of an open-source environment, which allows one to create their own scenes. Workshops are currently sketched out to be the following: 1) sound-walks with existing RJDJ scenes and brainstorming design session; 2) a programming session for composing one's own scenes; 3) a "make your own speakers/sound-parasites" DIY hacking workshop for turning any surface into a speaker – from junk boxes to windows in urban space. The last workshop will end with a performance in public space, with the everyday environment used as a resource for creation and an interface for performance. Besides taking pride in the creative potentials of the mundane of their neighborhood environment, this process aims to foster locally-rooted and original musical innovation which may give a sense of "representing" one's own community.

Throughout our collaboration with Generator in this phase of the SiDE project, we are interested in observing how young people interact with such creative interactive technologies and appropriate them, as well as explore how this makes them engaged in their environment and with others. Based on findings from this, the following phase will transition to the participatory design of interactive prototypes for creativity and social inclusion of young people, a process where the input of the participants will help them bring social capital in technology development that will be deployed at the scale of the whole region.

7 Discussion

It was important to create a strategy of partnership that could connect our work in SiDE with ongoing regional inclusion work, in a way that would yield mutual benefit. Doing so brings several pragmatic benefits besides the deeper benefits of forging meaningful collaborative partnerships. These include ready access to established user groups, consultation with experienced and approved facilitators.

Working with partners reveals a two-tiered structure, both institutionally and personally. Institutionally, the objects of study become as much the partner institution as the user group assembled by the partner. The latter in this view can be seen as "institutional" as it is an entity whose makeup is defined by the organizations in question and in this way are distinct from any group of users SiDE would assemble directly or that might emerge spontaneously.

The effectiveness of a working relationship is often influenced by institutional agendas. Community outreach and cultural sector organizations do not work in a research context, so the timescales for work and depth of enquiry are limited in this regard. Creating a fruitful research partnership where research extracts from the activity meaningful results is a not insignificant challenge.

At the user level, a two-tiered differentiation of beneficiaries emerges. Mediators and facilitators of the existing outreach activities have emerged as a crucial component in the delivery structure. The end user is the young person taking part in the workshop activity.

This has brought about an interesting dynamic in the participatory design activities. Facilitators are often quick to grasp the potential of SiDE technology and imagine the enhancement of activities they deliver. End users may lack the confidence to express themselves or think through a hunch or question they may have, but that creating an environment conducive to non-hierarchical discussion can bring out unexpected results.

The wish to compartmentalize these levels of user to better understand them is a natural tendency that brings up significant problems. It is attractive as a means to protect the end user from any institutional agenda that is represented by the presence of the mediator. However, ease of access, and the dynamics of trust would necessarily be impacted by isolating these user types.

Strategies for establishing partnerships and carrying out collaborative work feed directly into the research methodology. This can be summarized as:

1. Establishing criteria for partnership selection based on existing work, social benefit, and the potential for enhancement through digital technology
2. Identifying contribution to be made by SiDE through observation, participatory discussion, and pilot studies
3. Develop contribution by design, engineering, development, and deployment
4. Measure effect of contribution through observation, discussion, and analysis
5. Iterate

8 Conclusion

We have described the first field trial of the Creative Media group in the large scale project, Social Inclusion through the Digital Economy. In this trial, we partnered with Generator Music, a regional music development charity with an existing user base of young people from Newcastle upon Tyne. We put in place a process of acclimatization and participatory consultation that led to the conception of music technology sessions that introduced interactive music techniques to enhance an existing workshop program.

Our approach meant that the participants are working directly with materials that are the music they listen to. They re-appropriate and become pro-active with media they heretofore only passively consumed. The user group here, young people, represent an interesting challenge in digital inclusion and accessibility work. They are the born digital generation, so use of digital technology is not the problem. The problem is not technology use, but a sense of empowerment. Rather seeing mobile music as a consumer entertainment medium, we sought to communicate the simple message that with the right tools, music can be made interactive, and becomes a democratized medium for personal expression.

The enthusiasm that the young people demonstrated in the workshop sessions fulfills the hypothesis that novel forms of interaction with digital media can unlock access to creative practice processes for social benefit. This points to the possibility that from this we could identify forms of knowledge that are being shared that could result in the acquisition of transferrable skills that would permit the young people in question to engage more fully with broader aspects of contemporary digital society. In this way we consider that our approach has potential benefits in the area of social innovation.

This work applies the technique of triangulation across disciplines. We used participatory design methodology from human-computer interaction (HCI) research to introduce interactive music technologies from New Interfaces for Musical Expression (NIME) practice, and studied the outcomes from a social science perspective. This represented a form of action-based research situated in real life situations, in the wild. The use of advanced digital technologies was found to be attractive to both the young people as well as to the workshop facilitators. Carrying out the field trial hi-lighted higher level institutional differences between interactive media research and community arts outreach work that point to both potential benefits as well as issues to be resolved in future work. This provides initial results and reflection on the application of creative digital media practice in a social inclusion setting.

References

1. Schwarz, H.-P.: Media-Art-History: Media Museum. Prestel, Munich (1997)
2. Grau, O.: MediaArtHistories. MIT Press, Cambridge (2007)
3. Reisinger, G., Daniels, D.: Net Pioneers 1.0: Contextualizing Early Net-Based Art. Sternberg Press, Berlin (2010)
4. Dodge, C., Jerse, T.A.: Computer Music: Synthesis, Composition, and Performance. Schirmer Books, New York (1985)
5. Risset, J.-C.: Introductory Catalogue of Computer Synthesized Sounds. Bell Telephone Laboratories, Murray Hill (1969)
6. Poupyrev, I., Lyons, M.J., Fels, S., Blaine, T.: New Interfaces For Musical Expression Workshop. In: CHI 2001 Extended Abstracts (2001)
7. Silver, H.: Policies to combat social exclusion: A French-British comparison. International Institute for Labour Studies, Geneva (1995)
8. Compaine, B.M.: The Digital Divide: Facing a Crisis or Creating a Myth? MIT Press, Cambridge (2001)
9. Warschauer, M.: Technology and Social Inclusion: Rethinking the Digital Divide. MIT Press, Cambridge (2004)

10. Katz, J., Rice, R.: Social Consequences of Internet Use: Access, Involvement, and Interaction. MIT Press, Cambridge (2002)
11. Digital Britain. Department for Culture, Media and Sport, Department for Business, Innovation and Skills, London (2009)
12. Dench, G., Flower, T., Gavron, K.: Young at Eighty. Carcanet, Manchester (1995)
13. Social Inclusion through the Digital Economy, http://www.side.ac.uk
14. Abras, C., Maloney-Krichmar, D., Preece, J.: User-Centered Design. In: Bainbridge, W. (ed.) Encyclopedia of Human-Computer Interaction. Sage Publications, Thousand Oaks (2004)
15. Vredenburg, K., Mao, J.Y., Smith, P.W., Carey, T.: A survey of user-centered design practice. In: Proceedings of the SIGCHI Conference on Human Factors in Computing Systems, pp. 471–478. ACM Press, New York (2002)
16. Jasanoff, S.: States of Knowledge: The Co-Production of Science and the Social Order. Routledge, Oxford (2006)
17. Gibbons, M., Limoges, C., et al.: The New Production of Knowledge: The dynamics of science and research in contemporary societies. Sage Publications, Thousand Oaks (1994)
18. Oudshoorn, N., Pinch, T.: How Users Matter: The Co-Construction of Users And Technology. MIT Press, Cambridge (2003)
19. Leadbeater, C.: We-think: Mass innovation, not mass production: The Power of Mass Creativity. Profile Books, London (2008)
20. Jo, K., Tanaka, A.: The Music Participates. In: Schroeder, F. (ed.) Performing Technology: User Content and the New Digital Media. Cambridge Scholars Publishing, Newcastle upon Tyne (2009)
21. Arnstein, S.R.: A Ladder of Citizen Participation. Journal of the American Institute of Planners 35(4), 216–224 (1969)
22. Mackay, W.E., Fayard, A.-L.: HCI, Natural Science and Design: A Framework for Triangulation Across Disciplines. In: Proc. DIS 1997, Amsterdam, The Netherlands (1997)
23. Unterfrauner, E., Marschalek, I.: ICT and Mobile Phones as Resources for Marginalised Youth. In: Proc. Interaction Design and Children, IDC 2009 (2009)
24. Reality Jockey, http://www.rjdj.me
25. Gaye, L., Mazé, R., Holmquist, L.E.: Sonic City: The Urban Environment as a Musical Interface. In: Proc. NIME (2003)

Opening the Can:
Public Interaction with Ready-Made Contents

Shlomo Dubnov[1] and Philippe Codognet[2]

[1] Music Department,
University of California in San Diego
La Jolla, CA, USA
sdubnov@ucsd.edu
[2] CNRS / UPMC/ University of Tokyo
JFLI, Information Technology Center,
2-11-16 Yayoi, Bunkyo-ku
113-8658 Tokyo, Japan
codognet@jfli.itc.u-tokyo.ac.jp

Abstract. We present a system for public interaction during presentations of non-interactive readymade (canned) materials such as films or pre-composed performances. Using concepts of user back-channeling, moderator and shared canvas, the system allows a significant part of an art piece that is actually happing "in the heads" of the audience to be shared in parallel or in sequential manner with the main show. We also briefly present the historical background of the blind manipulation of symbols (canned contents) and argue that a new cognitive paradigm is at work with user interaction in computer-based entertainment and digital art.

1 Introduction

Most of the contents on the web are not interactive. Videos, music, images and other media are abundantly produced by professionals and amateurs and put on the web as readymade contents that express their creators' own voices. Even though most of these contents are available for reuse under various kinds of fair use licenses, only a small fraction of it indeed finds its way into other productions. User interaction with such contents is usually limited to search or recommendation of related contents and textual commenting. Even then, the sometimes dubious quality of recommendations and the shallow comments leave most of the contents unaltered in terms of how much a user can learn or benefit from other people impressions or from the activity that the surrounds the original creator's readymade idea. In this paper we are interested in exploring the question of reusing these readymade contents by turning them into a focal element of a larger production such as placing them in an interactive system that combines fixed contents with user interaction, creating a framework that actually encourages more active and sustainable user engagement. Using the term of "canned contents" to denote these readymade media, we consider ways of creating open systems that provide some combination of interoperability, portability and open

R. Nakatsu et al. (Eds.): ECS 2010, IFIP AICT 333, pp. 179–189, 2010.
© IFIP International Federation for Information Processing 2010

standards for applying these artifacts to creation of new cultural experiences. This also bears resemblance to open system of learning, where information is sourced from multiple sources to promote active learning that focuses the responsibility of learning on learners. There are several models of instruction that promoting discovery learning by encouraging learners to be engaged during learning and cognitively active.

In applying these ideas to entertainment in general and the arts and music in particular we face with several unique problems. On practical level there is a certain amount of professionalism, both in terms of the technical skills and artistic expression that is required for producing such contents that might be prohibitive to most of the users. One cannot expect large audiences to exhibit the same amount of control and awareness of the impact of media manipulations as someone who had the time and possibility to perfect those details. Moreover, we want to open the readymade contents to include expressions by audiences that might result in shift of attention from the contents themselves to what other audiences think about them. This shift towards social media is current with the burgeoning trend to segment the fans base for artistic creation into smaller groups rather than maintain a central sense of accepted quality and an overall established taste. But rather then considering practicalities, we would like to draw the reader's attention also to the broader questions of the significance and cultural role of public interaction with canned contents. We will show that interaction through commentary and other exegetic practices puts the audience in the role of "significance givers", a practice that had been already a dominant force in shaping cultural and religious thought in early scholastic practices.

2 The Binary Computer and "Blind Thought"

The current success of the computer as a universal information-processing machine essentially lies in the fact that there exists a universal language in which many different kinds of information (text, images, music, videos, etc) could be encoded and that this language could be fully mechanized. Computers are artifacts aimed at storing and manipulating information encoded in various ways, information being basically anything that could be algorithmically generated. In 1697, the German philosopher and mathematician G. W. Leibniz invented binary notation and considered his discovery to be *imago creationis*, that is, at the image of the Creation, see [3] for details. He used the motto *unus ex nihilo omnia* : "from nothing, the One creates everything"... Indeed, with the numbers zero and one only, all others could be constructed and therefore the whole universe of numbers, in the same way as, in Christian theology, God created the world from nothingness. This idea is perfectly at work in current computer entertainment systems and videogames, where complex virtual universes are built from simple (but long) strings of 0's and 1's. Therefore, digital computer technologies have been able to digest the whole world little by little, dimension after dimension, reifying indeed Leibniz' dream. Binary notation thus became the Universal Language to describe non only the linearity of numbers and texts, but also the flatland of images and, moreover, virtual environments in 3D.

The power of the computer lies in its ability to blindly manipulate symbols representing any encoded information; information that will be transmitted, reinterpreted and decoded later to become humanly intelligible. Indeed, this idea of performing, within a given symbol system, operations on symbolic objects in a purely syntactical manner, without reference to their usual meaning or modus operandi (for instance because their meaning is unknown) has also been proposed by Leibniz in the seventeenth century as the basis of combinatorics, and he named it the *cogitatio coeca*, that is, "blind thought". This reasoning process thus operates on atomic signs (that could not be further interpreted), as in mathematical algebra when the resolution of problem is conducted by a computation involving operations on symbolic variables and arithmetic terms, without any idea of what the variables actually refer to (e.g. in equation solving). Leibniz will use this paradigm in mathematics and combinatorial systems as an *ars inventendi* (art of inventing), and for laying the grounds of modern semiotic systems, but the roots of these concepts has to be dug out further back in the *ars magna* (great art) of the Franciscan monk Ramon Llull (1232 - 1316). Interestingly, some authors relate lullian systems to the Jewish Kabbalah, as the use of combinatorics is at the core of several processes in the Kabbalah, for instance in the ecstatic Kabbalah of Abraham Abulafia (1240-1291) [10]. Anyway, Llull's ground-breaking work was highly praised by many medieval and renaissance philosophers and there was an abundance of lullian treaties written up to the seventeenth century, in particular by Giordano Bruno (1548 - 1600) [12]. The importance Bruno gave to the syntactic form of signs over the semantics is clearly stated in the *De lampade combinatoria lulliana* (1586): "One should not pay attention to the properties of terms but only to the fact that they define an order, a texture, an architecture" [8]. For further details linking these pioneers to the birth of modern logic at the turn of the 20th century and, see [2].

3 Virtual Worlds, Interaction and Immersion

Computers are massively widespread in the contemporary society and are taking major part in our everyday life. They are certainly, in a subtle but nevertheless very concrete way, developing new cognitive abilities which open the public to a different perspective on the world. Portable wireless handheld devices and GPS-enabled smart objects let us foresee the so-called ubiquitous networking society that will soon be ours, surrounding us with a data-gas of information-filled radio waves, a new ecosystem to be decoded and understood by digital machines only. However let us first look at the last decade of the 20th century and the development of 3D virtual worlds, which popularized computer entertainment and video games and express an important paradigm shift, which is not without resonance with what was happening in contemporary art at the same time.

From the forgotten pioneering work of Morton Heilig (1926-1997) who patented, back in 1960, a device composed of two small TV monitors placed in front of one's eyes and Head Mounted Displays (HMDs), created at NASA in 1984 following the original ideas of Ivan Sutherland back in 1968 to the CAVE systems [4], an immersive system created by the EVL group at the University of Illinois in 1992, and today's advanced systems incorporating haptic devices, Virtual Reality technologies are getting closer and closer to the fantasy dream of the "Ultimate Display" [15]. The scientific experiments or artistic installations developed by using immersive 3D technology compel the spectator to enter within a simulated world instead of just watching it from the outside, as a mere series of photographs, a predefined movie or even a monitor display. On the small screen and in the domain of computer entertainment, the revolution of 3D games with a first-person point of view and subjective camera happened at the same period, with games such as Wolfenstein 3D (1992) and the magnificent Doom (1993). Despite an incredibly simple scenario (« hunt-and-kill ») and rudimentary graphics, the immersive effect was totally operational, maybe even too much for certain people, as the gamer was totally engaged - mentally if not physically - in the virtual universe. Then some innovative game design tricks appeared which would further enhance immersion, in particular the possibility to not only wander in the virtual space but also to interact and use objects. This was introduced by Half-Life (1998) through the use of the « E » key of the keyboard: by using this key and pointing on certain objects, the gamer could trigger some predefined action, such as calling an elevator, opening a valve, or even drive a railways bucket. This "manipulability" of the world, although extremely simple as each object contained its own teleology, induced nevertheless a deep feeling of immersion and of coherence in the virtual world. This was further achieved in games like the superb Metal Gear Solid (1999) and Deus Ex (2000) where clicking on an object could lead to some complex manipulation : virtual computers could connect to Internet and let you read your email (or hack someone else's) and virtual cash could be drown from ATMs ... Thanks to the increasing power of CPUs and GPUs, such interactivity has been vastly improved nowadays, with games incorporating impressive physics-based simulation engines making it possible to manipulate and use objects in a very realistic manner, cf. e.g. Half-life 2 (2004) or Metal Gear Solid 4 (2008).

Interestingly, immersive virtual worlds and 3D RFPS games amount to a shift from the cartographic paradigm, found for instance in board games such as Go, Chess or so-called God-games (*Sim City, the Sims, Back and White*, etc) to enter the ichnographic paradigm, that is, based on the notion of path. We move away from the metaphor of the map to the metaphor or the path, we move from the third person point of view (God's eye) to the first-person point of view (our eye). As Morpheus said to Neo in the blockbuster movie The Matrix (1999), "There is a difference between knowing the path and walking the path". We are thus leaving, in the virtual experience and exploration of an unknown artificial world, the Cartesian paradigm of the Euclidean, homogeneous and objective space in which points could be described in an allo-centric manner by coordinates (x, y, z) for a new paradigm of a more constructive, ego-centric, and indeed subjective space. This is somehow backtracking to the ideas of the French mathematician Henri Poincare, founder of modern topology, who considered that a point in space should be described by the transformation that has to be applied to reach it. Hence space is represented as a set of situated actions. No one knows the totality of the map; no one can picture or order the territory in any comprehensive way, even abstractly. The complexity of the structure ("graph" to follow the word of Michel Serres, "rhizome" for Deleuze, or "network" in the contemporary terminology) cannot be conceptually apprehended nor depicted. It is worth noticing that, by moving from a 2D to a 3D model, some information is in some way lost. Lost first is the idea of a comprehensive, full-blown representation – such as in the map. This is precisely what happens also with the Word Wide Web: no one is able to draw the whole map of the Web, maybe only can we store it on an army of data centers ... We can only explore the Web by following paths, references from one location to another and performing actions, which will open to new paths and possibilities, and so on so forth ...

4   Active Cognition

A key point in immersive environments and computer entertainment is the place of the spectator into the system and not outside, as can be found in normal computer-human interaction. The ability of games to lead to deep integration of the player into the gameplay and to therefore amount to cognitive immersion, by letting him perform intuitive and meaningful *actions*, is certainly the main novelty of this genre. In the paradigm of the interface, interaction has often been considered as a necessarily reduced and incomplete dialogue between the human and the machine, as a means of access that will always be frustrating since it is always limited and imperfect. Immersive virtual environments and now pervasive technologies are doing their utmost to devise interfaces that are more or less natural to allow for an improved interaction with the digital systems. However, one should not forget that immersion is cognitive before being perceptive, the virtual "reality" is clearly being re-invented and re-created by the viewer and not just perceived and undergone. As Marcel Duchamp put it in 1914, referring to his well-known Readymade artworks : "the viewers make the artwork" (in French: « *Ce sont les regardeurs qui font l'oeuvre* ») [7]. By performing actions in a virtual world, or by interpreting (i.e. creating the meaning of) a conceptual artwork, we are engaged in *active cognition*: we learn by doing. In the cognitive philosophy of [11,16], one key idea is the contingency of cognition: "living systems are cognitive systems, and living as a process is a process of cognition." [10]. Varela proposed the concept of enaction: in the enactive paradigm, the subject is always conceived as situated and interacting with his environment. Cognition is thus inseparable from the experience of the world, cognition is conceived as an embodied action. We should also remember, in the same line of thought, the words of the cybernetics pioneer Heinz von Foerster: "If you desire to see, learn how to act" [17]. For him, "perceiving is making" and all perception is therefore created by the subject's action upon his environment; perception is active. Experiments have shown that sensory organs (in animals and humans) can be trained to better perceive expected signals before the brain considers them. Therefore, by analogy, it would not be unreasonable to think that a key issue in understanding experiences in virtual worlds would be the ability to perform actions and observe their consequences in order to learn the rules governing the artificial environment – maybe simply by trial and error. This is obviously easier to do in a virtual world than in the real one, and this cognitive process is therefore put to use in many computer games and now intuitively performed by video-game-educated kids. It might be possible that this ability to develop cognition by action is indeed gradually replacing the more classical humanist tradition of learning by books and letters.

5   Exegeses and the Role of a Commentator

In his 1945 article [1], Vannevar Bush described a futuristic device "in which an individual stores all his books, records, and communications, and which is mechanized so that it may be consulted with exceeding speed and flexibility... When the user is building a trail, he names it, inserts the name in his code book, and taps it out on his keyboard. Before him are the two items to be joined, projected onto adjacent viewing positions. At the bottom of each there are a number of blank code spaces, and a pointer is set to indicate one of these on each item. The user taps a single key, and the items are permanently joined". The interesting thing about this device is that Bush envisioned a mechanistic method of combining memory trails that only requires a single click. The enactment is limited to some earlier recording of data into the computer that is personally meaningful, while the operation of extracting or creating new meaning is assumed to arise from manipulation of the syntactic form that this data bears, which could be "blindly" handled by a machine. With the advance of pattern matching and machine learning technologies, indeed some progress was made in terms of automatic recombination of cultural artifacts, such as imitation of a personal musical style through Leibnizian-like combinatorics [5]. The advance of artificial intelligence technology actually extended the concept of atomic signs to codebooks of arbitrary size that could be dynamically acquired from observing redundancies and collecting statistics from prerecorded digital artifacts. This mechanical recombination symbolizes the step of moving beyond replication of real life environments through virtual representations of physical objects, to representation of semantics that is encoded through some careful parsing of the same universal binary representation, but now relative to a specific domain, personal memory trail or statistically derived code book.

The act of joining two or more data records into a combined meaningful whole puts an exegetic pressure on the process of combining this data. In early religious traditions we witness the need for reconciliatory techniques that arose from the need to harmonize collections of conflicting canonical texts, generating abstract pantheons of gods, monotheistic deities or cosmological principles. Over many centuries Neo-Platonic, Neo-Confucian, Vedic and Talmudic traditions employed commentarial techniques to show unity in disjoint collections of texts, with increasingly complex and hierarchical visions of reality being constructed through hermeneutical approaches to scripture. Moreover, it is claimed that exegetical techniques are largely culturally invariant, with differences of producing monotheistic deities or linear time versus metaphysical principles or cyclical models of time being dependent on the text they were operating on [9].

6   The Opera of Meaning

The idea of opera of meaning (OoM) is combining the syntactic, "blind" manipulations of the universal binary language of the readymade presentation with enactment of a viewer / user, whose actions serve to validate the cognitive relevance of these digital artifacts. Implemented on the web, OoM employs a variety of exegetic techniques to direct a group of viewers in synchronized or semi-synchronized way towards more active perception and cognizance of the meaning of the "canned" story, while at the same time using the audience expressions to expand the scope of the presentation contents. Designed originally as a format of presentation of media contents, such as dramatic work, entertainment or lecture, it uses a realization of a script to push to the viewers a collection of electronic objects for interacting with the story meaning. Some of these object are created "on the fly" based on structural analysis of the canned contents and/or analytics of the audience inputs. As all art finally happens in the heads of the audience, the system allow to tap at "the silent conversation" that follows any concert or show, which is an essential element missed by a lot of interactive art. Through processes of linking, association, abstraction, correlation, syncretic fusion and mashup, the semantic scope of the presentation is constantly expanded and contracted, turning a passive viewing into a dynamic scenario of negotiating and contextualizing the meaning of the canned contents according to suggestions of the audience, controlled or orchestrated by a moderator. Exegetic techniques employed in OoM included textual commenting and threaded responses, voting through polls, ranking, image selection, linking and searching, text analytics, sentiment and topic analysis, summarizing, visualization and more. In principle, any web service that provides search, analytics and data mining, can be included in the presentation and triggered from the script at an appropriate moment. The results of these processes are then summarized and shared with the rest of the audience in parallel with the main show.

The following figure shows the elements of OoM, which comprise of several different modalities that keep evolving as we more scenarios to experiment with the system are developed. The main elements in the system are the canned contents, the audience back channel, the moderator function and the shared canvas. In the figure below the presence of the "canned" contents is denoted as "presentation". The presentation can be a visual, audio or textural rendering of a story that the audiences will perceive. This may be combined with a script that contains structural representation of the story, such as metadata or other descriptors of the canned elements. This information is essential in order to provide more knowledge to the moderator function, as will be explained below, as well as to automate the push of related contents and interactive widgets. In case this information is missing, automatic analysis, such as media semantic processing can be applied to the presentation to try to provide a model according to which the data from the users can be analyzed. For instance, in an ongoing project we use correspondence analysis of the text of a screen-play [12] to create a set of filters or rankings on audience comments "in the context" of the story narrative. In another project [6], association of the user input to the story line is proposed by creation of a metadata space in Mathematical Model of Meaning.

Once the relation between the audience input and the story are established, the communication are bound to shared canvas through a moderator, whose role as an information processing element is to negotiate and prioritize the display of user inputs, possibly by compact visualization or some other summarization process. The additional element of "artificial participant" suggests a possibility for a direct mechanistic intervention of a computational process in the user back channel without intervention of the moderator, as will be explained later.

In terms of functional description, one of the central features of Opera of Meaning is that the public can interact with related contents during the story presentation either privately, or by sharing it with other audiences by posting to designate publicly viewed display areas. The shared canvas provides a way for rendering the user communication in the "back channel" in parallel to watching the main story. Using associative search or semantic database management, additional contents that are relevant to the main story are made available to the users. These contents can be shared at predetermined times on private or shared canvas, depending on their purpose and available screen real estate. It should be also noted that the audience can not directly

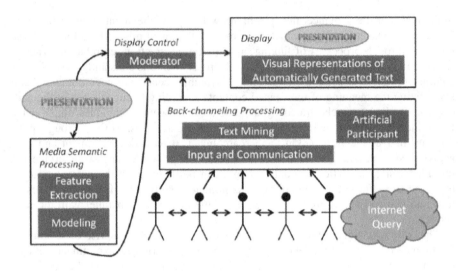

Fig. 1. System diagram describing the different OoM components

interact or modify the canned contents of the main presentation, except for cases where a specific role for the shared canvas had been integrated in the design of the main show. Examples of such integration could be use of shared canvas as a back drop in theatrical presentation as part of the set design, or including debate and media sharing episodes intermittently with the canned contents as part of a visual montage, or using audience input to create the remix or collage on the fly, and so on.

Another central role is that of a moderator who "listens" to the input from the presentation and the audience back channel and reports back its results on the shared canvas display, in parallel or in sequence with the canned presentation. To give a concrete example, the moderator can summarize the ongoing chat in the audience and post it to the shared display as a tag cloud. Moderator can also create a tag cloud from the text that accompanies the main presentation. In such a case the tag cloud representation might combine both sources of information – that of the main story and that from the audience. More sophisticated application that we currently explore are automatic creation of web mashups that are derived from topic analysis of the backchannel, through automatic search and keyword expansion "in context" of the semantics of the canned presentation.

In many cases, asking the viewers to post a comment might be the most difficult part in getting the discussion rolling. The role of the artificial participant is to "break the ice" by providing an initial input regarding the canned contents. An important distinction between the artificial participant and the moderator is that the moderator "summarizes" the overall activity that goes on in the back channel and uses that to alter or augment the presentation, while the artificial participant communicates privately with audience members, either through textual comments or graphical widgets, triggering responses and provoking participation.

An example of the screens and comments generated by OoM are given in Figure 2. This is one of multiple pages that were running during a panel session in the Theater Deparment in UCSD on activism in the arts. The central image represents a theatrical

Fig. 2. An example screen of OoM for an event regarding Art Activism

Fig. 3. Use of OoM as a backdrop and immpersive environment in a mixed music and media story telling show with audience participation

group called "Guerilla Gilrs", and it was brought up to demonstrate an example of feminist art activism, embedded from the web after searching for contents related to the topic of the main presentation [art activism, theatre, feminism]. The lower half of the screen shows the audience chat on the right and a dynamic text cloud on the left. Each one of the display elements comprises a separate object in the OoM system.

Other functions of the system include administrator functions for manual creation of web pages of the related contents, tools for creating polls and a control panel for arranging the different performance objects both in terms of their layout on the page and timing their appearance in synch with the main show.

As last figure we present a photo of a deployment of such system in a live concert situation. In this piece the deployment of the system was integrated with the design of the projection space in such a way that the displays used for related contents and shared canvas actually surrounded the audience creating an immersive experience. The main presentation is the performance in the middle, while the audiences with laptops interact with each other and with the system [13].

6   Conclusion

In this paper we presented a system for public interaction during presentations of non-interactive readymade (canned) materials such as films or pre-composed performances. Using concepts of user back-channeling, moderator and shared canvas, the system allows a significant part of an art piece that is actually happing "in the heads" of the audience to be shared in parallel or in sequential manner with the main show. Sharing audience impressions not only contributes to the experience and understanding of the work, but actually creates a new role for the viewer as a second person "significance giver". We discussed how this type of engagement changes the role of the spectator from being either third or first person, or being either a passive viewer or an direct operator of digital contents, into a second person role whose operative is one of a establishing the meaning of an artwork through a process negotiating with other viewers or addressing other associated contents. The setup allows mixed attendance modes that combine first person interaction among attendees directly or through a moderator, and a third person mode of viewing with regards to the main story, with its associated freedom of imagination and deliberation. This mixed operational mode has both advantages and disadvantages.

We also discussed the broader questions of the cultural role of public interaction with canned contents and showed that interaction through commentary and other exegetic techniques can become a dominant force in shaping cultural thought, such as the case with religious thought in early scholastic practices. The name "Opera of Meaning" is intended to emphasize the interplay of meanings and exchange of opinions that occur during performance of a story. This approach is related to works that explore social and educational roles of film and theater media, and is inspired by methods of debate and commentary that are common in traditional religious studious situations, as mentioned above.

References

1. Bush, V.: As We May Think. In: Atlantic Monthly (July 1945)
2. Codognet, P.: Combinatorics, Randomness, and the Art of Invention. In: Assayag, G., Gerzso, A. (eds.) New Computational Paradigms for Computer Music. IRCAM/Editions Delatour (2009)
3. Codognet, P.: Ancient Images and New Technologies: the Semiotics of the Web. Leonardo 35(1) (January 2002)
4. Cruz-Neira, C., Sandin, D.J., DeFanti, T.A.: Surround-Screen Projection-Based Virtual Reality: The Design and Implementation of the CAVE. In: Proceedings of SIGGRAPH 1993, pp. 135–142. ACM Press, New York (1993)
5. Dubnov, S., Assayag, G.: Universal Prediction Applied to Music Generation with Style. In: Mathematics and Music. Springer, Heidelberg (2002)
6. Dubnov, S., Kiyoki, Y.: Opera of Meaning: film and music performance with semantic associative search. In: Proceedings of Frontiers in Artificial Intelligence and Applications, Information Modelling and Knowledge Bases XX, vol. 190, pp. 384–391 (2009)
7. Duchamp, M.: Marchand du sel, texts collected and edited by M. Sanouillet. Editions Le Terrain Vague, Paris (1959)
8. Eco, U.: The Search for the Perfect Language. Wiley-Blackwell (1997)
9. Farmer, S., Henderson, J.B., Robinson, P.: Commentary Traditions and the Evolution of Premodern Religious and Philosophical Systems: A Cross-Cultural Model. In: Kolloquium zu historischen und methodologischen Aspekten der Kommentierung von Text. University of Heidelberg (July 1997)
10. Idel, M.: The mystical experience in Abraham Abulafia. State University of New York Press (1988)
11. Maturana, H., Varela, F.: Autopoiesis and Cognition: The realization of the living. Reidel, Dordrecht (1980)
12. Murtagh, F., Ganz, A., McKie, S.: The structure of narrative: the case of film scripts. Pattern Recognition 42, 302–312 (2009); See discussion: Merali, Z.: Here's looking at you, kid. Nature 453, 708 (2008)
13. Ramsey, D., Sutro, D.: An Opera of Meaning Integrates Live Performance, Internet, Multimedia and Audience Participation at UC San Diego, UCSD News (February 2008)
14. Shearman, J.: Only Connect...: Art and the Spectator in the Italian Renaissance. Princeton University Press, Princeton (1994)
15. Sutherland, I.E.: The Ultimate Display. In: Proceedings of IFIP Congress, pp. 506–508 (1965)
16. Varela, F., Thompson, E., Rosch, E.: The Embodied Mind: Cognitive science and human experience. The MIT Press, Cambridge (1991)
17. von Foerster, H.: Observing Systems. Intersystems Publications, Salinas (1984)
18. Yates, F.: Lull and Bruno. In: Collected Essays I. Routledge and Kegan Paul, London (1982)

Cultural Computing – How to Investigate a Form of Unconscious User Experiences in Mixed Realities

Matthias Rauterberg, Jun Hu, and Geert Langereis

Industrial Design, Eindhoven University of Technology, The Netherlands
g.w.m.rauterberg@tue.nl

Abstract. This paper presents a new direction of research in user experiences and cognitive science. The problem addressed is drawing on results from different disciplines: psychology, brain and cognitive sciences, physics, and interaction design. As main objective we plan the empirical validation of the claim: Cultural computing as enabling technology for social transformations. Cultural computing is based on a form of cultural translation that uses scientific methods to capture and represent essential aspects of a particular culture. Cultural computing will enable particular cognitive and emotional responses from users as reflections on and of their inner, subliminal consciousness. Cultural computing is not only integrating cultural aspects into the interaction but also allowing the user to experience an interaction that is closely related to the core aspects of his/her own culture. As such it is important to understand one's cultural determinants and how to render them during the interaction. We will address individually and collectively the cultural determinants of the Western culture. Based on the given narrative 'Alice Adventures in Wonderland' we have already built the first demo version and plan to build an optimized version of a mixed reality installation to provide and investigate cultural user experiences. To address the research questions we propose three main research lines: (1) designing a mixed reality environment to provide certain unconscious user experiences; (2) inducing and measuring the changes in the individual's unconscious knowledge structure; and (3) empirical validation of a fundamentally new synchronization mechanism for sharing individual changes collectively. We hypothesize that there eventually exists an interconnecting knowledge field at the foundation of reality that conserves and conveys information collectively. This knowledge field looks like a possible candidate for a required 'supra-natural' memory for cultural knowledge to tap into for social transformations.

Keywords: cultural computing, mixed reality, social transformation, user experience, unconsciousness.

1 Introduction

This paper presents a new direction of research in user experiences and cognitive science [1]. The problem addressed is drawing on results from different disciplines: psychology, brain and cognitive sciences, physics, and interaction design [2]. The

R. Nakatsu et al. (Eds.): ECS 2010, IFIP AICT 333, pp. 190–197, 2010.
© IFIP International Federation for Information Processing 2010

main objective is the empirical validation of the claim: Cultural computing as ena-bling technology for social transformations [3]. Cultural computing is based on a form of cultural translation that uses scientific methods to capture and represent essential aspects of a culture. Cultural computing will enable particular cognitive and emotional responses from users as reflections on and of their inner, subliminal con-sciousness [4]. Cultural computing is not only integrating cultural aspects into the interaction but also allowing the user to experience an interaction that is closely re-lated to the core aspects of his/her own culture [5]. Hence it is important to under-stand one's cultural determinants and how to render them during the interaction [6].

For the Japanese culture the existing ZENetic computer [7] is an innovative table-top application to address cultural computing in the East (see also [8]). ZENetic com-puter "brings a kind of 'awakening' within users' 'information selves,' and strives to stimulate their unconscious imagination. As the system 'classifies' the user's personal-ity based on the composition of her sansui landscape design, it generates a story for the user, drawing her into an alternate world through the display" [9]. The following three main research lines can be foreseen to address our main research questions: (1) How to design a mixed reality (MR) environment to provide certain unconscious user experiences for Westerners [10-12]; (2) how to induce and measure the changes in the individual's unconscious knowledge structure due to these unusual experiences trig-gered by cultural computing [13]; and (3) which synchronization mechanism exist to share these individual changes collectively? [14-15]

2   Designing a Mixed Reality Environment for Subconscious User Experiences

Assuming the intended individual unconscious effects might be small [16-17] we have to achieve a maximum in user immersion/presence and therefore a high impact on the user's unconscious knowledge structure. The amount of user's immersion is influenced by several factors: the amount of sensory involvement [18], the richness of the narrative [19], amount of engagement through action [20], and perceived realism of the situation engaged [21]. Hence a MR installation is the best choice for an ex-perimental test bed. MR installations are close to a realistic environment, provides sufficient experimental control and a maximum of user engagement through physical actions. But which narrative as design concept for such MR is most appropriate? The narrative should touch on deep cultural dimensions, should be widely accepted, and should provide unusual user experiences. After rigorous selection the narrative of 'Alice adventures in wonderland' [22] was chosen. Several scenes of this narrative are already partially realized in the ALICE installation at TU/e [23]. This MR installation is 10 meter wide, 10 meter deep and 7 meter high. Inside this cube are following stages foreseen: (stage-1) in the park (investigating the relationship of bore-dom/curiosity and behavior [24]), (stage-2) down the rabbit hole (investigating the cognitive mechanisms for perceived movement), (3) 5-side virtual reality cave with 'eat me' and 'drink me' (investigating the cognitive mechanisms for self-perceived body size and body image [18, 25]), (4) pool of tears (investigating the effects of 'water' on emotions), (5) encounter with caterpillar (investigating the self-concept and ego [26]), and (6) discussion with Cheshire cat (investigating the relation between

logic and emotion [27]). So far the achieved state of our MR installation was sufficient for demonstrations and small experiments, but a full experience over all stages
for experiments still needs developments in technology and measurement procedures.

3 Measuring User's Effects on His/Her Unconscious Knowledge

Recent investigation in cognitive psychology of consciousness and unconsciousness
are promising. Most of the brain's energy consumption is not used for processing
responses to external stimuli; but what is this brain energy then for? [28-29]. One
possible answer is for subconscious information processing to forcast the future.
Dijksterhuis, Bos, Nordgren, and van Baaren [29-30] could show the advantages of the
unconscious information processing, and therefore they open a door to a new view on
the relationship towards unconsciousness [31-33]. The possible effects of extreme user
experiences on their cognitive structure can be addressed as follows: (1) through
psychological measures (e.g. Implicit Association Test, [34]), (2) through unobtrusive
observation via cameras of user's shown behaviour (incl. facial expressions [35]), (3)
through physiological sensors on the human body or in the neighbourhood [36-37], and
(4) measuring emotionally influenced quantum effects through dedicated hardware (i.e.
Random Event Generator - REG [38-39]). The Global Consciousness Project [40-42]
builds on astonishing experiments conducted over the past years, demonstrating that
human consciousness interacts with REGs, so that they produce non-random patterns.
For measuring unconsious processes, it is ultimately important not to affect the person
under test by the infringement of observing hardware. Therefore, we would like to
implement the system with option (4) rather than option (3).

The Implicit Association Test (IAT) focuses only on the implicit (unconscious)
part of cognition [34, 43]. The IAT measures differential (unconscious) association of
two target concepts with an attribute. The two concepts appear in a binary choice task
(e.g., *self* vs. *others* names), and the attribute in a second task (e.g., *pleasant* vs.
unpleasant words for an evaluation attribute). When instructions oblige highly
associated categories (e.g., *self* + *pleasant*) to share a response key, performance is
faster than when less associated categories (e.g., *others* + *pleasant*) share a key. This
response time performance difference implicitly measures differential association of
the two concepts with the attribute. We used already the IAT version that especially
measures self-concept [26]. The IAT seems to be a useful measure for the effects of
unconscious experiences.

One of the research questions is to which extent humans can unconsciously process
semantically rich information [33, 44]. Although the state of art is controversial, we
assume that in rich settings (see R1) unconscious processing takes place. The challeng
is how to measure these cognitive processes in an unobtrusive manner, e.g. compared
to fMRI scans [17, 45]; portable Electroencephalography (EEG) and Random Event
Generator (REG) might be an option.

Three different REGs are used[1]. The REG electronics produces 'white noise' based
on completely unpredictable quantum fluctuations. PEAR-REG is based on Johnson
noise (extremely low-level fluctuations in electron flow in a resistor due to thermal

---

[1] See at http://www.psyleron.com/reg1.aspx

influences). It has a built-in logic transformation (XOR) of every other bit from 1 to 0 or vice versa for eliminating any bias of the mean output of the device. The MICRO-REG utilizes on the Field-Effect Transistor for the 'white noise'. The ORION-REG uses two diodes which independently produce a random bitstream each. Nelson et al. [39] found empirical evidence for a replicable effect on data from a global network of REGs that is correlated with designated periods of intense collective human activity or engagement (e.g. September 11, 2001), but not with any other physical sources of influence.

4 Investigation of Synchronization Mechanism for Disseminating Changes

If we acknowledge that people's individual norms may deviate from an established collective norm, than we should identify a way to address these relationships [46]. Culture can only exist on the collective level, beyond the individual. The cultural determinates are mainly unconscious [12]: Culture is always ambient to individuals as carrier of cultural knowledge and collective as a synchronisation mechanism for the behaviour of these individuals. The following metaphor helps to describe this double nature of culture: 'the drop is in the ocean, but the ocean is in the drop as well'. Jung [47] has seen this with remarkable clarity and provides a framework to describe the knowledge structure of the collective unconsciousness. But what might this 'collective unconscious' be? A possible answer can be drawn from quantum physics.

Quantum physics describes the properties of matter and energy at near atomic scale [17]: (1) Quantum coherence (individual particles yield identity to a collective, unifying wave function). (2) Non-local quantum entanglement (spatially separated particle states are nonetheless connected or related [48-50]). (3) Quantum superposition (particles exist in two or more states or locations simultaneously). (4) Quantum state reduction or 'collapse of the wave function' (super positioned particles reduce or collapse to specific choices) [51]. Of particular interest is the non-local quantum entanglement that shows there might be an interconnecting layer in nature, beyond the forces we are familiar with [50]. Information might be stored in some yet unknown way, and we might tap into this knowledge field, or exchange information with other minds, if the necessary conditions of 'sympathetic resonance' exist (see also the 'morphic resonance' concept of Sheldrake [52], and the Global Conscious Project [39]). Now the remaining question is how can a cognitive system interact with such kind of knowledge field? [53].

The Penrose–Hameroff 'OrchOR' model portrays consciousness as quantum computation in microtubules which collapse or reduce by an objective factor related to quantum gravity. Penrose [54-55] proposed a quantum gravity mechanism that following periods of preconscious quantum computation tubulin super-positions self-collapse at an objective threshold. During classical phases protein connections associated with microtubules provide input. The basic ideas are [56, p. 160-161]: (1) Conformational states of individual tubulins within neuronal microtubules are determined by quantum mechanical London forces within the tubulin interiors which can induce conformational quantum superposition; (2) in superposition tubulins 'communicate' with entangled tubulins in the same microtubule, and in other microtubules in the same neuron; (3) quantum states in microtubules in any given neuron may extend to microtubules in neighboring neurons, and through macroscopic regions of brain via tunneling through gap junctions; (4) quantum states of tubulin, resp. microtubules are isolated/protected from environmental decoherence by biological mechanisms which include phases of actin gelation, ordered water, coherent pumping and topological quantum error correction; (5) microtubule quantum computations, resp. superpositions are tuned or 'orchestrated' (Orch) by microtubule-associated proteins during a classical, liquid phase which with a quantum, solid state phase; (6) following periods of pre-conscious quantum computation (e.g. on the order of tens to hundreds of milliseconds) tubulin superpositions reduce or collapse by Penrose quantum gravity 'objective reduction' (OR). The classical output states which result from the OR process are chosen non-algorithmically ('non-computably') and then govern neurophysiologic events by binding of microtubule-associated proteins, regulating synapses and membrane functions etc.; (7) the reduction or 'self-collapse' in the orchestrated objective reduction 'OrchOR' model is suggested to be a 'conscious moment', (see Penrose's quantum gravity mechanism which ties the process to fundamental space-time geometry). According OrchOR model [57], quantum computation occurs in microtubules inside neurons. In the OrchOR model microtubules exist transiently in quantum superposition of two or more conformational states. Each OrchOR quantum computation determines classical output states of tubulin to establish starting conditions for the next conscious event [57-59].

We hypothesize that there eventually exists an interconnecting knowledge field at the foundation of our quantum reality that conserves and conveys information collectively. This knowledge field looks like a possible candidate for a required 'supranatural' memory for cultural knowledge to tap into for social transformations [60].

References

1. Nakatsu, R., Rauterberg, M.: Entertainment computing: Inaugural Editorial. Entertainment Computing 1(1), 1–7 (2009)
2. Nijholt, A., Bos, D.P.-O., Reuderink, B.: Turning shortcomings into challenges: Brain-computer interfaces for games. Entertainment Computing 1(2), 85–94 (2009)
3. Tosa, N., Matsuoka, S., Thomas, H.: Inter-culture computing: ZENetic computer. In: Elliott-Famularo, H. (ed.) ACM SIGGRAPH 2004 Emerging Technologies, p. 11. ACM, Los Angeles (2004)
4. Tosa, N.: Expression of emotion, unconsciousness with art and technology. In: Hatano, G., Okada, N., Tanabe, H. (eds.) Affective Minds, pp. 183–205. Elsevier, Amsterdam (2000)
5. Hu, J., Bartneck, C.: Culture matters: A study on presence in an interactive movie. Cyberpsychology and Behavior 11(5), 529–536 (2008)
6. Tosa, N.: Unconscious flow. Leonardo 33(5), 442 (2000)
7. Tosa, N., Matsuoka, S.: Recreating our selves: ZENetic computer. In: International Conference on Information Visualisation - IV 2003, pp. 614–618. IEEE Computer Society, Los Alamitos (2003)
8. Cheok, A.D., et al.: Confucius computer: Transforming the future through ancient philosophy. In: ACM SIGGRAPH 2008 New Tech Demos. ACM, Los Angeles (2008)
9. Tosa, N.: Cultural Computing: ZENetic Computer. In: Intelligent Agent 6.1.1, Kyoto (2006)

10. Nisbett, R.E., et al.: Culture and systems of thought: Holistic versus analytic cognition. Psychological Review 108(2), 291–310 (2001)
11. Nisbett, R.E., Masuda, T.: Culture and point of view. Proceedings National Academy of Sciences 100(19), 11163–11170 (2003)
12. Rauterberg, M.: Ambient culture: A possible future for entertainment computing. In: Lugmayr, A., Golebiowski, P. (eds.) Interactive TV: a shared experience - Adjunct Proceedings of EuroITV-2007, pp. 37–39. Tampere International Center for Signal Processing, Tampere (2007)
13. Rauterberg, M.: How to assess the user's experience in cultural computing. In: Bosenick, T. (ed.) Usability Professionals, pp. 12–17. Fraunhofer Informationszentrum Raum und Bau, Gelsenkirchen (2006)
14. Rauterberg, M.: Usability in the future – explicit and implicit effects in cultural computing. In: Heinecke, A.M., Paul, H. (eds.) Mensch und Computer im Strukturwandel, pp. 29–36. München, Oldenbourg (2006)
15. Peng, K., Nisbett, R.E., Wong, N.Y.C.: Validity problems comparing values across cultures and possible solutions. Psychological Methods 2(4), 329–344 (1997)
16. Merikle, P.M., Daneman, M.: Memory for unconsciously perceived events: Evidence from anesthetized patients. Consciousness and Cognition 5, 525–541 (1996)
17. van den Noort, M., Hugdahl, K., Bosch, P.: Human machine interaction: The special role for human unconscious emotional information processing. In: Tao, J., Tan, T., Picard, R.W. (eds.) ACII 2005. LNCS, vol. 3784, pp. 598–605. Springer, Heidelberg (2005)
18. Drascic, D., Milgram, P.: Perceptual issues in augmented reality. In: Proceedings of SPIE - Stereoscopic Displays and Virtual Reality Systems III, pp. 123–134. The International Society for Optical Engineering, Bellingham (1996)
19. Qin, H., Rau, P.-L., Salvendy, G.: Player immersion in the computer game narrative. In: Ma, L., Rauterberg, M., Nakatsu, R. (eds.) ICEC 2007. LNCS, vol. 4740, pp. 458–461. Springer, Heidelberg (2007)
20. Milgram, P., Kishino, A.F.: Taxonomy of mixed reality visual displays. IEICE Transactions on Information and Systems E77-D(12), 1321–1329 (1994)
21. Busselle, R., Ryabovolova, A., Wilson, B.: Ruining a good story: Cultivation, perceived realism and narrative. Communications 29(3), 365–378 (2004)
22. Carroll, L.: Alice's adventures in wonderland. Macmillan, London (1865)
23. ALICE. Project ALICE: Not just another interactive installation (2010), http://www.alice.id.tue.nl/
24. van Aart, J., et al.: Designing for experience: Arousing boredom to evoke predefined user behaviour. In: Desmet, P., et al. (eds.) Proceedings of the 6th Design & Emotion Conference, Hong Kong, pp. 1607–1611 (2008)
25. Schilder, P.: The image and appearance of the human body. International University Press, New York (1950)
26. Kooijmans, T., Rauterberg, M.: Cultural computing and the self concept: Towards unconscious metamorphosis. In: Ma, L., Rauterberg, M., Nakatsu, R. (eds.) ICEC 2007. LNCS, vol. 4740, pp. 171–181. Springer, Heidelberg (2007)
27. Sobol-Shikler, T., Robinson, P.: Classification of complex information: Inference of co-occuring affective states from their expressions in speech. IEEE Transactions on Pattern Analysis and Machine Intelligence (in Press)
28. Raichle, M.E.: The brain's dark energy. Science 314, 1249–1250 (2006)
29. Raichle, M.E.: A brief history of human brain mapping. Trends in Neurosciences 32(2), 118–126 (2008)

30. Dijksterhuis, A., et al.: On making the right choice: the deliberation-without-attention effect. Science 311, 1005–1007 (2006)
31. Nakatsu, R., Rauterberg, M., Salem, B.: Forms and theories of communication: From multimedia to Kansei mediation. Multimedia Systems 11(3), 304–312 (2006)
32. Dijksterhuis, A., Nordgren, L.: A theory of unconscious thought. Perspectives on Psychology 1(2), 95–109 (2006)
33. Dehaene, S., et al.: Imaging unconscious semantic priming. Nature 395, 597–600 (1998)
34. Greenwald, A.G., Farnham, S.D.: Using the Implicit Association Test to measure selfesteem and self-concept. Journal of Personality and Social Psychology 79(6), 1022–1038 (2000)
35. Barakova, E., Laurens, T.: Expressing and interpreting emotional movements in social games with robots. Personal and Ubiquitous Computing (January 16, 2010)
36. Taelman, J., et al.: Contactless EMG sensors for continuous monitoring of muscle activity to prevent musculoskeletal disorders. In: Proceedings of the first Annual Symposium of the IEEE-EMBS Benelux Chapter, pp. 223–226. IEEE Benelux chapter on Engineering in Medicine and Biology Society, Brussels (2006)
37. Ouwerkerk, M., Pasveer, F., Langereis, G.: Unobtrusive sensing of psychophysiological parameters. In: Westerink, J., et al. (eds.) Probing Experience: From Assessment of User Emotions and Behaviour to Development of Products, pp. 163–193. Springer, Dordrecht (2008)
38. REG. Random event generator design (2010),
    http://noosphere.princeton.edu/reg.html
39. Nelson, R.D., et al.: Correlations of continuous random data with major world events. Foundations of Physics Letters 15(6), 537–550 (2002)
40. Nelson, R.: The Global Consciousness Project - Part 2. The Golden Thread, 6–10 (August 2002)
41. Nelson, R.: The Global Consciousness Project - Part 3. The Golden Thread, 30–32 (November 2002)
42. Nelson, R.: The Global Consciousness Project - Part 1. The Golden Thread, 8–12 (May 2002)
43. Greenwald, A.G., McGhee, D.E., Schwartz, J.K.L.: Measuring individual differences in implicit cognition: The Implicit Association Test. Journal of Personality and Social Psychology 74(6), 1464–1480 (1998)
44. Naccache, L., Dehaene, S.: Unconscious semantic priming extends to novel unseen stimuli. Cognition 80, 215–229 (2001)
45. Noort, M.v.d., Bosch, P., Hugdahl, K.: Understanding the unconscious brain: Evidence for a non-linear information processing. In: Proceedings of the International Conference on Cognitive Systems, pp. 2254–2258 (2005)
46. Di Maggio, P.: Culture and cognition. Annual Review of Sociology 23, 263–287 (1997)
47. Jung, C.G.: Die Archetypen und das kollektive Unbewußte, Gesammelte Werke von C.G. Jung (Walter 1934)
48. Einstein, A., Podolsky, B., Rosen, N.: Can quantum-mechanical description of physical reality be considered complete? Physical Review 47(10), 777–780 (1935)
49. Aspect, A., Grangier, P., Roger, G.: Experimental realization of Einstein-Podolsky-Rosen-Bohm Gedankenexperiment: a new violation of Bell's inequalities. Physical Review Letters 49(2), 91–94 (1982)
50. Aspect, A.: Quantum mechanics: to be or not to be local. Nature 446, 866–867 (2007)
51. Woolf, N.J., Hameroff, S.R.: A quantum approach to visual consciousness. Trends in Cognitive Sciences 5(11), 472–478 (2001)

52. Sheldrake, R.: New science of life: The hypothesis of morphic resonance. Blond & Briggs (1981)
53. Noort, M.v.d.: The unconscious brain - the relative time and information theory of emotions. Citadel, Oegstgeest (2003)
54. Penrose, R.: The emperor's new mind. Oxford University Press, Oxford (1989)
55. Penrose, R.: Shadows of the mind: A search for the missing science of consciousness. Oxford University Press, Oxford (1994)
56. Hameroff, S., et al.: Conduction pathways in microtubules, biological quantum computation, and consciousness. BioSystems 64, 149–168 (2002)
57. Hameroff, S.R.: Quantum computation in brain microtubules? The Penrose-Hameroff 'OrchOR' model of consciousness. Philosophical Transactions Royal Society London A 356, 1869–1896 (1998)
58. Penrose, R., Hameroff, S.R.: What gaps? Reply to Grush and Churchland. Journal of Consciousness Studies 2, 98–112 (1995)
59. Hameroff, S.R., Penrose, R.: Conscious events as orchestrated space-time selections. NeuroQuantology 1, 10–35 (2003)
60. Rauterberg, M.: Entertainment computing, social transformation and the quantum field. In: Nijholt, A., Reidsma, D., Hondorp, H. (eds.) Intelligent Technologies for Interactive Entertainment - INTETAIN 2009, pp. 1–8. Springer, Heidelberg (2009)

Emotions as a Communication Medium between the Unconscious and the Conscious

Matthias Rauterberg

Industrial Design, Eindhoven University of Technology
Den Dolech 2, 5600MB Eindhoven, The Netherlands
g.w.m.rauterberg@tue.nl

Abstract. Emotions are conceptualized and framed as a separate entity in human's cognitive architecture. In this paper I present the different idea that emotions are the form in which the result from a high dimensional optimization process happening in the unconscious is communicated to the low dimensional conscious. Instead of framing emotions as a separate sub component of our cognitive system, I argue for emotions as the main characteristic of the communication between the unconscious and the conscious. Based on this holistic view I recommend a different design and architecture for entertainment robots and other entertainment products with 'emotional' behavior. Intuition is the powerful information processing function of the unconscious while emotion is the result of this process communicated to the conscious. Emotions are the perception of the mapping from the high dimensional problem solving space of the unconscious to the low dimensional space of the conscious.

Keywords: emotion, intuition, unconscious, conscious, mapping.

1 Introduction

A lot of concepts and frameworks about emotions are already available. In this paper I argue for a new holistic view of the relation between the unconscious and the conscious information processing part of our brain. Although a lot of research has been done since the 80ties of last century [1], still important questions are unanswered [2]. The most accepted view on emotion is a modular sub component of our cognitive system linked and related to a lot of cognitive functions [3]. This conceptualization is also leading the design and architecture of entertainment robots [4]. I will argue for a different view so that designers of such kind of systems are better supported than nowadays.

One of the main characteristics of emotions is their richness, heterogeneity, vagueness and openness for multiple interpretations [5]. This is one of the most interesting but also often overlooked and underestimated aspect of emotions. I will argue for a new way of how to conceptualize emotions as a central aspect between the unconscious and the conscious information processing.

R. Nakatsu et al. (Eds.): ECS 2010, IFIP AICT 333, pp. 198–207, 2010.
© IFIP International Federation for Information Processing 2010

2 Emotion, Unconscious and the Mapping Problem

In this chapter I discuss the state of art [1] and beyond for concepts about emotion, unconscious and mappings from high dimensional spaces to low dimensional spaces.

2.1 Concepts of Emotions: The State of Art

Several cognitive functions can be ordered according to their life-span (see Figure 1). Proper design of entertainment systems has the potential to stimulate and influence most of these functions. The primary cognitive functions are: *reflexes*, *sensations*, *thoughts*, *dreams*, *emotions*, *moods*, and *drives* (see also [1]).

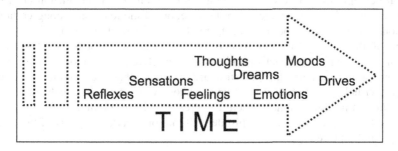

Fig. 1. Time scale of some cognitive functions (adopted from [6])

These different cognitive functions are linked to different control systems (bold black in Figure 2) of our body. In turn, these links help us design the right interaction (italic in Figure 2) through various body parts and control systems. To achieve users' emotional involvement, one needs to address these interactions with the right channels (as the examples given to the right of Figure 2).

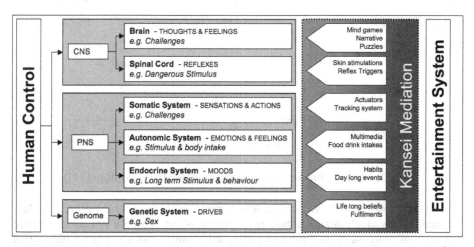

Fig. 2. From human control mechanisms to entertainment [CNS: Central Nervous System, PNS: Peripheral Nervous System] (adopted from [6])

The human unconscious can be framed by the genetic reproduction system, the peripheral nervous system (PNS) and the central nervous system (CNS). These three distinct systems contribute to unconscious information processing. Each of them has certain sub-systems which are directly related to emotional feelings (see Figure 2; [1]). One of the main differences between these subsystems is the cycle time to process incoming signals to actions executed (from milliseconds to hours; see Figure 1). All of these processes are related in one or the other way to emotions [1, 7].

Research in psychology has tried to structure prototypical emotional feelings into discrete basic categories [8-9]. Because emotions are complex, divers and with multiple facets there are different ways to construct these basic categories. The boundaries of the phenomenon *emotion* are so blurry that almost every feeling, mood and other internal perceptions can be categorized as an emotion. The phenomenon *emotion* is too broad to fit into one single scientific category. Emotions vary along certain dimensions (i.e. intensity, amount of pleasure, degree of activation, etc.).

One of the most prominent models is based on two dimensions: 'unpleasant-pleasant' and 'activation-deactivation' as the core affect [10]. "Emotion categories do not cluster at the axes, and thus the structure of emotion has been said to be a circumplex. Nevertheless, although we are among those who emphasize such findings, we now believe this dimensional structure represents and is limited to the core affect involved. Prototypical emotional episodes fall into only certain regions of the circumplex" [8, p. 807] (see Figure 3).

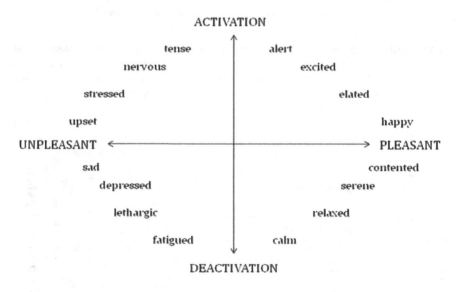

Fig. 3. The two dimensional core affect model (adapted from [11])

The combination of the two object-less dimensions 'pleasure-displeasure' and 'activation-deactivation' might capture most emotions but certainly not all. Cognitive information processing, intuition and behavioral planning can account for the myriad manifestations of emotions. The approach so far to capture emotions is dimensional and in addition limited. "The process of changing core affect is not fully understood, but the important point here is the complexity of the causal story" [11, p. 148].

Lane [12] goes even a step further by relating neural correlates to conscious emotional experience. He put forward a hierarchical model as follows [neuroanatomical structure/psychological function; however a one-to-one mapping between neuro-anatomy and psychology is not intended]: brainstem/visceral activation, diencephalon/action tendencies, limbic/discrete emotion, paralimbic/blends of emotion, and prefrontal cortex/blends of blends. I can conclude that emotions can be based on conscious and unconscious information processing. Both processes have influences on actual behavior, behavior control and internal adaptation through learning.

Although emotions are complex phenomena and rich in content, main stream psychology tries to capture them in less complex models and frameworks. If we want to maintain the richness in our understanding of emotions, we probably have to change our view. Before I come back to this I will first introduce the unconscious cognitive functions.

2.2 The Power of the Unconscious

When we think of being conscious, we think of being awake and aware of our surroundings (see for more at [13]). Being conscious also means being aware of ourselves as individuals. Mostly, people tend to think of being conscious as being alive. We tend to think that the person should be responsive to the surrounding environment to be conscious. Being in a coma is considered to be the opposite of conscious, so called non-conscious or unconsciousness. There are at least three forms of consciousness for humans: (1) the conscious state; (2) the subconscious state; and (3) the unconscious state. In the scope of this paper the unconscious state is fully operational and functional for a normal human living as a parallel background process of our mind and body, we are just not aware of (e.g. activities of the cerebellum). The subconscious can be turned into conscious (i.e. by paying attention to subconscious activities); the unconscious normally is not available to the conscious. The remaining question is how –if at all- does the unconscious communicate with the conscious?

The conscious part of the brain is investigated already for a long time. One of the important results is the limitations of the information processing capacity of the short-term memory [14]. In his classical paper Miller [15] found that the conscious information processing capacity is limited to seven (plus or minus two) chunks or dimensions [16]. This conscious part is mainly described as the short-term or working memory to emphasize its role in decision making and controlling behavior.

Consciousness is a topic for which either there exist no acceptable description, definition and explanation or, and this depends on one's point of view, there are far too many and far too divergent ones. Most definitions from the Western world are resulting in Descartes dualism [17]. This dualism has created a schism between mind and body that does not necessarily exist and that has been a key, not necessarily a correct one, in the Western world understanding of consciousness. Even today's literature is full of reference to the mind and the body as if it has been established beyond doubt that there was indeed a separation [18]. The illusory Cartesian self is more and more challenged by biological and neurofunctional evidences that point to consciousness as an emergent property of competing and successive brain processes. Unconscious and conscious play a role in the initiation and performance of voluntary actions [19]. Both action and expression originate in the unconscious [20]. They are probably then vetoed by emotions and moods. Actions and expressions not vetoed are then performed.

In the dualist approach advocated by Descartes, the mind is conscious and the body unconscious. Outside cognitive and brain sciences was and still is a primacy of conscious over unconscious [1]. The unconscious activities of the human mind are hidden under and are controlled by consciousness (the word oppressed is often used). In the emergent view however, there is no such separation between mind and body and consciousness is said to be an emerging property of unconsciousness. It is moving away from the concept of conscious oppression of perception and expression into the concept of emerging perception and expression. Nakatsu, Rauterberg and Salem [19] show a model of the different views of the relationship between human consciousness and sub-consciousness, now (dualist view) and in the future (emergent view).

An iceberg can serve as a useful metaphor to understand the unconscious mind [21-22]. As an iceberg floats in the water, the huge mass of it remains below the surface. Only a small percentage of the whole iceberg is visible above the surface. In this way, the iceberg is like the mind. The conscious mind is what we notice above the surface while the sub- and unconscious mind, the largest and most powerful part, remains unseen below the surface. The unconscious mind holds all awareness that is not presently in the conscious mind. All activities, memories and thoughts that are out of conscious awareness are by definition sub- or even unconscious. Scherer [22] assumes that a large part of emotions functions in an unconscious mode and only some parts will emerge into conscious. But how does this relationship between unconscious and conscious look like?

Recent investigation in cognitive psychology of the conscious and unconscious are promising. Most of the brain's energy consumption is *not* used for processing responses to external stimuli as usually assumed; but what is this enormous amount of brain energy then for? [23-24] One promising aspect of unconscious information processing is finding optimal solutions in the multidimensional sensor and knowledge space of the unconscious for controlling behavior by situated forcasting the near and far future. But how does the unconscious communicate these 'solutions' to the conscious? Before I can provide an answer, I have to introduce the 'mapping problem' from a high (i.e. unconscious) to a low dimensional (i.e. conscious) processing space. The following chapter is pure metaphorical, all introduces concepts have *no* specific technical meaning in the context of this paper.

2.3 Mapping from High to Low Dimensional Spaces

A standard problem in several research areas is the visualization of results found in a high dimensional space into the two dimensional (2D) space of plane paper. This problem is quite old and several solutions are already developed, depending on the particular mapping problem [25-27]. To introduce into these approaches I will shortly discuss this classical 3D-2D example. Abbott [28] wrote the book 'Flatland'. Flatland has only two dimensions, and is populated with lines (females), triangles, squares, polygons, and circles; these inhabitants perceive their 2D environment differently than we do perceive our three dimensional (3D) environment. The basic idea is to explain the main differences about a fourth dimension beyond our 3D world.

Flatlanders cannot understand a third dimension, and we have the same trouble with 4D, and definitively for higher dimensions. In Flatland for example is the ball from a 3D world perceived as changing diameters of circles, the 2D 'shadow' (see Figure 5).

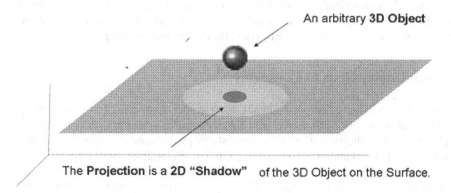

An arbitrary **3D Object**

The **Projection** is a **2D "Shadow"** of the 3D Object on the Surface.

Fig. 4. The projection of a ball shaped 3D object on a 2D surface results in its form of a flat circle (from http://mdchristian.com/Normal_Projections.html)

Rucker [29] goes beyond Abbott's idea by taking the 2D world of the Flatlanders into curved space, black holes, and beyond. Banchoff [30] describes the problem of mappings between different dimensional spaces in more technical terms, applying several mapping methods to the design of computer graphics and other graphical shapes. He uses techniques of slices, projections, shadows, and generalization. The most practical part is learning to count the number of faces, vertices, and edges in a 4D (and higher) hypercube.

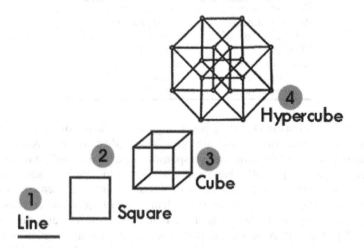

Fig. 5. Mapping a one dimensional line into two dimensions results in a square, a square into three dimensions in a cube, a cube into four dimensions in a hypercube (adopted from http://qunud.wordpress.com/)

The mapping downwards into a three dimensional space of a hypercube results in eight different cubes. Figure 5 cannot exist in the real world with a 3D space; in addition Figure 5 itself is the projection of higher dimensional objects onto two dimensions of this 2D paper surface. If I now assume that the unconscious information processing often described as intuition [31-32] takes place in a high dimensional space, then I have to question how the solutions found in this high dimensional space can be mapped into a low dimensional space, the conscious reasoning?

3   From Unconscious to Conscious

Decades ago, Dreyfus questioned already the rational approach of cognitivism by excluding intuition, etc. [33]. Since then luckily a lot of research – in particular in psychology –have shown the growing interests in phenomena like tacit knowledge [34], intuition [31-32] and the unconscious [35]. Scherer assumes that a large majority of cognitive processes related to emotions are unconscious and "that only some of these processes (or their outcomes) will emerge into consciousness for some time" [22, p. 312]. First I have to show that the conscious and the unconscious are separated but related. Kahneman clearly operates on the assumption that both systems are distinct [36], and the unconscious is fallible. He describes the unconscious as 'intuition' and the conscious as 'reasoning'; both systems have clear complementary characteristics (see Table 1). Dienes and Scott conclude that the structural knowledge is really divided between the unconscious and the conscious [37].

Table 1. The two primary cognitive systems: intuition/unconscious and reasoning/conscious. (Adapted from [36, p. 1451])

INTUITION	REASONING
Fast processing	Slow processing
Parallel processing	Serial processing
Automatic processing	Conscious controlled
Effortless	Effortful
Associative	Rule governed
Slow learning	Flexible, adaptive
Emotional / 'hot'	Neutral / 'cold'

Recent investigations in cognitive psychology of the nature of conscious and unconscious information processing are promising. Most of the brain's energy consumption is *not* used for processing responses to external stimuli; but what is this brain energy then for? [23-24]. One possible answer is for sub- or even unconscious information processing that guides behavior through situated forcasting. "Emotions are part of the biological solution to the problem of how to plan and carry out action aimed at satisfying multiple goals in environments which are not perfectly predictable" [10, p. 35]. According to the 'deliberation-without-attention' effect [38] it is not always advantageous to engage in intensive conscious decision making alone. On the basis of recent insights into the characteristics of conscious and unconscious thought, Dijksterhuis et al. [21] tested the hypothesis that simple choices produce better results after conscious information processing, but that choices in complex situations should be left to unconscious information processing. It was confirmed in several studies on consumer choice that purchases of complex products were viewed more favorably when decisions had been made in the absence of attentive deliberation. In addition, Dijksterhuis, Bos, Nordgren, and van Baaren [24, 39] could show the advantages of the unconscious information processing for complex processing, and therefore they open a door to a new view on the relationship towards the power of the unconscious [19, 38, 40]. Dienes and Scott showed in their experiments that conscious structural knowledge is associated with greater consistency in making errors than the unconscious [37, p. 348].

4 Discussion and Conclusions

The emotion experience and other cognitive activities are not separate, independent and distinctive processes, but should be conceptualized as a gradient in the interaction between cognitive activities (i.e. thoughts, memories, beliefs, etc.) [5]. "Brain structures at the heart of neural circuitry for emotion (e.g., the amygdale) impact cognitive processing from early attention allocation through perceptual processing to memory" [5, p. 390]. It seems not possible to explain how neural activities instantiates emotions if we conceptualize emotions as an independent cognitive process.

If we assume that emotions are perceived as important aspects in relation with other cognitive functions than we could go so far to conceptualize emotions as the appearance of these cognitive processes to our conscious. This is an internal perception loop about the own mental and bodily states [10, 41]. If we assume further that the information processing capacity of the unconscious is several magnitudes higher than the conscious, and both systems are somehow separate systems, I have to answer the question how do these two systems communicate with each other. My idea is that emotions can play this role as the 'voice of the unconscious' in telling the conscious the solutions found in a high dimensional space. But these emotions are not only to inform the conscious, they also communicate to the social context around us. Our whole body language is also part of the emotional expression space for the adjustment of social relations [10].

Applying this view to the design of entertainment systems, in particular entertainment robots with human like behavior, I recommend implementing a high dimensional processing unit (mainly sensor data input related to models of the systems itself as of the environment) that maps the found solution of situated forecasting into a low dimensional action control unit, instead of implementing a separate emotion unit [3-4]. This mapping is 'colored' as emotions, primarily for external purposes in social communication expressed via the nonverbal behavior of the entertainment system.

References

1. Ortony, A., Clore, G.L., Collins, A.: The cognitive structure of emotions. Cambridge University Press, Cambridge (1988)
2. Ortony, A., Turner, T.J.: What's basic about basic emotions? Psychological Review 97, 315–331 (1990)

3. Dörner, D., Hille, K.: Artificial souls: Motivated emotional robots. In: IEEE International Conference on Systems, Man and Cybernetics: Intelligent Systems for the 21st Century, pp. 3828–3832. IEEE Press, Piscataway (1995)
4. Itoh, K., et al.: Mechanisms and functions for a humanoid robot to express human-like emotions. In: Proceedings of the IEEE International Conference on Robotics and Automation, pp. 4390–4392. IEEE Press, Los Alamitos (2006)
5. Feldman-Barrett, L., et al.: The experience of emotion. Annual Review of Psychology 58, 373–403 (2007)
6. Salem, B., Nakatsu, R., Rauterberg, M.: Kansei mediated entertainment. In: Harper, R., Rauterberg, M., Combetto, M. (eds.) ICEC 2006. LNCS, vol. 4161, pp. 103–116. Springer, Heidelberg (2006)
7. Rolls, E.T.: Precis of The brain and emotion. Behavioral and Brain Sciences 23(2), 177–234 (2000)
8. Russell, J.A., Barrett, L.F.: Core affect, prototypical emotional episodes, and other things called emotion: Dissecting the elephant. Journal of Personality and Social Psychology 76(5), 805–819 (1999)
9. O'Rorke, P., Ortony, A.: Explaining emotions. Cognitive Science 18, 283–329 (1994)
10. Oatley, K., Johnson-Laird, P.N.: Towards a cognitive theory of emotions. Cognition and Emotion 1(1), 29–50 (1987)
11. Russell, J.A.: Core affect and the psychological construct of emotion. Psychological Review 110(1), 145–172 (2003)
12. Lane, R.D.: Neural correlates of conscious emotional experience. In: Lane, R.D. (ed.) Series in Affective Science, pp. 345–370. Oxford University Press, Oxford (2000)
13. Rauterberg, M.: Hypercomputation, unconsciousness and entertainment technology. In: Markopoulos, P., de Ruyter, B., IJsselsteijn, W.A., Rowland, D., et al. (eds.) Fun and Games 2008. LNCS, vol. 5294, pp. 11–20. Springer, Heidelberg (2008)
14. Baddeley, A.: The magical number seven: Still magic after all these years? Psychological Review 101(2), 353–356 (1994)
15. Miller, G.A.: The magical number seven, plus or minus two: Some limits on our capacity for processing information. The Psychological Review 63(2), 81–97 (1956)
16. Simon, H.A.: How big is a chunk? By combining data from several experiments, a basic human memory unit can be identified and measured. Science 183(4124), 482–488 (1974)
17. Descartes, R.: Discours de la méthode pour bien conduire sa raison, et chercher la vérité dans les sciences. Leiden, Ian Maire (1637)
18. Dreyfus, H.L., Dreyfus, S.E.: From Socrates to expert systems: The limits of calculative rationality. Technology in Society 6(3), 217–233 (1984)
19. Nakatsu, R., Rauterberg, M., Salem, B.: Forms and theories of communication: From multimedia to Kansei mediation. Multimedia Systems 11(3), 304–312 (2006)
20. Libet, B.: Can conscious experience affect brain activity? Journal of Consciousness Studies 10(12), 24–28 (2003)
21. Dijksterhuis, A., Nordgren, L.: A theory of unconscious thought. Perspectives on Psychology 1(2), 95–109 (2006)
22. Scherer, K.R.: Unconscious processes in emotion. In: Feldman-Barrett, L., Niedenthal, P.M., Winkielman, P. (eds.) Emotion and Consciousness, pp. 312–334. Guildford, New York (2005)
23. Raichle, M.E.: The brain's dark energy. Science 314, 1249–1250 (2006)
24. Raichle, M.E.: A brief history of human brain mapping. Trends in Neurosciences 32(2), 118–126 (2008)
25. Tufte, E.R.: Envisioning information. Graphics Press, Cheshire (1990)

26. Tufte, E.R.: The visual display of quantitative information. Graphics Press, Cheshire (1983)
27. Tufte, E.R.: Visual explanations. Graphics Press, Cheshire (1997)
28. Abbott, E.A.: Flatland: A romance of many dimensions. Dover Publications, Mineola (1992)
29. Rucker, R.: The fourth dimension: A guided tour of the higher universe. Houghton Mifflin, Boston (1984)
30. Banchoff, T.F.: Beyond the third dimension: Geometry, computer graphics, and higher dimensions. W.H. Freeman & Company, New York (1996)
31. Khatri, N., Ng, H.A.: The role of intuition in strategic decision making. Human Relations 53(1), 57–86 (2000)
32. Witteman, C., et al.: Assessing rational and intuitive thinking styles. European Journal of Psychological Assessment 25(1), 39–47 (2009)
33. Dreyfus, H.L.: The Socratic and Platonic basis of cognitivism. AI & Society 2, 99–112 (1988)
34. Reber, A.S.: Implicit learning and tacit knowledge. Journal of Experimental Psychology: General 118(3), 219–235 (1989)
35. Naccache, L., Dehaene, S.: Unconscious semantic priming extends to novel unseen stimuli. Cognition 80, 215–229 (2001)
36. Kahneman, D.: Maps of bounded rationality: Psychology for behavioral economics. The American Economic Review 93(5), 1449–1475 (2003)
37. Dienes, Z., Scott, R.: Measuring unconscious knowledge: distinguishing structural knowledge and judgment knowledge. Psychological Research 69, 338–351 (2005)
38. Dijksterhuis, A., et al.: On making the right choice: the deliberation-without-attention effect. Science 311, 1005–1007 (2006)
39. Coutrix, C., Nigay, L.: Mixed reality: A model of mixed interaction. In: Proceedings of International Working Conference on Advanced Visual Interface - AVI 2006, pp. 43–50. ACM, New York (2006)
40. Dehaene, S., et al.: Imaging unconscious semantic priming. Nature 395, 597–600 (1998)
41. Rauterberg, M.: About a framework for information and information processing of learning systems. In: Falkenberg, E.D., Hesse, W., Olivé, A. (eds.) Information System Concepts: Towards a Consolidation of Views, pp. 54–69. Chapman&Hall, London (1995)

Emotional Expression of Korean Dance Assisted by a Virtual Environment System

Taeyoung Uhm[1], Hanhoon Park[2], Mi-Hee Lee[3], Un-Mi Kim[3], and Jong-Il Park[1]

[1] Mixed Reality Laboratory, Department of Electronics and Computer Engineering,
Hanyang University, Seoul, Korea
[2] NHK Science & Technology Research Laboratories, Tokyo, Japan
[3] Research Institute of Korean Traditional Dance, Department of Dance,
Hanyang University, Seoul, Korea
{uty02,hanuni}@mr.hanyang.ac.kr,
{A029019,kimunmi,jipark}@hanyang.ac.kr

Abstract. Korean dance, which is one of the traditional Korean performing arts, has been a common way of expressing Korean peculiar emotion including "han", "heung", and "mut". This emotional presentation discriminates Korean dance from Western dance. In this paper, we try to understand what "han" is and assist the emotional expression of a representative Korean dance "salpuri" with empathy for "han" using a virtual environment system. Qualitative and quantitative analysis results demonstrate that "han" is related to being more dynamic and expressive and better empathy and expression of a dancer can be expected by using the virtual environment system.

Keywords: Virtual environment system, Korean dance, emotional expression assistance, qualitative and quantitative analysis.

1 Introduction

The traditional Korean arts involve Korean peculiar and implicit emotions and characteristics. In particular, Korean dance is the most typical way for expressing these emotions and characteristics. However, it has been directly passed down only through personal communication among people. Therefore, there has been a difficulty in training and expressing Korean dance with empathy for the emotions and characteristics that cannot be explained by words. Therefore, it would be very helpful if a system of assisting to express Korean dance visually and aurally and analyzing the expression is provided. Thus, in this paper, we construct a virtual environment system that:

- is a three-planes CAVE-like projection-based system and provides visual and aural information, i.e. video and music related to Korean dance, thus enhances strongly the sense of immersion of the performer.
- includes a motion analysis system that was devised for analyzing and recognizing emotional performance.

and demonstrate its effectiveness through qualitative and quantitative analysis.

R. Nakatsu et al. (Eds.): ECS 2010, IFIP AICT 333, pp. 208–213, 2010.
© IFIP International Federation for Information Processing 2010

1.1 Related Work

Research for training using virtual environment has been important for helping boost motivation to exercise and train sports skill and has been mainly focused on motion analysis from user's body parts [2, 3]. In the medical field, Pieper *et al.* [4] and Maekawa *et al.* [5] made it possible for user to train medical surgery and treatment by using virtual environment system.

However, existing systems were only for helping users train physical skills using virtual environment. To the best of our knowledge, there has been no virtual environment system that assists to train emotional expression, in particular from Korean traditional dance performance.

2 Korean Peculiar Emotions and Korean Dance "Salpuri"

In fact, it is not easy to define Korean emotions with several specific words because they are complicated, delicate, mixed, and so on. However, Korean peculiar emotions which are expressed by Korean dance are usually categorized into three classes ("han": close to understated sorrow, "heung": close to excitement, "mut": close to spruce-up). In this paper, we deal with "han" which is the most representative Korean peculiar emotion, which is started as sorrowful regret and ended in the excess of mirth by Korean dance performance.

Korean dance is roughly formed A-B type which is changed from static A to dynamic B, or A-B-A' type which is ended another static A' for becoming light-hearted and is suitable for expressing "han". The "salpuri" that is originally aimed at exorcism is a typical Korean dance performance of A-B-A' type. Therefore, we use "salpuri" to understand "han".

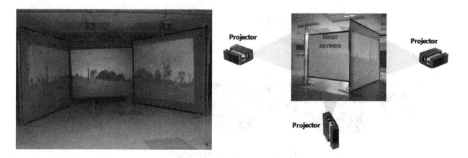

Fig. 1. Our virtual environment system

3 Virtual Environment System

A virtual environment system was created as shown in Fig. 1. The system has three sides (rear screens) where video images are projected by three rear projectors, and it is surrounded by speakers and lighting lamps, and thus can provide an immersive virtual environment. A single camera is used for calibrating the system and capturing the scene. The captured images are used for the motion analysis which will be explained in Section 3.2. The projectors and camera were synchronized with the v-sync signal of video output from a laptop. The synchronization is required for user region extraction which will be explained in Section 3.1. The geometric calibration and radiometric calibration [1] were done once in an initial step.

3.1 User Region Extraction

In our environment system, a single camera image (C) consists of two regions: one is a projection region (R_O) and the other is a non-projection region (R_X). And, each region consists of a foreground region (a part of user region) and a background region as follows.

$$C = R_O + R_X + N \tag{1}$$

Where
$$R_O = F_O + B_O, \; R_X = F_X + B_X.$$

Here, F, B, N indicate the foreground, the background, and the environmental noise, respectively. This is also illustrated in Fig. 2. The separation between R_O and R_X can be done by the geometric calibration [6] that informs us where the projected background is in the camera images. From the two regions, user region is extracted precisely and in real-time by a cooperative method [7]. Figure 3 shows the results of extracting the real dancer's region in our virtual environment system.

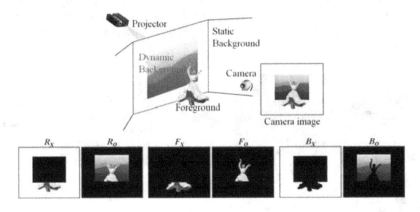

Fig. 2. User region extraction

3.2 Motion Analysis

After extracting user region, we extract low-level features, that describe the 2D motion of a rectangle circumscribing the user region in 3D space which consists of space-, time-, and energy-axis based on Laban's theory, from the user region and outliers are eliminated using a spatial normalization and clipping method [8]. By comparing the distribution of the low-level features extracted from different dance performances, we can recognize how different the dance performances are.

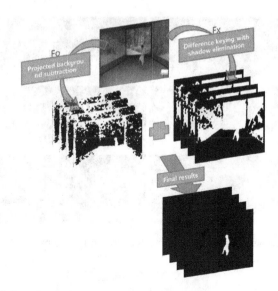

Fig. 3. Results of extracting user region using a cooperative method [7]

4 Experimental Results

We exploited the virtual environment system to analyze the characteristics of Korean dance. Its effectiveness in learning Korean dance is also tested. Six students, who have never learned any Korean dance performance, learned the "salpuri" intensively in a short period. When their learning curve was almost saturated, they performed the "salpuri" in the system twice as shown in Fig. 4. At the first trial, the virtual environment system was turned off. At the second trial, the system was turned on.

Background music for "salpuri" and "janggu" (double-headed drum with a narrow waist in the middle) beats were played and performed to provide rhythmical tune during performance. For the second trial, the real sounds such as the lapping of the waves or the rustle of leaves were provided additionally through the virtual environment system.

4.1 Qualitative Analysis

We deeply interviewed the students on the spot and had a general discussion about the validity of the virtual environment system. Through a hermeneutical approach, we could know that the virtual environment system had two important positive effects:

1. With the virtual environment system, the students were easily and more absorbed in an emotional expression.
2. The application of virtual environment system helped the students express well "han" inside them with empathy and finally clear up the sadness.

Fig. 4. Camera images of capturing "salpuri" performed by six students

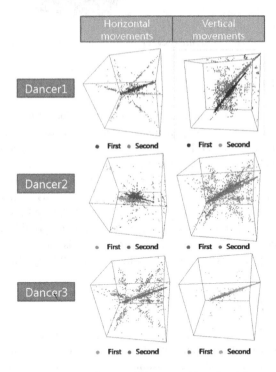

Fig. 5. Example of showing the distribution difference of low-level features between different emotional performances

4.2 Quantitative Analysis

We analyzed the difference between spatial distributions of low level features extracted from two sets of performances performed by each student. Figure 5 shows a part of results that is the distribution of activity, velocity, and acceleration in the horizontal and vertical movement of their performing region. In the result, their second performance with our system on was more dynamic and expressive than the first performance. We also asked several dance experts to evaluate the performances and found that the ones with the virtual environment system obtained better scores. Therefore, we arrive at the conclusion that expressing "han", which includes both sorrow and mirth, with empathy is related to being more dynamic and expressive and the virtual environment system is useful for dance training.

5 Conclusion

In this paper, we tried to understand the Korean peculiar emotion "han" and assisted to express well it by performing the Korean traditional dance "salpuri" in a virtual environment system. From the qualitative and quantitative analysis results, we could know that "han" was related to being more dynamic and expressive and the virtual environment system was useful. In the future, we will focus on more detailed quantitative analysis of the emotional characteristics of "salpuri". For this research, we currently consider to use bio-signal sensors and motion sensors.

Acknowledgments. This research is supported by Ministry of Cultuure, Sports and Tourism(MICST) and Korea Creative Content Agency(KOCCA) in the Culture Technology(CT) Research & Development Program (2010).

References

1. Park, H., Lee, M.-H., Kim, S.-J., Park, J.-I.: Surface-Independent Direct-Projected Augmented Reality. In: Narayanan, P.J., Nayar, S.K., Shum, H.-Y. (eds.) ACCV 2006. LNCS, vol. 3852, pp. 892–901. Springer, Heidelberg (2006)
2. IJsselsteijn, W., de Kort, Y., Westerink, J., de Jager, M., Bonants, R.: Fun and Sports: Enhancing the Home Fitness Experience. In: Rauterberg, M. (ed.) ICEC 2004. LNCS, vol. 3166, pp. 46–56. Springer, Heidelberg (2004)
3. Tsuji, T., Sumida, Y., Kaneko, M., Sadao, K.: A Virtual Sports System for Skill Training. Journal of Robotics and Mechatronics 13(2), 168–175 (2001)
4. Pieper, S.D., Delp, S., Rosen, J., Fisher, S.S.: Virtual Environment System for Simulation of Leg Surgery. In: SPIE, vol. 1457, p. 188 (1991)
5. Maekawa, Y., Ishiguro, K., Yasuo, O.: Simplified Apparatus for the Abdominal Breathing Exercise. The Journal of Japanese Physical Therapy Association 22(7), 413–416 (1995)
6. Pingali, G., Hampapur, A.: Geometric Image Masking for Segmenting Dynamic Projected Imagery. In: International Conference on Image Processing (2003)
7. Uhm, T., Park, H., Lee, M.-H., Park, J.-I.: User Region Extraction from Dynamic Projected Background for Virtual Environment System. In: The 2nd International Conference on Digital Image Processing, pp. 75462I-1-6 (2010)
8. Uhm, T., Park, H., Park, J.-I., Kim, U.-M.: Quantitative Analysis of Korean Dance Performance Based on a Vision-Based Emotion Recognition System. In: International Symposium on Ubiquitous VR, pp. 113–114 (2006)

Machine-Made Puzzles and Hand-Made Puzzles

Hiroshi Higashida

Graduate School of Human and Environmental Studies, Kyoto University, Japan
cheva-teiri@coral.broba.cc

Abstract. Originally puzzles were not for recreation, but serious questions you might be killed if you couldn't solve them. But in modern times, puzzles had become a sort of recreation, decreasing the seriousness and religiousness gradually. Now, the 'rule creators' of puzzles began to attract notice. I, as a rule creator, published a book, *Kyoto University Student, Higashida's Puzzles.* I'll show several puzzle examples from my inventions. In the puzzle world, the importance of not only making problems but also inventing rules has been insisted. But, unless the mass-producing system of the new rule puzzle is constituted, the rule will disappear at once. It is usually hard to remake puzzles into computer games or videogames. But the puzzle world, where new rules are created in succession, shouldn't be left behind the times.

1 Introduction

Puzzles have existed since the history of human beings began. They have been and will have been created continuously, changing their shapes or structures variously. Especially since the industrial revolution, puzzles have been invented and produced one after another by gaining 'rules,' and sometimes even have driven the world crazy. These days they are often remade to be sold as computer-games. In fact, puzzle games have a great share of iphone application software and Nintendo DSiWare. This paper studies puzzles as a cultural activity from a view of a puzzle (or its rule) creator, showing some examples of my original ones.

2 The History of Puzzles with Rules

Puzzles originated in ancient Greek or ancient Egypt. The description, like a numerical formula, on papyrus in ancient Egypt, or the riddle, 'What goes on four feet, on two feet, and three, but the more feet it goes on the weaker it be?' which the sphinx questioned in the ancient Greek myth, *Oedipus Tyrannos*, is thought as the oldest one. Mazes, which are often categorized into puzzles, bore religious meaning accompanied by various superstitions all over the world. In ancient Greek, puzzles are sometimes presented in the form of oracles by gods.

Researching the birth of puzzles tells us that originally they were not for recreation, but serious questions you might be killed if you couldn't solve them, represented by the myth *Oedipus Tyrannos*. Also in the ancient China, Chinese historical document *Sengoku Saku* says, wire puzzles were assigned a role of ascertaining the degree of

R. Nakatsu et al. (Eds.): ECS 2010, IFIP AICT 333, pp. 214–222, 2010.

intelligence of the enemy's king. This fact means that the original seriousness of puzzles was not only in the West, but also in the East. In addition, Many puzzles had born religiousness strongly and been given mysterious rules because of the covered mystery of their answer. 'Magic square' is the representative. Puzzles pursuing this nature reached a climax being inseparable from arts when Rabanus Maurus, a theologian in Karolingische Renaissance, devoted to the empire the puzzle text, *a book about praise of sacred cross.*

But after that, puzzles had become a sort of recreation, decreasing the seriousness and religiousness gradually. Consequently, puzzles had come to be created by *geniuses* from among human beings instead of God. The representatives are Sam Loyd and Henry E Dudeney, who are the big two in 19th puzzle world. on the other hand, tangram, whose origin is argued between Japan and China, had formed a new puzzle genre in which everybody could participate as a puzzle creator, by gaining 'rules' that many current puzzles also have. In modern times, when the existence of God who had formed the rules of the world was doubted, puzzle creation had shifted to the task of geniuses or the activity based on given rules; anyway, puzzles became products of human beings.

After the Industrial Revolution, the first triumph as a puzzle with rules was achieved by 'crossword puzzles,' which is even now very popular. It was the dawn of the 'pencil and paper puzzle' which would become the center of the 20th puzzle world. Crossword puzzles, which can be printed on paper, soon spread all over the world because of the cheap cost of production. they were so widespread that Roger Caillois predicted in *Les jeux et les hommes* that crossword puzzles would decline to end up as a evanescent boom. Now we can say that his prediction was quite wrong. On the contrary, crossword puzzles have cultivated a new puzzle field, in place of the field of mechanical puzzles which had been the center of the puzzle world before then. I predict that crossword puzzles will have been the center of the puzzle world for a while, for they can be easily ported to computer games because they can be shown on a plane.

Japanese puzzle creators are good at pencil and paper puzzles, the genre born of crossword puzzles. 'Number place,' which was born in America and now is the most popular pencil and paper puzzle, was named '*sudoku*' in Japan and now even American people call it '*SUDOKU,*' which tells Japanese people have grown and developed the puzzle. In addition, because various rules of pencil and paper puzzles are invented in Japan, Japanese puzzles are occupying the attention of the whole world. The Japanese language has an abundant letters combining ideograms and phonograms so is suited for word puzzles by nature. Moreover, the two facts in Edo period that *Jingoki,* a mathematical book by Mitsuyoshi Yoshida, was a best seller and ordinary people dedicated their achievement of mathematics to shrines, tell that Japanese people have had familiarity with number puzzles since the old days.

Hiroshi Higashida, the author of this paper, is a creator of pencil and paper puzzles. I have not only made puzzles with existent rules, but also developed new rules. I have invented puzzle forms which can be made easily and yet by which puzzle creators can give various expression. In the next chapter, as a puzzle researcher and at the same time as a puzzle creator, I'll tell my theory about puzzles.

3 What's Puzzle?

It's difficult to define 'a puzzle,' but we can approximately decide the category through the comparison with neighboring notions like a quiz or a game. While a quiz is a question to which we can answer right away if we know its answer, a puzzle is a question to which we cannot answer right away even if we know its answer. But for example in a quiz competition using quiz buzzers, though usually called 'quiz,' participants often guess the question sentence which haven't been read completely yet, so the process of thinking is very similar to a puzzle. Conversely, in solving a crossword puzzle, though usually called 'puzzle,' the process of thinking in which solvers think about a word to fill the grid from each clue is often similar to a quiz. Therefore, it is difficult to delineate the boundary between a quiz and a puzzle. If any, there would be gradual difference at most. But it is the undoubted fact that the mechanism of deduction is necessary for solving a puzzle, not for answering a quiz, and it is also the undoubted fact that clear rules are needed to deduce rightly in each puzzle.

A game, like a puzzle, also has clear rules. Violation of rules is regarded as a foul, and if you committed such a foul, you would never be judged to be a winner in both a puzzle and a game. But we can distinguish the two to some extent. While a game has elements which a player cannot handle just as he or her hopes, like chance or opponents, a puzzle doesn't have such elements. The reason why computer games played alone are 'games' is that enemies appear at unpredictable time, and that players cannot manipulate the controller completely just as they hope. Here, we must take into account toys which require cleverness, like cup and ball or mazes with balls. When doing cup and ball, it is difficult to say that we can handle it as we desire. On the other hand, it seems to be less complex to manipulate and to have less intervention of chance than a computer game. So Slocum's classification, which is one of the most well-known classifications of puzzles, contains such toys into 'puzzle,' calling them 'dexterity puzzles.' It is undeniable, however, that such toys are quite similar to games, so it should be discussed more.

Anyway, we can say that a puzzle is a question which challenges people to solve, requires their deduction based on its rules to win, and doesn't depend on chance or other people's action. You cannot defy rules which are, so to speak, 'absolute authority.'

Puzzle creators, not only solvers, mustn't defy rules, either. Especially, in puzzles which can be made easily one after another like crossword puzzles, we might say that rules control the creators and rules even form the works. It is a curious paradox that puzzles, which seem to be independent of the control of chance or other people, are in fact already controlled at the stage of creation by rules someone made. Rules which appear in the 20th century uncovered this paradox in the puzzle world and thereby altered nature of puzzle creators.

4 I, as a Rule Creator

In 20th century, numerous creators of pencil and paper puzzles appeared. This genre, from crossword puzzles to Sudoku, shows us various scenes, because rules of a puzzle by which creators can make it easily are made one after another. Creators can express their creativity in their works there, displaying their originalities obeying existent rules, just as haiku poets create their works under the rule of seventeen syllables in the 5-7-5 form.

At the same time, the 'rule creators' of puzzles began to attract notice. Some puzzle magazines positively accept contributions of puzzle rules. Now rules in themselves are coming to be recognized to be valuable. In 2010, these two puzzle books were published in succession in Japan; *Puzzle Brain,* by Naoki Inaba, Odysseus, in which 24 sorts of new puzzles are included, and *Kyoto University Student, Higashida's Puzzles,* by Hiroshi Higashida, Kadokawa Gakugei, in which 18 sorts of new puzzles are included. Before, there weren't any books in which only puzzles with new rules by one author are collected. These two books tell us the importance of invention of rules in current puzzle world.

In one of the two, my *Kyoto University Student, Higashida's Puzzles,* eight sorts of puzzles which depend on Japanese language and ten sorts of puzzles which don't depend on Japanese language are included. The former puzzles don't have international penetration because we cannot solve them if we don't know Japanese characters or vocabularies. But we can rediscover Japanese nature through solving them and seeing Japanese abundant expressions with characters from various angles. By contrast, the latter puzzles can be played by people all over the world since numbers or signs are used in them. The worldwide boom in Sudoku proves that. Certainly, crossword puzzles, which depend on language, seem to spread in the world. But for example in China, where kanji is used, it is hard to make them, so they don't have perfect penetration just as it is. On the other hand, puzzles which don't depend on language have demerits, for expression creators can give is limited and originality they can display is hard to see in those puzzles.

I've invented rules of both language-dependent and language-independent puzzles. I might be a 'rule creator,' as opposed to a 'puzzle creator' who makes puzzles under existent rules. Especially, there weren't many eager rule creators of language-dependent puzzles. Inaba's book I've referred before, without exception, consists of only language-independent puzzles. There are few people who can invent both of the two sorts one after another. This is because the two require different way of thinking; language-dependent puzzles are intuitive, while language-independent puzzles are logical. So, working of many puzzle creators inclines to one of them. My today's working as a 'rule creator' reaps great benefits from my lucky nature of being able to enjoy both puzzles.

5 Higashida Puzzles

Now, I'll show several puzzle examples from my inventions. From my book, *Kyoto University Student, Higashida's Puzzles,* first, I'll introduce a few language-independent puzzles. In *room light*, you must put a light (a circle) in each room divided by bold lines (Fig.1). The numbers on the outside of the grid indicate how many lights must be put in that row or column. In easy problems, you'll find numbers like 0 or 7, which tell clearly whether there are lights or not in that row and column, and from there you can proceed. In difficult problems, you'll have to seek a cell where a light is certainly or never placed, wherever a light is put in another $1 \times n$ room. This puzzle is comparably simple, for there are few more difficult solutions. If I had wanted the puzzle more complex, I would have added this rule, 'no two lights can be in adjacent cells.' But in fact I didn't, and retained the simplicity. This is because I wanted to avoid increasing fatigue of solvers by adding one rule. Though *room light* is the simplest puzzle, even then it maintains the essence of the real attraction of mathematical puzzles. Here are two problems, one is easy, and the other is difficult. Please challenge them.

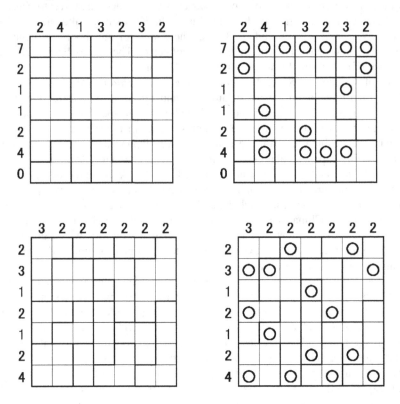

Fig. 1. left: problem right: solution

In '*Alphabet block,*' you must divide the grid into blocks which contain four cells, provided that different alphabets mustn't be included in one block (Fig.2). Though this puzzle is also quite simple, the rule deciding how many cells each block has effectively enables us to create difficult problems. In this puzzle too, if I had added the rule, 'no two blocks which contain the same alphabet can touch, except at corners,' the puzzle would have become more complex. But actually I didn't, under this concept, 'the simpler the rule is, the better.' Even then we can create more difficult problems of this puzzle than *room light*.

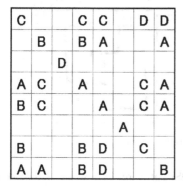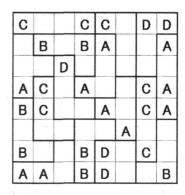

Fig. 2. left: problem right: solution

As the last example of language-independent puzzles, I'll introduce *'connect number,'* which was remade into Nintendo DSi software later. In this puzzle, you must connect all pairs of numbers with continuous lines, provided that you mustn't cross lines (Fig.3). The idea, to link pairs, has existed in puzzle world since before I was born. *'Number link'* is one of the forms of the idea, which has been published in the books or magazines of Nikoli, Japanese puzzle publishing company. But in *number link,* the addition of the rule, 'you can draw only one line on a cell,' makes the puzzle too difficult for puzzle beginners to solve (Fig.4). So I tried to remove 'grid,' which had long fixed pencil and paper puzzle world since the invention of crossword puzzle. After considering various possibilities, I discovered the way of adding the place where lines cannot pass (wall). Thereby in *connect number,* while the grid rules are removed, we can create from easy problem to difficult. This puzzle will please all people. For beginners, the rules are easy, and for experts, drawing lines freely is fresh.

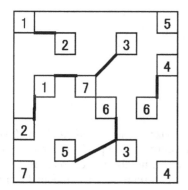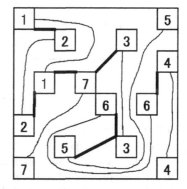

Fig. 3. left: problem right: solution

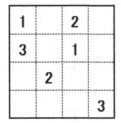 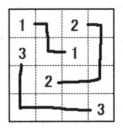

Fig. 4. left: problem right: solution

This puzzle was remade into Nintendo DSi software, as I wrote before (Fig.5). Pencil and paper puzzles are suitable for Nintendo DS which we manipulate with a touch pen, and this puzzle is no exception. But in the game edition, it was altered in a few points: first, to change numbers into pictures; second, to set a time limit; finally, to allow more than one solution. The reason of first alteration is that at the game solvers perhaps think they must connect from 1 in order by misunderstanding. The second is to enhance solvers' seriousness to the game. A problem with plural solutions, the final alternation, is allowed because the game machine can judge whether solvers finished or not and so they can be sure of their completion. This alternation for the game produced a new way of playing, playing by finding another solution that is effective for speed-up.

Fig. 5.

Next, I'll introduce my language-dependent puzzles. See '*compound word maze*' (Fig.6). In Japanese language, many compound words made up of four kanji are used, and they often have a special meaning like proverbs. In this puzzle, you must go from the start to the goal, picking up just four kanji to constitute such a compound word. In this puzzle, puzzle creators can control the level of their problems, by increasing or decreasing tricky kanji and obstacle walls. Also, Japanese people's name often consists of four kanji, so the rule can be altered to constitute the name of historical figure, for example. Because the structure of mazes is not so complex, this puzzle can appear on TV programs. In fact, I have shown this puzzle on TV a few times.

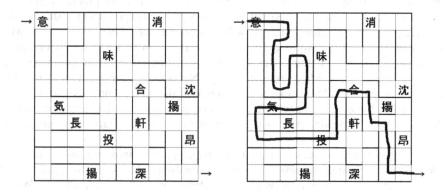

Fig. 6. left: problem right: solution

The last puzzle I introduce is '*kanji katakana cohabitation.*' See fig.7. Japanese is a language which has numerous characters, kanji, katakana, and hiragana, used according to circumstances. Above all, words compounded of kanji and katakana are mixed words, in which coexist words of Japanese origin (written in kanji) and words of foreign origin (written in katakana) , and interest puzzle creators. To take such words into my puzzle, I decided to adopt a rule of '*number crossword*'' which originated in English language sphere. '*Number crossword*'' is a sort of crossword puzzle in which solvers fill the grid under this rule: 'each letter is replaced by a number.' It is unexpected that this rule is suited for kanji-katakana words, but certainly it is. Consequently, the first puzzle of kanji-katakana words in Japan (of course in the world) was completed. The puzzle form in which only kanji is appearing and katakana should be filled in spaces is quite unique.

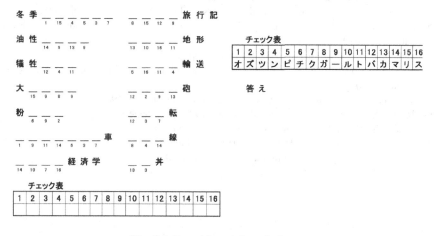

Fig. 7. left: problem right: solution

6 Conclusions

Thus, in the puzzle world, the importance of not only making problems but also inventing rules has long been insisted. But, unless the mass-producing system of the new rule puzzle is constituted, the rule will disappear at once. One of the reasons why *Sudoku* have driven the world crazy is that creators can make problems one after another by computer programs. But it is often said that problems by computers are inferior to that by hand. Mass production of problems of inferior quality may ruin the attraction of puzzles. The auto-making programs should be improved. Today, the system which has advantages of both computers and hand-made has been considered. These new ways of making puzzles are expected to become a trigger of inventing new rules.

It is usually hard to remake pencil and paper puzzles into computer games or videogames, because of the restriction of their hardware. Above all, to remake kanji puzzles, kanji recognition systems of the hardware are still underdeveloped. While digitization of books is developing rapidly, the puzzle world, where new rules are created in succession, shouldn't be left behind the times. Just like the case that *'connect number'* was digitized, the pursuit of pleasure only in electronic mediums should be aimed.

Movement, order, and time are hard to realize on paper. In electronic medium, puzzles which contain such elements can be realized. If the medium changes, the restriction on making rules also changes. The puzzle rules only for computers or videogames will show us the new puzzle world in the future. The demand for 'rule creator' is certainly increasing now.

References

1. Akiyama, H.: Chinese Rings Book, Shinkigensha (2003) (in Japanese)
2. Akiyama, H.: Picture and Shape Puzzles Book, Shinkigensha (2005) (in Japanese)
3. Caillois, R.: Les jeux et les hommes. Gallimard (1967)
4. Danesi, M.: The Liar Paradox and the Towers of Hanoi. Wiley, Chichester (2004)
5. Higashida, H.: Kyoto University Student, Higashida's Puzzles. Kadokawa Gakugei Publisher (2010) (in Japanese)
6. Inaba, N.: Puzzle Brain, Odysseus (2010) (in Japanese)
7. Shibata, T., Tanikawa, S., Yagawa, S.: World Riddles Encyclopedia, Taishukan (1984) (in Japanese)
8. Slocum, J., Botermans, J.: Puzzles Old and New, Washington (1986)
9. Takagi, S.: Puzzle Encyclopedia, Kodansha (1985) (in Japanese)
10. Takagi, S.: Play Puzzle, Heibonsha (1981) (in Japanese)
11. Takagi, S.: Play Puzzle 2, Heibonsha (1982) (in Japanese)
12. Zumthor, P.: Langue Texte Énigme. Editions du Seuil, Paris (1975)

Cultural Computing – Creative Power Integrating Culture, Unconsciousness and Software*

Naoko Tosa

Kyoto University
Yoshida Nihonmatsu-cho, Sakyo-ku, Kyoto, 606-8501, Japan
tosa@media.kyoto-u.ac.jp

Abstract. The author is carrying out technology studies to explore and expand human emotions, sensibility, and consciousness by making innovative use of artistic creativity. We develop interfaces for experiencing and expressing the "essence of culture" such as human feelings, ethnicity, and story. History has shown that human cultures have common and unique forms such as behavior and grammar. We suggest a computer model for that process and a method of interactive expression and experiencing cultural understanding using IT called "cultural computing". We particularly examine Japanese culture, although it is only a small subject of computing.

Keywords: Communication, Software, Information System, Cultural Computing, Interactive Art.

1 Introduction

"The ethnic crisis, the urban crisis, and the education crisis are interrelated. If viewed comprehensively all three can be seen as different facets of a larger crisis, a natural outgrowth of man's having developed a new dimension – the cultural dimension – most of which is hidden from view. The question is, How long can man afford to consciously ignore his own dimension?" This phrase is from "The Hidden Dimension" by cultural anthropologist Edward T. Hall, 1966.

Nowadays, computers play an important roll in various ways in our life. Cellular phones, e-mails, websites, games as well as PCs are almost parts of our life, and they became the daily items or media. Computers were only 'machines to calculate something' at first, but now they are 'media for thinking and memorization support.'

Let us see the relation between traditional customs and computers. Computers are typically used for calculation to restore something or for historical simulation. Archiving the fading cultures with using computers are barely in the use of thinking and memorization support, but it isn't an effective application of the ability of computers which now treats multimedia and are connected in network. The present ages often communicate with someone who has another cultural background, so they are needed to understand the history of their culture and other cultures. Because the typical way

---

* Published in '10 Spring Forum of Society of Automotive Engineers of Japan, May 00, 2010.

R. Nakatsu et al. (Eds.): ECS 2010, IFIP AICT 333, pp. 223–232, 2010.

to understand them is to read the books or to go to the museum, understanding another culture with picking appropriate information is not so easy. Can we understand the culture using computers as 'media for thinking and memorization support'which became more suitable for network, mobile, and two-way communication by the development of information technology? This paper describes basic methodology of cultural computing, that is, to treat the essences of the deep-inside culture like sensitivity, national traits, or narratives. And it integrates them into verbal and nonverbal information, proposing the prosperity of the field that treats the experience of exchange between cultural experiences and culture models by using computer. The cultural computing, which is essential for the communication ability of future computer, introduces you to this new field which defines what humans have stored in each culture and it's history in forms of actions or grammars are sharing common or peculiar forms by showing some concrete methodology and some examples.

2 Media for Thinking and Memorization Support

2.1 The Transcending Artist

What is the aim of arts? This is very huge and heavy question, but if I dare to answer, it is 'the visualization of the status of someone's heart' in a word.

The value of arts is in contrary of the one of technologies. Great art works are having universal values that have not faded yet. On the other hand, old technologies are often selected and surpassed by other new ones. Media arts does transcend them, making new relationship between art and technology, and affecting to other various fields. In other words, arts transcend technologies and technologies transcend arts.

I was conscious of my way as a transcending artist, and determined to obtain global viewpoint instead of local, Japanese culture as the next step. I moved my base of research activity to Massachusetts Institute of Technology, USA. However, I faced the difference between cultures there. I noticed that there were the differences not only in our daily life, but also in the feelings, memories, sign, unconscious communications that are strongly related to their cultures. I noticed that extremely Japanese-characterized expressions as well as global express had also been used in my works, although I had tried to express my artworks generally.

I have tried to assimilate myself into America at first, but it was difficult and I strongly realized that I am Japanese. I paid attention to actions and grammars that are seemed as 'Japanese culture' in America. I tried to expression the difference between American behaviors or grammars and Japanese ones in the arts.

At that time, I have met Sansui ink paintings (Japanese landscape paintings) of Sesshu. Sansui paintings are not landscape painting, but they are imagined scenery. This is in relation to the unconsciousness of occidental Jung's psychology. I discovered the way of unconscious communication to understand other cultures by using the components of unconsciousness in Sansui paintings.

I succeeded to create an interactive artwork, 《ZENetic Computer》 by modeling the structure of Zen and Sansui, which are thought the very Japanese culture. After that, I created the Kanji inspiration 《i.plot》 which gives relations between psychological associations and graphical images of ideograms. Furthermore, I produced 《Hitch Haiku》 system which supports creating the Haiku from several Kanji (Chinese character) input, using the template of 5 − 7 − 5 characters.

Surprisingly, when I exhibited these works in overseas, for example MIT, many Americans understood these works. This shows that these arts, transcending the time as history or culture, and the space as nations, became the media which people in other culture can understand, by picking up the structure of peculiar traditional Japanese culture through the computer.

2.2 Cultural Poiesis

By continuing these studies, I discovered that I could precede the methods of art and technology. That is, interactive works with computer modeling of Japanese culture can be brand new media that enable everyone to understand other cultures by touching them. Thus, obstacles between Japanese traditional culture that was thought as peculiar and other cultures were slowly disappeared.

To express a core of a culture based on the traditional culture model, by using computer. Many people from around the world can create their own Haiku or Zen, and send them to the world by the computer using traditional cultural model through the metaphor. Of course, computers can model not only Japanese cultural metaphor but also the world theater of Shakespeare, and it is possible to create Kabuki composed by the metaphor of the Globe Theatre. I think this can be called as the creation of the culture, the cultural computing.

I noticed that computers have a feature appropriate to create the new culture. Computer processes are divided into algorithms and data. We can seem them as types and contents! Handling the culture by the computer would lead to the creation of the new culture. The culture in that context is a poiesis (that means creation in Greek) of communication between different cultures.

3 From Occidental Unconsciousness to Eastern Sansui Paintings

3.1 《Neuro-Baby》 Connects *Here* and *There*

I am a postwar generation with plenty of American cultures for TVs available when I was born. The effect is great that unconsciously I had an interest in surrealism of adolescence and Jung's unconsciousness of psychoanalysis. After that, I began to express something invisible, like consciousness or feeling. That is why I started to create computer characters, computer characters exist "there." On the other hand in virtual reality, and human exist in this world "here" Sometimes through "there." We can communicate each other.

At that time, computers were in evolution from workstation to the personal computer. When I saw a personal computer at first, I knew by intuition that this item has functionality like human's one. I wanted to create a grown-up human, and make him/her talk through the feelings, by visualizing the internal consciousness as my theme of expression.

In the fields of AI, many researchers studied computers that can talk with humans as one field of technology. But their conversations are almost conventional, or a verbal exchange which is programmed in advance. So we can't help feeling that we are forced to talk along some patterns. Conversations should be more fresh, free and enjoyable.

I created a work 《Neuro-baby》 based on these ideas. The baby computer character cries, laughs, or does some actions from the user's voice expression of talk.

When I announced it in the international conference, it became the center of the attention of researchers in the fields of AI and robots. I did not know why, but now I think my work hit a blind spot in the point that it had an aim to exchange the feelings by the conversation, instead of their aim, to exchange the information.

The exhibition titled 'Artificial Life' took place at Als Electronica in 1993. Studies and works with computers and robots aiming at simulation of Lifelike evolution or humanize by using the theorem of biology or neural networks. There, I met an strange foreigner who was watching the 《Neurobaby》 many times, and talking to it in funny tone. After a casual greeting, I knew he was Rodney Brooks, a worldwide authority of MIT in the fields of AI and robots.

AI and robot technology met with Interactive art. I felt that technologies were approaching to arts in a new way. I also met Thomas Ray who were studying artificial life at ATR in the position of biology. At that time, few people created interactive arts, and there're no concrete way in this field.

I met Yoichi Tokura, who was the director of ATR (Advanced Telecommunications Research Institute International) Human Information Communication Research Laboratories and studied a sound using baby at ATR, and got the position of a guest researcher in new laboratory, Media Integration & Communications Research Laboratories of ATR. And among many technological researchers, I had studied the mechanism of the communication of feeling from 1995 to 2001.

Is it the technology using the method of art? Or is it an art using the method of technology? Looking back upon it, I focused on the essential component which is inherent in the human communications, rather than their technologies. I think I spend more time to visualize in artistic method using the technology. Communication is an action deeply related in our instinct, and includes many interesting phenomena. First, I focused on handling nonverbal information like feeling started in 《Neurobaby》 , and second I focused on handling the story.

A typical example of nonverbal information is feeling, and it contains much information widely spread from simple feelings like happiness, anger, sadness and comfort, sensitivity to the unconscious sense. So tackling these problems can make us enable the interactive visualization of feelings, sensitivity, and unconsciousness.

3.2 MIT CAVS

After I had quit ATR Media Integration and Communications Research Laboratories, I stayed Boston as the fellow of MIT Center for Advanced Visual Studies from 2002 to 2004.

The history of art & technology started from the avant-garde art group, EAT which was active in later half of 1960s. The main members of the group were engineers who engaged in Bell Telephone Laboratory of AT&T. Famous artists, Robert Rauschenberg, Robert Whitman and John Cage participated in, and carried out activities crossing the borders of arts, dances, music, videos, pursuit of the borderline between art and technologies by setting the foothold to New York. EAT is the mother group of Center for Advanced Visual Studies (CAVS) established in MIT, 1967. Gyorgy Kepes, who had defected to America and became a professor of the department of architecture, was there. He invented large movements in various fields like urban life, environment and life, the fusion of art and science, as well as the architecture. Kepes founded the CAVS, and became as a director of it. It was 1968, when whole America had hoped for new arts. CAVS has the longest history as a laboratory of art & technology (and it is now at 3F above the main gallery of MIT Museum). It was an pioneer of performance and collaboration, and its effect to post generations is so large.

Artists like Namu June Paik, Charlotte Moorman who is cellist and collaborated with Paik, Scott Fisher who invented 'Head Mount Display', which created virtual reality (VR) technology are typical members of it.

I worked as a fellow from 2002 to 2004, invited by Prof. Steven Benton who was the 4th director of it. He was a recognized authority on a study of holography, and he invented the rainbow holography. He is also one of those founded MIT Media Laboratories. He took me in so that CAVS can change its motto from "art and science" to "art and computer", that means, from analog to digital. My expected role was to blow Asian wind of digital arts on CAVS, which had been deep-rooted in European culture.

3.3 We Cannot Take Our Culture Off

Have you had impatience about communication and thought, "Communications usually succeed, but why do they occasionally fail?" It fails because you communicate with someone supposing that they should be able to understand you. Communications are needed, however, for they cannot understand you. If you get it, you will find how to communicate with them calmly.

If we have understood all of us already, we do not need to communicate with each other. Japanese people has a strong pride of homogeneous race, so we apt to have relatively the same feelings, impressions and opinions about someone's actions, phenomena and a course of our society. As they typically call it a 'direct communication from mind to mind (Ishin-denshin in Japanese)', we are prone to think something supposing that they should understand us.

The characteristic of Japanese becomes obvious when we go abroad. That's because we face the condition that we cannot make ourselves understood even if we have thought they should be able to understand. Many other Japanese looks hard to be normal, like herbivorous animal living with carnivorous animals.

In America, however, especially Anglo-Americans often communicate with considering that a person cannot understand them, I think. Actually, I had colleagues from Germany, Greece, Lebanon, Japanese, Chinese, French and Anglo-America. Southern Europeans usually use a nonverbal communication like Japanese, which makes me feel a sense of closeness. However, Anglo-Americans keep a distance when they communicate. Somehow, they do not open their hearts, or they tend to hesitate at showing their feelings. This fact shows that they communicate with considering that a person cannot understand them.

The same situation sometimes occurs when we communicate with a computer as well as a person.

In Boston, audio response systems often answer when we call to enter into contracts with a telephone or a gas service. Computers ask us, "My name is Alice (e.g.), please answer me to register." "May I ask your name, please?" "May I ask your address?" Those questions continue. And what is worse, the speech recognition sometimes fail. Then the computer says, "I couldn't recognize, please repeat that again?" Answering it three times will be the limits of our patience. One of what are good about American frontier spirit is this big-hearted and trendy disposition.

"Do people here really patient about computer operators?" I asked my friend and she advised me, "In that case, you should wait while human operator appears." She says that various things (computers or humans) meddle in phenomena, and extended the time we decide something. This analysis also shows the difference between Japanese who accustomed to communicate tacitly and Americans who accustomed not to communicate tacitly.

While I stayed at Boston, I realized by my experience that we should think communications occur only when people can't understand each other, considering the difference of their culture. Many times I experienced satisfaction of sympathy with someone whom I thought was not understandable, which is beyond expression. We cannot communicate freshly without this moment. If we communicate not only with discovering our errors, differences or sympathies but also with exchanging and amplifing our knowledge and feelings, the communication will transchend each cultures.

We obtained global comunication by adopting medica technologies in face-to-face communication which had been limited to a small community. E-mails, social networks, blogs enabled us to communicate more easily with people from around the world, beyond barriers of distance and culture. On the other hand, many people feel communications being more and more shallow these days. Rather, these shallow communications brought a recent typical face-to-face conversation, "Did you read my message?" Communications may be turning into extremely superficial communications, with taking off the tastes of cultures.

Ignoring this tendency will cause the decline in our communication ability which we have had as the basic instinct from ancient times. We immediately need the new communication media which can convey one's depth of feeling crossing the border of cultures. I knew it is realizable during my 2 years stay in Boston.

I wanted to create the communication media with which we can communicate deep feelings transcending the culture. As the result of my stay in Boston, I had this strong idea.

3.4 Technologies Combined with the Spirit

I visited Western China for 10 days, in the later July 2002. The aim of this trip was to discuss with Tibetan doctors and philosophers, and to complete the fieldwork for my research theme that looks for the problems about arts, technologies and hearts.

First, I visited Xining, the capital of Qinghai province. Gelug who consider the religious precepts highly important prosper there, and the founder, Tsongkhapa, and 14th Dalai Lama are also from there.

Many tulkus, including 14th Dalai Lama, practiced asceticism in the Kumbum Monastery (Ta'er), one of the 6 biggest temples of Gelug. I inspected the temple in where 4,000 monks practiced asceticism, and felt great energy or a sense of many people's mind flowing inside the temple where many pagodas (stupas) standing.

Tibetans naturally have an idea that the medicine and the philosophy is the same. Doctors are philosophers, and are Buddhist priests at the same time. I was impressed by the nature that doctors see what is wrong in patient's heart at first.

Tibetan philosophy has an faith to give freedom to all the afflicted lives. Their thought is deeply related to consciousness, feelings, the space and lives, centering the bowels of mercy and wisdom. The cosmic view has to do with our essential problems, the wheel of life and the existence. Many cultures in Tibet include Buddhist Tantrism as the appreciation of the idea that life cycles.

South of Xining is Guide (貴徳), which is famous for its hot springs. A 3,800 meters highland is nearby it. We visited a Tibetan tent (yurt), and they offered us butter named 'tsampa', milk of yak and dishes using barleys. We entered Tongren (Regon in Tibetan) and crossed a huge dam with a ship.

We went back to Xining and visited Arura Tibetan Medical Center. We discussed with five people including famous Dr. Denchi, the hierach and Buddhist philosopher, and Dr. Tanjinja who is nyingma (specialists for sadhana in Tibetan cabala). When we referred our spirituality of arts and the possibility of fusion between art and technology, they identified with us and said, "It is a possible idea as one of the figure of future religion." This encouraged us so much.

Tibetan Buddhists set the sprit of bodhisattva very important. This means to put off their tenacity to themselves and self-love, to have altruistic love. I noticed that this spirit is deeply related into interactive art.

Interactivity in art is shallow and the value is low if the purpose is up to self-assertive or communication of feeling. What is important is the interaction with having the sprit of bodhisattva and altruistic love. That is, if computer systems succeed to interact with having the sprit of bodhisattva, the interactivity of the system can deeply resonate the high spirit with other people.

I knew in my visit to Tibet that the Buddhism, which was born in India, has stayed in Tibet adjusting to the climate there and that the global consciousness is remaining there. I was impressed with the fact that we Japanese and Tibetan Buddhist are able to understand each other at a deep side of our spirit. I hoped to create something that Westerners can also understand the Buddhism, as a media expression using technologies. I just met the Sesshu, which critically affected my artworks after that.

3.5 Meeting the Sansui

I met the Sesshu at the exhibition "Sesshu – special exhibition at 500th anniversary of his death" (Kyoto National Museum, 2002). I was fascinated with the world Sesshu had created. I did not have a special interest in Japanese culture before. For some reason, the Sansui world of Sesshu in that exhibition seemed a virtual reality which expressed his heart!

In old China, a Sansui picture was once about a landscape we wanted to watch forever, a place we wanted to go to play, a place we wanted to live, and a hometown of our heart in which we wanted to pass away. The Sansui picture is imagined scenery like that. Its bleeding, cracked, feathering lines of ink brush draw the movement of the heart. It makes us feel the color even if it is monochrome.

I had an inspiration to compute the Sansui picture typically by Sesshu and the world of Zen which was expressed in Sansui picture. Zen makes us feel Japanese culture by its absence of absolutes, beauty sense of "Wabi-Sabi", and getting rid of the water from the Chinese garden with taking the Asian culture in. Many elements in Japanese culture are gathered in Sansui, like the Ume-Sansui (Sansui with Japanese aprlicot). I wanted to express the Sansui picture and Zen culture, centering the Japanese Zen.

Cultures consist of 'the God, the Buddhist image, a view of Life, a view of world'. They have been created, changed, opposed and fused with each other, and are irrational and rational. They, which have both irrationality and rationality, have seemed difficult to handle.

Almost all the existent media art works featured traditional contents like Noh and Kabuki, and added interactive function to them. These were seemed as only superficial digital expressions, though these are extensions of texts, images, videos, and their combinational multimedia that explain the traditional culture. They are only a explanations and not new arts. They are on the stage only to treat the surface, than to approach directly to the culture.

There was no research to make use of the hierarchy of Japanese culture to the computer logic in the existent computer technology. This is the reason why there are no arts expressing the deep historical 'culture' in large scale yet. Another reason is that everyone have paid attention to the uniqueness of Japanese culture and seemed the Japanese culture as Japanese superficial expressions.

On the other hand, technologies finds the mechanism of phenomena, and analyzes the elements of them with the structure. And the study finds new relationship between different things and constructs them, by reconstructing them, trying some combination of them and comparing them.

What we can make use of in creating new media arts are extracting the basic structure or thoughts of Japanese culture, modeling them or using them as tools with using the technology. Fresh media works or art works would likely be created by that. This method will bring about a great possibility to the advancement in media arts and interactive arts hereafter.

Thanks to the cooperation of Seigo Matsuoka, who is a researcher of Japanese Culture in Editorial Engineering Laboratory, we took a little advantage in this difficult challenge that we reconstruct the world of Zen which was expressed in Sansui picture on the computer. Though we needed three years, we reached to the unique system named 《ZENetic Computer》 as the result.

We succeeded to construct the extremely futuristic interactive system by projecting a part of allegory or symbol in Sansui pictures, Yamato-e (Japanese traditional paintings), Haikus, Kimonos that reminds of the Japanese culture – the structure of the oriental thought, the structure of Buddhist philosophy and the mechanism of Japanese traditional culture – which rarely have featured by the computers before.

This system uses various symbols and allegories that are included in Buddhism, an oriental thought and the Japanese culture. This is because they include a plenty of implications, and they have extraordinary terms, figures or colors. There are many rules in Sansui pictures and the world of Zen. We discovered that computers can handle them, if we can select and extract them. For example, there are 'San-En' which is an expression of Sansui pictures, and 'Go-Un' (five elements which form a self-existence) which is a function to recognize the human in Buddhism and so on.

The first exhibition of this system was in MIT museum. I wondered whether Westerners understand it or not. As a result, however, it was accepted by many Westerners and won the great popularity. Westerners had felt that Sansui pictures and Zen is extremely oriental and hard to approach, but they gave me impressions that they could understand them through the interaction with this system. I myself had an impression that we could achieved the initial goal to express Japanese culture in media, when I saw a American child interacting joyfully with this system.

After that, it was exhibited in SIGGRAPH, the international conference of CG, and Kodaiji, a Zen temple in Kyoto. Each exhibition won great popularity. This success of the experiment using this system made me certain that the 'cultural computing' which computes the culture is reasonable to set to my research goal.

4 Structure of the Culture Becomes a Communication Technology

4.1 An Interaction to Reach the Racial Memory

I was encouraged by the success of 《ZENetic Computer》 , and felt that interaction that reaches the deep-inside racial memory was the research I wanted to realize as the next stage. From the dry interaction of computers to the friendly and impressive interaction. How to realize this challenge?

I tried to classify the types, structures and relationship of what supports racial memories in Japanese culture with my co-researcher, Seigo Matsuoka. Below is the detail:

1. Japanese natural climate
    Japanese transient weather and nature, thought of transience like 'Monono-Aware', beauty senses like 'Wabi-Sabi', existential thought that loves present situation.
2. Relationships between Japanese culture and Asian one (Japanese own method to take over the Asian culture)
    Transformation from Chinese Sansui pictures to Japanese ones, Chinese gardens and grove gardens to the Japanese Rock Garden.
3. The syncretization of Shinto and Buddhism
    The cultural structure that was reconstructed as a belief system, mixing the native faith and the Buddhism.
4. Characteristics of Japanese language
    Waka poem, Haiku poem, Noh thater, and the script of Kabuki. And as applications, Honka-Dori, Uta-Makura, Kakari-Musubi, etc.
5. Japanese Design
    Japanese designs are the most popular. Two-dimensional designs are Mon (armorital bearings), Ori (pattern of textiles), colors, paper patterns, lines for example. Three-dimensional dynamic designs are the design of Noh, Kabuki, etc.

On these bases, we can consult on various racial types of Japanese culture and the rear communication.

4.2 Computers Do Not Have a Cultural Information Hierarchy

Scientific technologies have developed Web2.0 like Google, Youtube, Wikipedia and SNS by which we can send our information more easily. Robot technologies are also developing new basic techniques to realize the superior functions that living things have. More specifically, they are global communication technologies including the movement functionality, manipulation system, distributed autonomous system for upgrading the intelligence.

There is, however, no cultural information hierarchy that is needed to live with humans. Adding the local cultural information by cultural computing to here may contribute to create higher-level communication systems.

5 Conclusion

These methods of 'cultural computing' enables us to model and structure the deep-inside essentials of culture like sensitivity, intuition, racial characteristics and narratives that we have not able to quantification. I have set my goal to realize the communication that moves one's racial characteristic expanding the present computer's communication ability to have an ability to reflect the difference in feelings, consciousness and memories, based on the culture. If these systems are realized, social practical and cultural information expression systems through the languages, voices and movies will be realized in various fields.

References

1. Tosa, N.: Cultural Computing. NTT Publishing (2009) (in Japanese)
2. Barbara Maria Stafford, Visual Analogy: Consciousness as the Art of Connecting. The MIT Press (2001)
3. Tosa, N., Nakatsu, R.: Life-like Communication Agent -Emotion Sensing Character "MIC" and Feeling Session Character "MUSE". In: The Third IEEE International Conference on Multimedia Computing and Systems (ICMCS), pp. 12–19 (June 1996)
4. Minsky, M.: Society Of Mind. Simon & Schuster (1988)
5. Hall, E.: The Hidden Dimension, Anchor (1990)
6. Nakatsu, R.: Future of Communications: How can technology Contribute the Spiritual Aspect of our Communications. Ohm-Sha Publishing (2010) (in Japanese)
7. Tosa, N., Matsuoka, S.: ZENetic Computer: Exploring Japanese Culture. The Journal of the International Society for Arts, Sciences and Technology: LEONARDO 39, 205–211 (2006)

Entertainment and Its Future

Ryohei Nakatsu

Interactive & Digital Media Instutite, National University of Singapore
21 Heng Mui Keng Terrace, I-Cube Building Level 2,
Singapore 119613
idmdir@nus.edu.sg

Abstract. Various new forms of entertainment using information and media technologies have emerged and been accepted among people all over the world. Casual and serious games, as well as communication using mobile phones, blogs, and Twitter, are such kinds of new entertainment. It is important to discuss the basic characteristics of such entertainment and to understand the direction to which these new forms are leading human societies. This paper provides a comparative study of entertainment between developing countries and developed countries, and between ancient times and the present day. The future relationship between entertainment and society is also described.

Keywords: Entertainment, logic, emotion, logos, pathos, communication.

1 Introduction

New network, information, and media technologies are rapidly changing our society, including human relationships, lifestyles, and communication. Entertainment is one area that these new technologies are strongly influencing. One good example is games. Playing computer and video games is a common daily activity for people, especially for younger generations. In particular, online games have become very popular in both the U.S. and Asian countries. Another good example is communication. People communicate with their families and friends through e-mail, mobile phones, texting, Twitter, and other means. Until the 1980s, communication media such as telephones were mainly used for business communication. Today, however, communication extends beyond business conversations and has become a form of everyday entertainment.

There are many discussions on these phenomena, but most of them merely observe what is happening in society and report the fact that more people are spending more time on these new forms of entertainment. Unfortunately, however, there has been little consideration of the basic reasons why these new forms have been accepted by people all over the world. One fundamental questions is whether this a totally new phenomenon within our long history. Another question is which aspects of society are changing through the introduction of these new forms of entertainment, and how much those aspects are changing. Another, more difficult question is the direction to which such entertainment is leading our society. In other words, what will be the

R. Nakatsu et al. (Eds.): ECS 2010, IFIP AICT 333, pp. 233–242, 2010.

future of our society, where people are expected to spend more time on entertainment than they do now.

In this paper, I try to answer these questions by starting from the question of what entertainment is. It will be clarified that over the long course of human history, people have tried to clearly separate logical and emotional aspects of our behaviors, in other words, the logos and pathos, respectively. Consequently, we have succeeded in confining the great power of emotion to only the private aspects of our lives.

New media such as games and mobile phones, however, have strongly affected this relationship between logos and pathos and have partly destroyed it. Today, people are showing the emotional aspect of their behaviors even in formal situations. A more distinctive point is that this tendency is more obvious in Western countries.

Finally, given these considerations, I anticipate the direction to which our society is headed. I also discuss what we should do to maintain our basic identity as human beings.

2 The Nature of Entertainment

2.1 What Is Entertainment?

At least one billon people currently face starvation all over the world. For these people it is crucial to obtain food for tomorrow or even today. This problem has been one of the most serious topics at global conferences and meetings such as World Economic Forum [1].

On the other hand, in developed countries new types of entertainment have emerged, such as chat on mobile phones and games on game systems and PCs. People in those countries are tending to spend more and more time enjoying such forms of entertainment. There have been significant concerns and complaints about this trend. The basic logic of such complaints is that compared with other human activities, such as education, business, industrial production, and so on, entertainment is not productive. In other words, the complaints suggest that entertainment is only a waste of time.

An important question, however, is whether this is actually true, when the established entertainment industry is huge and includes the movie, game, sports, and other businesses. Another question is why the demand and markets for such entertainment are so huge. The issue of whether entertainment is a waste of time clearly requires care.

2.2 Origin of Entertainment

What is happening now is not a totally new phenomenon. In earlier times, human life was simple. Humans farmed or hunted to survive. When people were not occupied with these tasks, they entertained themselves by various means. In other words, we can say that food is strongly related to our physical sustainability, yet at the same time, we can point out that entertainment is related to our mental and spiritual sustainability.

Then the era of civilization began. People introduced various novel types of activities, such as art, business, learning and teaching, and religion. Because of these activities, entertainment came to be considered as a secondary activity in human life.

Although entertainment remained a certain part of our everyday life, it has not been considered an essential part. Figure 1 illustrates these changes in our physical and mental sustainability.

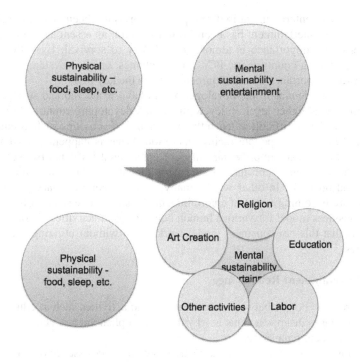

Fig. 1. Changes in the physical and mental sustainability of human beings

2.3 Our Life and Entertainment

Even now sometimes that fact that entertainment is an important part of our life becomes apparent. Consider passengers on an airplane. During a flight, most people sleep, eat, or entertain themselves by watching movies, reading novels, and so forth. Only a few people work during a flight. This means that in a simple situation, our lifestyle consists of three basic activities: sleeping, eating, and entertaining ourselves.

What is happening now is, in one sense, an "entertainment renaissance." The introduction of new technologies, especially interactive technologies, into traditional forms of entertainment has totally renewed and strengthened those forms. People are again noticing the basic strength and meaning of entertainment and recognizing that it is a substantial part of their lives. This is a key point in trying to understand such substantial issues as the role of entertainment in developed and developing countries and the future direction of entertainment.

3 Entertainment in Developing and Developed Countries

3.1 Entertainment in Developing Countries

The importance of entertainment in developing countries has been underestimated. As described above, entertainment has been, from its origin, an essential part of our life. In once sense, its importance is almost second only to survival. Even though few people in developing countries use PCs, mobile phones, or game systems, they intuitively know the importance of entertainment. This is the key point.

Leaders and academics in the developed world have wondered and struggled with how to introduce a higher level of development into developing countries. For example, it was considered difficult to teach the importance of activities such as education, religion, and business to people facing starvation. What is happening in developed countries, however, can simplify this. In developed countries it is observed that an emerging phenomenon of the merger of entertainment with other activities such as education and business. In other words, many activities commonplace in the developed world are becoming forms of entertainment. This is, in one sense, a fundamental change in business model for various human behaviors and activities. Another important point is that this new business model works even without utilizing cutting-edge technologies.

3.2 An Entertainment Renaissance

In other words, the border between entertainment and activities such as education and business is going to disappear. This is why the current phenomenon could be regarded as an "entertainment renaissance."

This means that many serious human activities contain the essence of entertainment and could be enjoyed. This could make it easier to promote such activities as various types of entertainment to people in developing countries. This would lead to greater participation in activities such as education and business, because these activities could now be interpreted as a form of entertainment and would thus be more familiar.

On the other hand, we should carefully examine the new forms of entertainment enthusiastically accepted by younger generations in developed countries. The question is whether these are actually new types of entertainment or not. When we examined new entertainment types in detail, we found that most of them have their origins in older forms of entertainment. For example, the experience of playing role-playing games is almost the same as the experience of reading fantasy novels. Another good example is new types of communication. Communication via chat, texting, or Twitter, using mobile phones, is actually a reshaped form of everyday conversation among family members and friends.

This means that new information and media technologies have reshaped traditional entertainment while keeping the same basic concept. Because of this, while the game market expanded with surprisingly great speed in the early days of video and PC games, it has now apparently reached a certain level of saturation, and various new forms of entertainment face the problem of sustainability. We should probably understand the core concept of entertainment and the future directions of the game industry by studying how people in developing countries entertain themselves.

4 Logos, Pathos, and Entertainment

4.1 Logos and Pathos

What is happening in developed countries is actually deep and substantial. Through the emergence of new forms of entertainment, our societies and lifestyles are experiencing a fundamental change.

Here, we recall the ancient Greek origin of Western philosophy. Plato compared the human spirit to a carriage with two horses and one driver in his *Republic* [2]. Here, as illustrated in Fig. 2, the driver is a metaphor for the rational aspect of the human spirit, called the "logos." On the other hand, the two horses are a metaphor for the emotional aspect, called the "pathos." The former could be linked to the formal parts of our lives, and the latter, to the private parts. Furthermore, one of the horses represents passion, while the other represents the instinctive aspect of emotion.

Plato admired logos as the basis of rational human behaviors. As for pathos, passion was admired as the source of creative behaviors, but instinct was despised as undeveloped and representing the dark side of behavior. Plato also expected that logos could control the dark side of pathos, instinct, with help from the bright side of pathos, passion.

This definition and statement by Plato determined the initial direction of philosophy and morality in the Western world. Since the ancient Greek era, people have been trying to separate logos and pathos in their lives. In other words, they have been trying to separate the logical and emotional aspects of living.

Logos   *Pathos*
Bright side: Passion
Dark side: Instinctive
desire

Fig. 2. Logos and pathos

4.2 Formal and Informal Aspects of Life

In the long history of Western society, starting with Plato's philosophical considerations, logos has been considered related to the formal aspects of human behaviors, in social situations and in business scenes, for example. On the other hand, pathos has been related to the private aspects of human activities. Westerners have long and eagerly sought to clearly separate these two aspects. In addition, people have tried to emphasize the importance of logos while neglecting pathos.

Asian languages also make such a distinction. For example, in Japan the formal aspect of behavior is called *honne*, while the informal aspect is called *tatemae*. In terms of *honne* and *tatemae*, Japanese people have been accused of having a double standard of behavior. As the above observation of Western society shows, however, this is not correct. All humans have both formal and private aspects of their behavior, in other words, *honne* and *tatemae*. The problem is that because people in Asian societies have not been very conscious of these two aspects, they have not been good at clearly separating these two types of behavior. In other words, Japanese people could be said to present confusion of the formal and private aspects of behavior.

One good example is that of the former prime minster, Mr. Asoh. He once declared at the Japanese parliament that he was actually against privatization of Japan's Post Office when he was a member of the previous Koizumi cabinet. The problem with his behavior is that, because he was a member of the cabinet and this formal decision was made within the cabinet, it was inappropriate to express his private opinion in a formal situation. What was worse was that he thought he was being honest by expressing his private opinion and could not understand why people accused him of expressing honne.

4.3 Approach between Logos and Pathos

In contrast with the above situation, the introduction of new media and forms of entertainment has invaded deeply into our lives and changed our behaviors. It was long considered civilized and sophisticated to act logically and hide the emotional aspect of behavior. Now, however, people tend to expose their emotions even in the formal parts of their lives. A good example is means of communication. It has become common for people to communicate even with close friends or family members by using mobile phones or PCs even during meetings or during dinner. This is surprising because communication with people close to us has typically been a private, emotional behavior.

This means that in our everyday life emotional behaviors have again become influential and can play a major role, after long years of separation between logos and pathos and the higher priority of logos over pathos in formal situations. In one sense, our behaviors are returning to those in ancient times. Moreover, this phenomenon has another important aspect. In observing the phenomenon, we notice two fundamental, distinctive features. First, human behaviors in the Western and Eastern worlds are becoming more similar. Second, human behaviors in developed countries and developing countries are also becoming more similar. In other words, differences in human behavior styles between Western and Asian countries, and between developed and developing countries, are disappearing. People are beginning to share the same ways of thinking and cultural principles and rules. In one sense, this is good because it will lower barriers between different people and countries. At the same time, however, we are losing the local features of cultures, which have long been preserved over the course of history.

5 Media and Entertainment

5.1 History of Media

It is important to consider why we are losing the separation between formal and informal aspects of our behaviors. As indicated above, the arrival of new media strongly influences this phenomenon.

To explain this, consider the history of significant media inventions. The two most impactful media inventions are written characters and the invention of printing typography. These remarkable inventions have enabled people to think, memorize, discuss, and describe by using language. In other words, these inventions have made people more left-brain dependent. It is noteworthy that this mainly happened in Western countries, as shown by the long history of Western philosophy, as represented by Plato. What happened in Asian counties is somewhat different. Somehow people did not try to clearly separate rational and emotional actions. The reason for this is an interesting research topic and is discussed elsewhere. In any case, however, for Asian people the concept of separation between logos and pathos has not been so clear.

5.2 Influence of Movies and Telephones

Two more impactful inventions in the recent history of media are telephones and movies. Today we tend to focus on recent inventions such as video games, mobile phones, e-mail, blogs, and Twitter. Unfortunately, we have almost forgotten the major impact telephones and movies have had on the basic changes in our behavior.

Before the invention of the telephone, the formal and emotional aspects of our behavior were clearly separated. For emotional behaviors, mental distance and special distance were closely related. When we are together with people to whom we are close, such as family members and friends, we expose our private, emotional behaviors. We have a strong instinct to be connected with familiar people. Before the invention of the telephone, however, when we were spatially separated from such people, because we had no method of communicating with them, we had to hide our emotional aspects and behave formally, as in business situations. Then, after the telephone was invented, it enabled us to be connected to familiar people even though we were spatially separated. Since that time, people have gradually tended to mix the formal and emotional aspects of our lives. This is the fundamental reason why now, even during meetings, dinner, or other situations, people want to continue communicating with people to whom they are close by using mobile phones and smart phones. In other words, the telephone has initiated confusion between the rational and emotional aspects of our behavior. The development of mobile phones and other recent media is only accelerating this trend.

The invention of movies has had a similar effect. Before the invention of movies, people were trained to be left-brain dependent, and reading and writing were the major intellectual and communication behaviors. The invention of movies, however, introduced images as an important communication medium. Images have a strong power to directly influence the emotional part of the brain, the right brain. Therefore, after long years of training to rationally use the left brain, people began to depend more on using the right brain. This means that people have gradually become emotionally dependent instead of rationally dependent. The recent trend toward excessive use of computer graphics and animation originated with the invention of movies. These newer technologies are merely accelerating the trend.

5.3 Future of Entertainment and Media

As described above, after long years of separation between logos and pathos in human behavior, these two aspects are moving back together, we can expect that they will merge again in the future, as illustrated in Fig. 3.

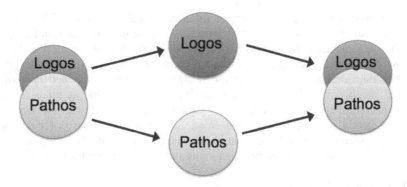

Fig. 3. Transitions of the relationship between logos and pathos

Regarding what this means for the future, it can be pointed out that an interesting and important phenomenon would happen. That is the behaviors of Westerners and Asians could become more alike and even become identical. As described above, in Asian countries a clear separation of logos and pathos has somehow not reached conscious awareness or discussion. Because of this, Asian people have been accused of being underdeveloped as human beings. In Western countries, however, people's behaviors are becoming more like those of Asian people [3]. A good example is communication behaviors. Today, even during such formal events as classes, meetings, discussions, or dinner, people often tend to check e-mail on their mobile phones and try to communicate with people to whom they are close. When a plane lands and arrives at a gate, the first thing many people do is take out their mobile phones, turn them on, and check e-mail or start calling family members. In this regard, there is no distinctive difference between the behaviors of Westerners and Asians.

5.4 Future of Human Beings

In one sense, this phenomenon is good, as various gaps between the West and Asia have long been headaches for cultural understanding. We can probably regard this as a bright side of globalization, but on the other side there is a danger. Each country and each ethnicity has developed its own culture, resulting in a rich variety of cultures all over the world. This is a major human accomplishment. The merger of behaviors between the West and Asia, however, could destroy this rich variety of cultural differences among different countries [4]. It is difficult to anticipate a future in which there are no cultural differences and people all over the world are connected to the network all the time and repeatedly receive and send shallow text messages. It could be like the virtual reality shown in the movie *The Matrix*.

There is another interpretation of the merger of logos and pathos. Animals lack any distinction of logos and pathos; rather, the two are tightly merged. Therefore, the merger of logos and pathos might mean that human beings will revert to an animal-like state. This would another bad outcome, in which we return to a very ancient time when human beings was not yet well developed and our behaviors were almost the same as those of other animals.

Instead, we probably should learn from our history. In both the Western world and the Asian world, there were eras when logos and pathos were not so clearly separated, yet people used to live fully human lives. For example, in the era of Homer's *Iliad* [5], logos and pathos were not clearly separated but the characters behaved honestly, bravely, and heroically. We should compare the behaviors of heroes and heroines in classical antiquity with those of modern people and determine from such comparisons what our behaviors should be in the future.

On the other hand, in Japan we have *The Tale of Genji* [6], the world's oldest novel. In once sense, the behaviors of the heroes and heroines in this novel are somewhat similar to those of current, younger generations. In the classic novel, men and women frequently exchange short poems, called *waka*, as a method of communication. Similarly, young people today frequently exchange short messages or post to Twitter accounts by using mobile phones. Probably the biggest difference, then, between these ancient and modern behaviors, is that the exchange of poems is a form of art creation, whereas message exchange using e-mail and Twitter does not involve art. The major question is how we can ennoble the communication behaviors of people in the network age. A good outcome would be to achieve the way of life described in *The Tale of Genji* but over a network using new media.

6 Conclusion

Various types of new entertainment, such as games and mobile phone applications, have been introduced into our society, rapidly changing our lifestyle. It seems we are in the era of chaos, and it is not certain what kind of lifestyle and society we will have in the future. In this situation, it is important to carefully observe the phenomena happening around us and extract findings, trends, tendencies, and so forth.

In this paper, by trying to answer the question of what entertainment is, I have tried to clarify the basic trends underlying various surface phenomena. It was first clarified that human behavior consists of two aspects, the logical and the emotional, and that entertainment is closely related to the emotional aspect.

Then, I discussed how Plato tried to separate the logical and emotional aspects of human behavior. Plato's efforts originated the long history of Western philosophy. Because entertainment is closely connected to the emotional side of behavior, it has been considered an informal aspect of behavior and thus hidden, even though entertainment is an essential aspect of our lives, like eating and sleeping.

It was also pointed out that the recent development of information and media technologies has raised the importance of the emotional aspect of life. In this sense, we are experiencing an entertainment renaissance. On the other hand, this means that logos and pathos, which have been clearly separated through history, are approaching each other and could even merge together.

There are several dangers in this trend. One is that the cultural differences that have enriched human history might fade away. Another is that human behaviors could revert to those of animals.

So far, there are no clear solutions to overcoming these dangers. One way to address this difficult situation, however, is to look back and learn from our history. There have been several eras when logos and pathos were joined together, as in the times described in the *Iliad* and *The Tale of Genji*. By learning from the behaviors detailed in these famous classics, we could perhaps imagine the future to which we are headed.

References

1. http://www.weforum.org/en/index.htm
2. Ptato: The Rebublic. Penguin Classics
3. Tosa, N.: Cultural Computing. NTT Publishing Co. (2009)
4. Nakatsu, R.: Future of Communications Empowered by Technologies. Ohm-sha Publishing Co. (2010)
5. Homer: Ilias. Hackett Publishing Company, Inc. (1997)
6. Murasaki, S.: The Tale of Genji. A Divition of Random House, Inc. (1976)

Author Index